Reconstructing Political Theory

To our Families

Reconstructing Political Theory

Feminist Perspectives

EDITED BY

Mary Lyndon Shanley and Uma Narayan

Polity Press

First published in 1997 by Polity Press
in association with Blackwell Publishers Ltd.

Editorial office:
Polity Press
65 Bridge Street
Cambridge CB2 1UR, UK

Marketing and production:
Blackwell Publishers Ltd
108 Cowley Road
Oxford OX4 1JF, UK

ISBN 0-7456-1796-4
ISBN 0-7456-1797-2 (pbk)

A CIP catalogue record for this book is available from the British Library.

Typeset in Garamond on 11/13 pt
by Best-set Typesetter Ltd., Hong Kong
Printed in Great Britain by TJ International Ltd, Padstow, Cornwall

This book is printed on acid-free paper.

Contents

List of Contributors

MARTHA ACKELSBERG is Professor of Government and Women's Studies at Smith College, where she teaches courses on urban politics, political participation, political theory, and feminist theory. Her writings include *Free Women of Spain: Anarchism and the Struggle for the Emancipation of Women* (Indiana University Press, 1991), and a variety of articles on women's activism, democratic theory, reconceptualizing families and family life in the modern period, Spanish anarchism, and Jewish feminism. She is currently working on issues of gender and citizenship.

ANITA ALLEN is Associate Dean for Research and Professor of Law and Philosophy at Georgetown Law Center. She has a special interest in jurisprudence and the right to privacy. Her publications include *Uneasy Access: Privacy for Women in a Free Society* and *Privacy: Cases and Materials*, a co-authored textbook. Her professional activities include advisory positions with numerous philosophy, bioethics, health and legal organizations.

KIMBERLÉ CRENSHAW is Professor of Law at UCLA Law School and Columbia Law School. She has lectured and written extensively on civil rights, black feminist legal theory, and race, racism and the law. Her work has appeared in the *Harvard Law Review, National Black Journal, Stanford Law Review* and *Southern California Law Review.* She is founding coordinator of the Critical Race Theory workshop, and co-editor of a forthcoming volume, *Critical Race Theory: Key Documents that Shaped the Movement.*

JEAN BETHKE ELSHTAIN is Professor in the Divinity School of the University of Chicago. She is the author of *Public Man/Private Woman, Meditations on Modern Political Thought,* and *Women and War.* She has edited numerous anthologies, including *The Family in Modern Political Thought, Power Trips and Other Journeys*, and *Just War Theory*.

NANCY FRASER is Professor of Political Science at the Graduate Faculty of the New School for Social Research. She is the author of *Unruly Practices: Power, Discourse and Gender in Contemporary Social Theory* (University of Minnesota Press, 1989), a co-author of *Feminist Contentions: A Philosophical Exchange* (Routledge, 1994) and the co-editor of *Revaluing French Feminism: Critical Essays on Difference, Agency and Culture* (Indiana University Press, 1992). Her most recent book is *Justice Interruptus: Critical Reflections on the "Postsocialist" Condition* (Routledge, 1997).

LINDA GORDON is Professor of History at the University of Wisconsin – Madison. She has written several books concerning the history of public policy, with particular concern for gender and family issues. Her most recent books are *Heroes of Their Own Lives: The Politics and History of Family Violence* (Viking Press, 1988) and *Pitied But Not Entitled* (The Free Press/Harvard University Press, 1994).

NANCY J. HIRSCHMANN is Associate Professor of Government at Cornell University, where she teaches political theory and feminist theory. The author of *Rethinking Obligation: A Feminist Method for Political Theory* (Cornell University Press, 1992) and co-editor with Christine Di Stefano of *Revisioning the Political: Feminist Reconstructions of Traditional Concepts in Western Political Theory* (Westview Press, 1996), she is currently writing a book on the concept of freedom.

ELIZABETH KISS is Director of the Kenan Ethics Program at Duke University. She is completing a book entitled *Rights As Instruments*. She has published extensively and continues to work in the areas of rights theory, feminist theory, and East Central European politics.

MARTHA MINOW is Professor of Law at Harvard Law School. She is the author of *Making All the Difference: Inclusion, Exclusion, and American Law* (Cornell University Press, 1990) and *Not Only for Myself: Identity, Politics and Law* (The New Press, forthcoming). She has edited *Family Matters: Readings on Family Lives and the Law* (The New Press, 1993) and co-edited *Law Stories* with Gary Bellow (University of Michigan Press, 1996). Her scholarship includes articles about the treatment of women, children, persons with disabilities, and members of ethnic, racial and religious minorities.

UMA NARAYAN is Assistant Professor of Philosophy at Vassar College. She works in the areas of ethics, philosophy of law, social and political philosophy and feminist theory. She has written articles on topics such as punishment, homelessness, affirmative action, surrogacy and colonialism. She is working on a volume of feminist essays tentatively entitled *Dislocating Cultures* for the Thinking Gender series, Routledge.

MARY LYNDON (MOLLY) SHANLEY is Professor of Political Science on the Margaret Stiles Halleck Chair at Vassar College, where she teaches courses on the history of political philosophy, feminist theory, and women and the law. She is author of *Feminism, Marriage and the Law in Victorian England* (Princeton University Press, 1989) and co-editor, with Carole Pateman, of *Feminist Interpretations and Political Theory* (Polity Press, 1990). Her current research concerns ethical issues in contemporary family law.

ELIZABETH V. SPELMAN, Professor of Philosophy at Smith College, is the author of *Inessential Woman: Problems of Exclusion in Feminist Thought* (Beacon Press). "The Heady Political Life of Compassion" adumbrates some themes central to her forthcoming book *Fruits of Sorrow: Use and Abuse of Suffering* (also Beacon).

ANNA YEATMAN is Professor and Chair of Sociology at Macquarie University, in Sydney, Australia. She is the author of two books: *Bureaucrats, Technocrats, Femocrats: Essays on the Contemporary Australian State* (1990) and *Postmodern Revisionings of the Political* (1994); she is co-editor of *Justice and Identity: Antipodean Practices* (1995) and *Feminism and the Politics of Difference* (1993). Her research interests cover feminist theory, the implications of globalization for the polity, the restructuring of the professions, and higher education.

Editors' Note

Chapter 2 is a revised and shortened version of an article which appeared in *Signs: Journal of Women in Culture and Society*, vol. 19, no. 2 (Winter 1994) under the title "A Genealogy of *Dependency*: Tracing a Keyword of the U.S. Welfare System."

Chapter 5 is a revised version of an article which appeared in *Hypatia*, vol. 11, no. 1 (Winter 1996) under the title "Relational Rights and Responsibilities: Revisioning the Family in Liberal Political Theory and Law."

Chapter 6 originally appeared in *Feminist Interpretations of Hannah Arendt* (ed. Bonnie Honig) published by Penn State Press (1995) and is reproduced by kind permission of the publishers.

Chapter 8 is a substantially revised version of an article which appeared in *Women's Studies Journal* vol. 10, no. 1 (1994) under the title "Women and Power."

Chapter 10 originally appeared in a longer version in the *Stanford Law Review*, vol. 43, no. 6 (July 1993) under the title "Mapping the Margins: Intersectionality, Identity Politics and Violence Against Women of Color."

Chapter 11 is a shortened version of an article which appeared in *Frontiers: A Journal of Women's Studies*, vol. 16, no. 1 (November 1995) under the title "Domestic Violence and the Theoretical Discourse of Freedom."

Introduction: Contentious Concepts

Uma Narayan and Mary Lyndon Shanley

In the decades since the early 1970s feminist political theory has come of age. Theorists have not only reread canonical texts and rethought many traditional concepts in order to reveal the relevance of gender to political theory, but have also argued for the importance of neglected texts and thinkers and attempted to expand the range of problems and concepts that have been regarded as central to political theory. The present volume, which contains essays that engage in feminist clarifications of important concepts, was envisioned as a companion to the earlier anthology, *Feminist Interpretations and Political Theory*, edited by Mary Lyndon Shanley and Carole Pateman. The earlier volume both subjects mainstream theoretical works by thinkers such as Plato, Locke and Rawls to feminist re-readings and incorporates the works of writers like Wollstonecraft and de Beauvoir into the history of Western political theory. This volume, in similar fashion, subjects to feminist re-examination concepts such as rights, power, freedom and citizenship that have long been central to the concerns of political theory. It also calls attention to concepts and concerns such as family, dependency, compassion, the intersectionality of race and gender, and the place of children in political life. These have not been central to mainstream political theory but are important to feminist projects of a reshaping political theory in a direction that is more fully responsive to women's interests, concerns and problems.

Feminist political theory is increasingly a multidisciplinary terrain, and contributors to this volume include philosophers, legal scholars, and political scientists. Despite the different disciplinary perspectives of the authors and the range of concepts they discuss, three general concerns emerge from these essays as being of particular importance to a feminist understanding of the gendered facets of political life: independence and dependency, public and private, and citizenship and political empowerment. These multifaceted and interlinked sets of concerns seem to us to capture not only the major themes that link the essays in this volume, but important sites within the ongoing feminist rethinking of the core concepts of political theory.

The essays by Elizabeth Kiss, Nancy Fraser and Linda Gordon, and Uma Narayan all show the ways in which ideas of rights and citizenship have long been associated with those of self-sufficiency and independence, and how such notions have been constructed so as to denigrate or dismiss the importance of different groups of women to the life of the polity. Kiss's essay, "Alchemy or Fool's Gold: Assessing Feminist Doubts about Rights," analyzes the feminist misgivings about rights that stem from the ways in which "rights-talk" seems to separate and distance one person from another, to emphasize possible encroachment rather than cooperation and mutual support, and to produce, as Simone Weil remarked, a shrill nagging of claims and counter-claims. This criticism of rights as simply boundary markers is flawed both practically and conceptually, Kiss believes. Practically, even rights as boundaries are valuable for the vulnerable such as abused or battered women. Conceptually, the denigration of rights ignores the many ways rights function in addition to serving as boundaries. For example, rights establish obligations for others and recognize the importance of certain relationships, as in the right to marry, to procreate, to educate one's children. But since most theories of justice continue "the centuries-old neglect of basic issues of child-rearing and care for dependents," any satisfactory theory of rights will, in Kiss's view, first have to remedy this neglect by "constructing principles of justice and frameworks of rights that take more seriously the facts of human dependency, neediness and vulnerability and hence the moral value and social importance of care." Kiss insists, however, that while many feminist critiques uncover problems with particular understandings of rights, they are mistaken if they think that these problems are endemic to all frameworks that take rights seriously and conclude that rights-talk is incompatible with a feminist politics. The feminist struggle over rights, then, must entail a struggle to conceptualize rights in a manner that is more responsive to our various responsibilities and ties to others, and to the facts of human interdependency.

Nancy Fraser and Linda Gordon continue the investigations of the connections between rights and independence through their examination of welfare rights. They analyze the ways in which changing historical understandings of "dependency" have helped shape our understandings of welfare rights and influenced attitudes regarding various groups of citizens who receive state support. Fraser and Gordon reconstruct the genealogy of the concept of "dependency" in US discussions of welfare rights, arguing that "dependency" is an ideological term. They analyze the historical shifts in the deployment of this term, revealing the sources of its current connotations with respect to gender roles, work, citizenship, the causes of poverty and the sources of entitlements. Their essay charts the disappearance of "good" dependency and the increasing association of dependency with pathology, which has culminated in the unmarried, teenage, Black mother becoming the stigmatized icon of welfare dependency in the United States.

In "Towards a Feminist Vision of Citizenship: Rethinking the Implications of Dignity, Political Participation, and Nationality," Uma Narayan echoes Fraser's and Gordon's concern with welfare rights and with protecting those who are made vulnerable by any one of numerous dependencies. Narayan goes on to argue that both "positive" and "negative" rights should be understood as means to minimize human vulnerabilities and preserve human dignity, grounded in feminist concerns to create a society that is responsive to the needs of all members of the national community. Welfare rights, she asserts, should therefore be severed from notions of "social contribution." She further claims that a feminist political concern with increasing representation for members of marginalized groups should move beyond a narrow concern with political representation to addressing such issues as education, affordable childcare, reduction of economic disparities and equal access to the workplace, all of which are connected to enabling participation in national life. Narayan points out that using "citizenship" as a term that grounds feminist political demands can be problematic in a world where non-citizens frequently reside for long periods of time in nations of which they are not citizens. Arguing for feminist attention to the interests of all those who are ongoing members of the national community, Narayan cautions that feminist concerns with women's second-class citizenship should not occlude attention to the predicaments of non-citizens, immigrant women in particular.

Kiss, Fraser and Gordon, and Narayan all make it clear that dependency is a normal and inevitable condition of many people at certain phases of their lives. Together, their essays challenge the notion that "independence" or self-sufficiency is a defining characteristic of the democratic citizen. Since the time of Aristotle, the realm of democratic participation has been portrayed as the arena of activity for independent and equal (male) citizens. The expansion of the electorate in the nineteenth and twentieth centuries in both Britain and the United States entailed overturning exclusions based explicitly on property, race, and sex. Suffragist and feminist attacks on the exclusion of women from public life due to their responsibility for children and hence their presumed lack of independence challenged the conflation between independence and citizenship. In different ways, Kiss, Fraser and Gordon, and Narayan all argue against that conflation and also insist that the state has responsibilities to provide for dependents and their caretakers. The state must insure that the work of caring for dependents does not impede caregivers from access to valuable forms of social activity, including paid work and participation in public debate and decision-making. These essays do not, however, reject independence as an important value; rather, they insist on understanding independence in terms other than that of self-sufficiency. Freedom from material want and deprivation as well as a range of life-options and choices in important areas of life, guaranteed by a well-functioning system of rights, constitute a kind of independence important to the welfare and flourishing of all political subjects. Furthermore, some forms of dependence might well facilitate other forms of independence – for instance, dependence on state-provided welfare may enable some women to achieve independence from an abusive spouse. Attention to the lives of different groups of women helps to underscore that it is neither helpful to see independence and dependence as polar opposites nor appropriate to cast dependence as always a problematic and avoidable condition.

Just as feminist theory has challenged the dichotomous thinking categorizing individuals as either independent or dependent, so it has attempted to break down the rigid demarcation between public and private without obliterating the distinction between those domains. Early in the second wave of feminism, thinkers pointed out the inadequacy of cordoning off family concerns from political life and consigning them to the private realm. While nearly all the essays in this volume touch on the public/ private distinction in some way, four involve sustained analyses of the strengths and limitations of this distinction. Each of these sees the boundary as more permeable than traditional theory, particularly liberal theory, held. But all regard privacy as an important value to protect both individuals (for example, women seeking to exercise reproductive choice) and intimate associations (for example, same-sex couples seeking the right to marry, or parents seeking to raise children without undue interference from the state).

Anita Allen's essay, "The Jurispolitics of Privacy," focuses on the concept of privacy as embodied in US constitutional and tort law. As Kiss is concerned with what she sees as some feminists' overly hasty dismissal of "rights" as a useful legal tool and category of analysis, so Allen argues for the importance of privacy as a protection against both the government and other citizens. Privacy jurisprudence, she asserts, was important in obtaining favorable constitutional decisions on abortion and reproductive rights. And while the United States Supreme Court used a notion of privacy and individual responsibility in its ruling that the federal government was not obligated to use public funds to pay for abortion, Allen argues that an understanding of privacy-related liberty could be employed to support public funding for abortion. Allen ends by arguing that the privacy tort, though historically rooted in concerns about feminine modesty, has significant potential in helping women address issues such as sexual harassment in the workplace. In Allen's eyes, then, the legal right to privacy functions as one of those boundary markers that Kiss sees as important to struggles to protect, and ultimately to empower, the vulnerable.

Like Allen, Martha Minow and Mary Lyndon Shanley examine how law both reflects and shapes the ways members of a community understand their institutions and social practices. In "Revisioning the Family: Relational Rights and Responsibilities," they argue that three factors have contributed to the deep contestation about what constitutes a family and what family policy and law should be: collapse of the common law paradigm of the unitary, patriarchal family; sociological changes like the increase in divorce and children born to unmarried women; and new reproductive technologies like in vitro fertilization and embryo donation. Minow and Shanley reject two current ways of conceptualizing the family, one as a purely contractual association and the other as an institution that reflects community standards and practices. Unlike contractarians they do not regard private ordering as an appropriate way to determine the responsibilities of family members to one another. Unlike communitarians, they resist shaping family law according to community norms alone. Rather, they suggest that families must be thought of above all as a configuration of relational rights and responsibilities involving ties both between adults and, particularly, between adults and children. Like Allen, they see the usefulness of invoking rights (including the rights to privacy and non-interference) to protect certain family forms and practices. Like Kiss, they believe that certain rights, like the right of adults to marry or raise children, and of children to be cared for and educated, do not separate and isolate individuals but strengthen relational ties.

The relationships between parents and children, and families and political communities, also concern Jean Elshtain. In "Political Children: Reflections on Hannah Arendt's Distinction between Public and Private Life," Elshtain contemplates what circumstances, if any, justify involving children in political action such as public marches and demonstrations, civil disobedience, and even armed confrontation. Using as a point of departure Hannah Arendt's essays, "Reflections on Little Rock" and "Crisis in Education," which criticized the tactic of putting children on the front lines of some battles in the Black civil rights movement in the United States, Elshtain considers what circumstances might legitimate (or require) children's political activity, even when such activity entails physical danger. She makes a distinction between children who are mobilized by the state (often by being yanked out of or alienated from their families), and those who act with their parents or their religious, ethnic, or other community. She presents a nuanced view of childhood, and argues that whether a child should be sheltered from or engaged with political struggle depends in part on the nature of the political context in which that child lives. Elshtain challenges Arendt's distinction between the public discourse of adults and the pre-political lives of children; her attention to childhood shows how difficult it is to draw any hard line between the public and private realms of human activity, but in no way renders the distinction futile or meaningless.

Elizabeth V. Spelman, in "The Heady Political Life of Compassion," is also critical of Arendt's definition of what may appropriately be regarded as "political." Arendt excluded compassion for another's suffering as a political sentiment, regarding personal pain as too idiosyncratic to be made a topic for public discussion and deliberation, the heart of political activity. Using Harriet Jacobs' account of her life in slavery, *Incidents in the Life of a Slave Girl,* Spelman argues, by contrast, that Jacobs was right to regard her suffering as a matter for public debate. The nature of the indignities and sufferings she witnessed and endured, including rape, flogging, and separation from family members, constituted part of her indictment of slavery. Moreover, both Jacobs and Spelman see Jacobs herself as agent as well as victim, assuming as much responsibility for the course of her life as the oppressive constraints of her circumstances allowed. Spelman discusses not only the ways in which Jacobs tried to be self-determining even as a slave, but also the techniques Jacobs used to shape her readers' responses to her story so that those reactions would transcend pity for an individual sufferer to include outrage at the institutional practices and legal constructions of slavery. Spelman's reading of Jacobs' account leads her to conclude, like Elshtain, that while the privacy of family life is an important value, the boundary between private and public worlds is less fixed and more permeable than Arendt thought. The responsibility to trace and define the implications of that boundary arises for political actors in a broad range of circumstances.

Each of these essays complicates, in interesting and different ways, the notion that any "bright line" separates the public from the private realm. Both Allen and Minow and Shanley emphasize the ways in which the privacy involved in reproductive choices and in the formation of family relationships are crucially dependent on legal and public policy decisions that secure different women's abilities to enjoy the benefits of such domains of privacy. Both essays also point to the ways in which considerations of privacy intersect with considerations of justice, both within the family and in the public world of work and community. Spelman's essay emphasizes how "private" suffering can and should be a matter for public debate and political engagement, especially where such suffering is facilitated by publicly endorsed institutions like slavery and by lack of public knowledge and concern about such suffering. While Spelman points out how private suffering is relevant to public politics, Elshtain's essay underlines the ways in which public historical and political contexts profoundly affect the ways in which families as private institutions can and should shelter their children from public political conflicts. Collectively, these essays underscore the variety of normative considerations that contribute to the boundary between public and private realms being both porous and open to contestation.

Feminist rethinking of the traditional distinctions between independence and dependency and traditional demarcations between private and public domains are closely related to underlying concerns about the empowerment of women and members of other marginalized groups. Increasing the representation of various groups within the structures of representative and participatory democracy, safeguarding political and civil rights for all members of the national community, and creating non-hierarchical democratic structures within which everyone's interests are adequately represented are important components of a feminist program to increase equitable access political power. Giving wives and mothers equal legal status with husbands and fathers and extending some protections of family status to unmarried men and women in committed relationships (for example, allowing them access to Family Court in cases of abuse, or allowing partners of gay or lesbian biological parents to establish co-parenting rights) are all steps that promote more equitable power in family relationships. The essays in this volume underline the degree to which different women's inequality with respect to the rights and responsibilities of citizenship or within the family act as an impediment to equality in the other domain, emphasizing the need for all women's empowered participation in both family and public life. (Inequality in the paid labor force also affects women's empowerment in both public and familial life, but that topic is not taken up directly by the essays in this volume.) While the empowerment of different groups of women and members of other marginalized groups is clearly an important concern for all the essays in this volume, it is a predominant concern in the final four essays.

Anna Yeatman's essay, "Feminism and Power," considers three facets of feminism's relationship to power: power as coercion, power as protection, and power as capacity. Considering power as coercion, Yeatman warns against a tendency among emancipatory movements to conflate power and domination. Cautioning against a feminist politics of *ressentiment* that casts powerlessness as moral virtue, Yeatman argues that feminists must be sensitive to differences between democratic and undemocratic uses of "power over" in order to accord reality to democratic achievements and to engage with the task of developing modern democratic institutions. In discussing power as protection, Yeatman criticizes protectionist conceptions of power that cast women as "innocent victims" and occlude women's capacities for agency. Yeatman urges that feminist concerns about paternalistic protection of vulnerable groups instead recognize that all individual agency must be socially constituted and supported. With respect to power as capacity, Yeatman advocates a feminist discourse that recognizes the full range of women's agentic capacities, including that of violence, and which recognizes the need for a democratic state that not only protects, but also respects, women's rights.

Martha Ackelsberg continues Yeatman's project of rethinking power and empowerment in her essay, "Rethinking Anarchism/Rethinking Power: A Contemporary Feminist Perspective." Ackelsberg examines the linkages between the political concerns of communalist anarchism and those of contemporary feminism. While arguing that the anarchist critique of power relations and domination is significant for feminists, Ackelsberg argues that the anarchist distinction between "formal" and "informal" power is problematic for feminists concerned about the empowerment of all those who are marginalized and excluded, as is the anarchist advocacy of the "annihilation" of power. Ackelsberg also examines the similarities and differences between anarchist and anti-state perspectives and contemporary feminist perceptions of state power. Ackelsberg shows how anarchist concerns with resistance and empowerment by means of participation in local, collective and non-hierarchical action are related to feminist views of the connections between the personal and the social, and delineates ways in which feminist practice provides resources for anarchist theory.

In addition to these analyses of the concept of political power, other essays show how various women's position in the family affects their power. The theorists represented here combine an insistence on the importance of family relationships and of women's domestic work and childcare labor with attempts to ensure that women are not victimized and constrained by their family roles and responsibilities. Attention to the boundaries between intimate and political worlds is of central concern to Kimberlé Crenshaw in "Intersectionality and Identity Politics: Learning from Violence against Women of Color," where she explores the ways in which violence against women is shaped by race and class as well as by gender. These multiple sources of identity make much political activity difficult or problematic for many women of color because the descriptive contents of these categories and the narratives on which they are based privilege some experiences and marginalize or exclude others. Not only are women of color often absent from dominant narratives about domestic violence constructed by white women, but women of color may themselves be divided by class, national origin, religion and so forth. Domestic violence highlights the importance such differences make: the ways in which a community allocates resources to deal with such violence reflects whose stories it hears and how it responds to those accounts. Women's abilities to resist and extricate themselves from private situations of domestic violence are affected by options that they have in the public world, and those options are profoundly shaped by race and class and sexual orientation as well as by gender. At stake in understanding these divisions and formulating theory to reflect them is not simply conceptual inclusiveness, but many women's well-being and sometimes their very lives.

In "The Theory and Practice of Freedom: The Case of Battered Women," Nancy Hirschmann uses discourse about domestic violence to develop her argument that the traditional concepts of "negative" and "positive" liberty, "freedom from" and "freedom to," are inadequate to capture all dimensions of women's experience. Trying to understand what "freedom" might mean to a victim of battering who remains with her husband leads Hirschmann to challenge the dichotomy between internal and external barriers to freely chosen activity. The traditional distinction between internal and external barriers rests on an understanding of the woman as an autonomous, separate individual, whereas Hirschmann finds that what is commonly thought of as internal, as pertaining to the woman's psyche alone, is in fact mediated and generated by external events and actions. She finds that the freedom of self-definition necessitates interaction with and the support of a community. By formulating theory out of and in response to the concrete experiences of women Hirschmann believes we can see women's lives more clearly, and also rethink and refine our understandings of freedom and independence, and individual and community.

In addition to shared themes, the conceptual rethinking common to these essays grows out of an engagement with real-world phenomena inadequately accounted for by traditional categories. Such conceptual rethinking is often responsive to ongoing legal and policy issues, to what is happening "on the ground." Sensitivity and responsiveness to real-life situations, especially to those crucially affecting the interests and well-being of women, emerges as a normative standard that is broadly shared by all these attempts to rethink important political concepts in feminist terms. The project of conceptual rethinking common to these essays regards the important concepts of political theory as politically charged and contested. These essays are themselves interventions in the ongoing public debate about the meaning, salience and value of political concepts. They attempt both to critique understandings and deployments of concepts that are detrimental to women's interests, and to reinforce or construct understandings and deployments that protect and promote women's interests.

These rethinkings of the important concepts of political theory are aware that the notion of "women's interests" is itself normatively charged and politically contested. The essays attempt to respond to the plurality of women's experiences and are concerned that their analyses encompass the problems and interests of women who are marginalized in virtue of features such as class, race, and sexual orientation. For example, Fraser and Gordon's essay demonstrates how the politics of associating dependency with pathology operates on class- and race-inflected stereotypes of gender. Minow and Shanley's arguments against contractarian and communitarian conceptualizations of the family reveal how these models are particularly inimical to the interests of those women marginalized in terms of class, race, and sexual orientation. Many of these essays also point to other aspects of identity that affect women's lives that are pertinent to political theory. For instance, Narayan considers how the lack of citizenship status affects women both within immigrant communities and in the overall national contexts of the countries in which they live. Crenshaw's essay, while focusing on the predicaments of women of color who are victims of domestic violence, also reveals how women's immigrant status as well as their non-mainstream linguistic and cultural backgrounds can result in their being inadequately served by prevalent political understandings of and institutional responses to domestic violence.

Feminist political theory appears increasingly to have a dual aspect. On the one hand, there is an ongoing commitment to challenging mainstream political theory in those areas where it is seriously inattentive to the implications of gender. On the other hand, feminist political theory increasingly contains significant debate with and critical responses to other feminist positions. Many of the essays in this volume enter into ongoing debates among feminists, debates that range from questioning the usefulness of certain concepts to feminist political visions to debates over how particular concepts might be deployed to best serve women's needs and goals. For example, Kiss and Allen take issue with various feminist attempts to argue that "rights" and "privacy" are concepts that have little value for women, or that may even be inimical to women's interests. Yeatman, for her part, challenges that feminist perspective that casts powerlessness as a moral virtue.

The rich diversity of perspectives represented in this volume make it clear that this is not the historical moment of "grand theory," but rather of careful attention to details and nuances of political categories and individual and group experiences that would have to be accommodated in any theory. Feminism, once thought to be a unified critique of the mainstream, or tied to traditional schools of thought such as Marxism or liberalism, is multifaceted. Not only are there differences in perspective among the essays in this volume, but even some individual essays are ambivalent about the usefulness of various concepts and approaches to feminist political theory. These differences and ambivalences seem to reflect the coming-of-age of feminist political theory. The essays in this volume permit neither complacency nor self-satisfaction. They force us to rethink issues that we thought we understood, and to reexamine the implications of settled positions. The feminist theory in this volume is "contentious" in the best sense of the word, that is, it invites critical and open-ended inquiry into what Plato called "the most important questions," questions about how we are both to understand and to order our lives in the political community.

Alchemy or Fool's Gold?
Assessing Feminist Doubts About Rights

Elizabeth Kiss

Introduction: Feminism's Uneasy Relationship to Rights

Should rights play an important role in feminist theory and practice? The answer is not as self-evident as it may appear to be, because contemporary feminism has a profoundly ambiguous relationship to rights. So many feminist goals have been expressed as demands for rights that a central role for rights within feminism's vocabulary seems assured. Yet many feminist theorists, especially among those employing more distinctively feminist approaches to ethics and political theory, express misgivings about or even outright hostility to rights-talk.

Demands for rights have figured prominently in the rhetoric of women's movements from the beginning. Feminism traces its lineage to social movements opposing absolutist and aristocratic rule in the seventeenth through nineteenth centuries, movements that have bequeathed to us the modern vocabulary of rights in its distinctively egalitarian and universalist form. To be sure, many rights champions preached the equal dignity of all while systematically denying it to most. But feminists turned the masters' tools against them, using the rhetoric of rights to press for women's full participation in political, professional, and economic life, for control over their reproductive lives, and for equality within marriage.[1] From Mary Wollstonecraft and Olympe de Gouges to the drafters of the Seneca Falls Declaration, the Equal Rights Amendment, and the International Convention on the Elimination of all Forms of Discrimination against Women, many feminists have made demands for rights central to their cause.

Their record of success has, of course, been mixed. In the lives of women (as in so much else) ours is an age less of rights triumphant than of continuing and massive wrongs.[2] Only very recently, for example, have women's groups begun to achieve a measure of international consensus around the view that abuse and subordination of women is a major and badly neglected human rights problem.[3] Nevertheless, struggles by women to claim and vindicate rights have altered social relationships, practices, and institutions, and have changed the way many women perceive themselves. Small wonder, then, that some theorists have ascribed a transformative power to rights, a power Patricia Williams likens to alchemy.[4]

A less positive picture of rights emerges from much of the recent literature in Anglo-American feminist theory, however. This is not to say that feminist theorists deny that women have achieved significant gains over the past century through struggles for rights.[5] But in looking to the future, many adopt a skeptical or even negative attitude toward rights. The language of rights, they claim, cannot adequately express women's experience, nor can it articulate the moral and political problems and goals of greatest concern to feminists.

Indeed, the most striking aspect of feminist doubts about rights is that they arise from so many otherwise disparate viewpoints. For feminism is not, of course, a monolithic movement, but a diverse and contentious field of inquiry and action, and doubts about rights abound. Feminists who embrace an ethic of care contrast their approach with an ethic of rights which they seek to supplement or even supplant.[6] Cultural feminists and feminist communitarians criticize rights for being overly abstract and impersonal and for reflecting and endorsing a selfish and atomistic vision of human nature and an excessively conflictual view of social life.[7] Feminist legal scholars argue that rights analysis obscures male dominance,[8] while feminist post-structuralists charge that rights language is bound up with socio-linguistic hierarchies of gender and with the outdated patriarchal fiction of a unitary self.[9] Finally, many theorists argue that feminist political strategies should not be centered around rights, claiming that such an approach reinforces a patriarchal *status quo*[10] and, in effect, abandons women to their rights.[11] Far from being the moral equivalent of alchemy, these arguments suggest, rights are fool's gold. To focus on rights is to abandon an effective commitment to women's emancipation and empowerment. For these critics, taking gender seriously raises grave doubts about the nature and value of rights.

Are feminist critics of rights right? Or do they misunderstand rights and misjudge their value? The answer, I believe, is both of the above. An assessment of feminist doubts about rights reveals some valuable insights and promising directions of research and political action, but also serious problems of overstatement, inconsistency, and political naiveté. At their best, feminist critiques demonstrate how sensitivity to the harms and deprivations women experience by virtue of their gender reveals the limitations of some traditional images of rights and approaches to rights activism, particularly those which cast states as the sole source of rights violations and courts or legislatures as necessary and sufficient guarantors of rights. Feminist theorists have also championed other moral concepts and approaches, reminding us that, whatever value rights have, it is impoverishing to view them as occupying the entire moral realm. At their worst, feminist critics fail to distinguish between the concept of rights in general and particular aspects or uses of the concept. Or they bemoan how rights function, ignoring their practical importance for members of subordinate groups, including women.

We should draw three lessons from the strengths and weaknesses of feminist critiques of rights. First, feminist political theory needs a more refined model of rights and a fuller understanding of how rights structure relations and institutions. Such an understanding would counteract the tendency to give up on rights too quickly and would put theorists in a better position to assess the powers as well as the limitations of rights. Second, while rights have more to offer feminist theory and practice than many feminists realize, the converse is also true. Attention to the injuries of gender and to the texture of women's lives can help us to think more acutely about what rights are and how they work, to construct a richer understanding of rights. Third, although feminists should not turn their backs on rights, some aspects of the feminist project do transcend the realm of rights-talk. In their efforts to imagine and create new life possibilities for women and men, feminists have to confront substantive questions about human values, meanings and ideals which rights-talk cannot fully capture.

Feminist doubts about rights can usefully be divided into those that are primarily *conceptual* and those that focus on *practical* or strategic concerns. I will examine each in turn.

The Feminist Critique of Rights as Boundaries

Perhaps the most common feminist criticism of rights is the charge that rights entail morally undesirable images of self and society. This claim is usually presented as a conceptual critique directed at the general category of rights rather than against any particular substantive rights theory. The concept of equal rights, Nancy Hirschmann argues in a recent example of this view, says we must respect one another not because we are connected but because of rights which highlight the lines of demarcation between us. Rights provide us with a language of distrust and competition rather than of relationship.[12] Other theorists agree, arguing that as rights-bearers we are separated and distanced from each other so that to respect a person's rights is to keep one's distance from him or her.[13] Rights construct us as bounded selves requiring protection from the encroachments of others, who are seen as threats to our autonomy and integrity. The concept of rights implies a moral absolutism in which the self exists in glorious isolation, unencumbered by obligations to others.[14] As the paradigmatic language of individualism, rights-talk legitimates aggressive selfishness and denies community, producing, as Simone Weil complained half a century ago, a shrill nagging of claims and counter-claims.[15]

care

Such arguments lead some feminists to conclude that the moral vision of self and society associated with the concept of rights is characteristically masculine and morally unattractive. Echoing Carol Gilligan's influential contrast between two moral voices, an ethic of care and an ethic of rights, feminist critics contrast a feminist (or feminine) self, conceived as connected to others, with the rights-bearing self, which is (or at least thinks it is) separate from others. It is no coincidence, they suggest, that Joel Feinberg, in his well-known essay "The Nature and Value of Rights," in which he linked rights to human dignity, wrote: "Having rights enables us to stand up like men, to look others in the eye, and to feel in some fundamental way the equal of anyone."[16] Women, these rights critics suggest, shouldn't strive to stand up like men, but rather should contest the masculine image of the typical rights bearer as an isolated self insisting on his boundaries.[17] Moreover, whether or not rights-bearing selves are characteristically masculine, some argue, an emphasis on rights is morally undesirable. Rights-talk evokes the image of a Hobbesian war of all against all. Indeed, a few theorists portray the dangers of rights rhetoric in almost apocalyptic tones. For them, the rights-bearing person is self-destructive and lives in a grim and socially fragmented world which threatens to collapse into a Kafkaesque nightmare of solitary individuals.[18]

Conceptual and Practical Flaws of the Boundary Critique

The feminist critique of rights as boundaries has serious flaws. Its chief conceptual flaw is that it ignores the many ways rights function besides serving as boundaries. Its chief practical flaw is that it overlooks the importance of the boundary-marking features of rights for vulnerable people, including women.

Equating rights with boundaries dramatically underestimates the range of functions rights possess, and the diversity of moral and political views that employ rights. This critique reduces the concept of a right to one category of rights, negative rights to non-interference. In the process it also reduces the rich variety of substantive views that embrace rights to libertarianism. Thus what bills itself as a sweeping criticism of all rights is in fact directed at a particular political ethic employing a narrow range of rights.

It is certainly true that one archetypal image of a right is that of a claim to be left alone, protected from interference by others. The image is particularly associated with the classical liberal triad of natural rights to life, liberty, and property. But even in the context of classical liberalism this represents a one-sided picture of rights, since it does not fit many traditional liberal rights like the right to vote or to a fair trial. Moreover, for the past century or more, rights theorists have recognized that rights encompass a broader range of functions. Wesley Hohfeld's influential typology of rights, developed in 1919, distinguished between four primary functions of legal rights: they can confer *liberties, immunities, claims,* and *powers.*[19] While contemporary rights theorists often modify or expand Hohfeld's categories,[20] his work clearly demonstrated that rights are internally complex and that they function as normative relationships, prescribing what others must or must not do.

As Hohfeld showed, rights can serve to separate and protect us from others; this is, roughly, the function of liberty and immunity rights. But rights also confer claims on others and powers to alter normative relationships. Rights as claims entitle people to expect and demand the help of others in the form of goods or services (such as a right to a fair trial or to free public education). Rights as powers authorize people to alter legal and moral relationships – as in the right to vote, to marry or divorce, to form associations, or to enter contracts.

In condemning rights as isolating and conflictual, feminist critics ignore the many ways in which rights institutionalize schemes of mutual obligation. There is nothing isolating about a right to vote, to form associations, or to receive free childhood immunizations. And while many rights, like political rights and rights to free expression, do enable people to express conflicts, they also create a framework for social cooperation.[21] Indeed, ascribing rights to someone implies a moral connection to her or him. Rights define a moral community; having rights means that my interests, aspirations, and vulnerabilities matter enough to impose duties on others.[22]

It is true that appeals to rights have been used to justify selfishness, privilege and moral indifference in the face of human suffering and deprivation. But while rights-talk figures prominently in views that seek to minimize the legal and moral claims people can make on one another, there is no necessary or exclusive link between the concept of rights and a substantive moral and political position like libertarianism. Rights also play a central role in arguments supporting more inclusive and egalitarian social arrangements.

In linking the concept of rights with a libertarian political ethic, some feminists appear to think that libertarians possess a monopoly over the legitimate meaning of rights. But we have no reason to accept this either as historical description or as theoretical argument. Through a rich history of political struggle and of legal and philosophical argument, the scope of moral and legal rights has expanded and diversified dynamically. We can, of course, argue over which rights are justified or valid. But any effort to evaluate the *concept* of rights must take into account the full range of rights that have currency today. The conceptual critique of rights as boundaries fails to do this.

However, the conceptual critique of rights is problematic even if we recast it as an explicit argument against the liberty and immunity rights celebrated by libertarians. For one thing, liberties and immunities, like other rights, prescribe what people can do or expect from others and hence define rather than simply deny relationships. Liberties and immunities can radically alter the balance of power within social, economic and political relationships. For instance, recognition of an immunity right against coerced marital sex profoundly alters marriage, giving wives new power and making them into more than performers of duties within marital sexual relations. But this immunity does not deny or destroy the relationship of marriage; it redefines it and makes it better.

The example of immunity rights against coerced sex[23] points to a deeper practical problem with feminist critiques of rights as boundaries: these critiques underestimate the importance to women of the boundary-marking functions of rights. Many feminist struggles have sought to guarantee women's capacities to set boundaries. Efforts to repeal the laws of coverture, to criminalize marital rape, to make sexual harassment a justiciable offense, and to protect women from forced sterilizations and other coercive medical procedures fall into this category. Feminists who issue sweeping denunciations of rights to non-interference as atomistic and isolating ignore the ways in which women need precisely these sorts of rights. As Marilyn Frye argues, total powerlessness is being unconditionally accessible. The slave who decides to exclude the master from her hut is declaring herself not a slave.[24] Vulnerable and stigmatized people often have the most to gain from the protection that abstract and impersonal frameworks of rights can provide, and from the strong images of integrity and self-assertion associated with rights.[25] When a woman is still struggling for a room of her own, as Frances Olsen argues, she is unlikely to complain that rights isolate her.[26] An abstract preference for connection over separation ignores the reality that, for the less powerful members of any society, connection often means invasion and intrusion rather than intimacy.[27] And worries about how rights reinforce the fiction of the unitary, assertive self ignore the fact that women everywhere remain systematically disadvantaged and disproportionally subject to violence and, in many countries, still lack basic enforceable rights of contract, inheritance, and education.[28] In a world in which many women are vulnerable to abuse, especially abuse by those claiming connection to them through bonds of love, family, religion, or culture, they need more, not fewer, powers of self-assertion. Feminists who uncritically celebrate connection at the expense of demarcation commit a utopian fallacy. In its strongest versions, which claim or imply that women should *abandon* the language of rights, the critique of rights as boundaries reflects a chasm between theory and practice, condemning rights from a perspective totally divorced from the lives of the majority of the world's women.

Feminist Sources of Skepticism and Insight

Why have many feminists found this overstated critique of rights compelling? Why, in other words, might attention to women's lives encourage skepticism toward rights, especially those rights associated with traditional liberal or libertarian views? The answer points to some of the ways in which feminism can help generate valuable insights about rights.

As many feminist theorists have stressed, traditional liberal conceptions of rights often deal inadequately with the injuries and deprivations experienced by women. Indeed, liberal rights theory has sometimes obscured and even legitimated women's injuries. The classic example of this is the way relationships of abuse and exploitation within marriage have been given moral and legal protection by liberal conceptions of a right to immunity from state interference within the private realm. Feminists have persuasively criticized traditional liberal understandings of the public/private distinction, stressing how politics shapes these boundaries and how oppressive power relationships can persist within them.[29]

Yet the problem is not with rights as such, but with the tendency to cast the state in the role of exclusive rights violator, ignoring the many ways in which non-state actors, like employers or spouses, can threaten people's freedom or well-being. Because the distinctive injuries of gender do not fit the images of state oppression that shaped traditional liberal understandings of rights,[30] attention to women's lives highlights two lessons of great importance for rights theory. The first is that we need to be skeptical about arguments that claim natural, metaphysical, self-evident, or in any other sense final validity for any particular set of rights. Rights are practices and should be assessed by whether they actually make a difference in people's lives. If a beating administered by a soldier counts as a rights violation, but one administered by a spouse does not, something is wrong with our account of rights. The second lesson is the need to recognize the limitations of the citizen/state dichotomy in conceptualizing rights. While the state remains the primary enforcer of rights, the diversity of social sources of harm and deprivation and the ubiquity of inequalities of power means that people need rights in a variety of social contexts. Rights must begin, as Eleanor Roosevelt said, in small places, close to home.[31] Thus attentiveness to women's lives highlights the need for a more contextual and dynamic understanding of rights, encompassing not only law-making and litigation but also the claims and expectations that shape the texture of everyday life.[32]

Obviously, these lessons are not exclusively linked to the experiences of women. They do, however, tend to be lessons best grasped by those who analyze social arrangements and norms on the basis of their effects on the less powerful. It is not surprising, then, that a number of scholars – Martha Minow, Jennifer Nedelsky, Elizabeth Schneider, Patricia Williams and others – have constructed innovative arguments about rights in work informed by a commitment to feminism. While their views differ in many other respects, all of these authors conceive rights as practices or relationships that arise out of political action and should be evaluated by their impact on people's lives.[33]

Beyond Rights: Care, Trust and Other Values

Some feminists are less concerned with what rights-talk says than with what it leaves unsaid. Their doubts about rights arise from a conviction that moral theory should pay more attention to concepts besides rights. This strand of feminist thought reflects a number of dissatisfactions with contemporary ethics: that it is excessively dominated by a legalistic, impartial and rationalistic model of morality, and that it systematically ignores or underplays the moral relevance of activities, relationships and attitudes that have traditionally been associated with women. The first dissatisfaction is shared by other critics of the Kantian–utilitarian mainstream of modern ethics, such as Bernard Williams and Alasdair MacIntyre.[34] The second is more distinctively feminist; it seeks to construct alternatives to what it views as the one-sidedness of contemporary ethics by drawing, in part, on a critical but appreciative theoretical encounter with women's lives.

Care

This shift in moral focus is exemplified by feminist work within the ethics of care, work inspired in large part by Carol Gilligan's *In a Different Voice.* Gilligan described a distinctive moral voice, the ethic of care or of relationships, which she claimed was employed more commonly by women than men and which she argued was as coherent and mature as the theoretically paradigmatic ethic of justice and rights.[35]

Care ethics has become the focus of lively debate within feminist theory.[36] Its proponents argue that dominant modern approaches to ethics ignore or underplay the relevance of intimate human relationships and of emotional responses like compassion as a source of theorizing about moral life in favor of a model of ethics based on impartial reasoning and public legislation.[37] As a result, personal connections, and the care, attentiveness and responsibility that is the first virtue of central human relationships like those between parents (especially, given traditional gender roles, mothers) and children, have not received the theoretical attention they deserve. The result has been an excessively rationalistic and legalistic model of moral life. Much of the work within a feminist ethics of care seeks to redress this imbalance.

It is easy to see how the shift in moral perspective taken by care theorists would make them attentive to the limitations of rights. In relationships with children, partners, friends and colleagues, we regard an attitude defined by and limited to concern for the other person's rights as morally problematic precisely because it constitutes a failure of intimacy or collegiality. Compared to a self-conscious ethic of rights and duties, an ethic of care may often be, as Kent Greenawalt suggests, superior at the personal level.[38]

Care ethics is only one example of this trend in feminist theory. Some theorists, inspired by Simone Weil, have focused on attentiveness to others as a foundational moral virtue.[39] Annette Baier has embarked on an effort to construct an ethics centered on trust, rather than on obligation or rights, and has argued, drawing on David Hume, that corrected (sometimes rule-corrected) sympathy, not law-discerning reason, is the fundamental moral capacity.[40]

trust

A full discussion of feminist arguments for care, trust and other values is beyond the scope of this essay. Many versions of care ethics have been rightly criticized on a number of counts: for relying on essentialized gender stereotypes, for ignoring the ways a history of subordination may have shaped women's behavior, for privatizing ethics and ignoring the ethical dilemmas raised by our relations with strangers, and for confusing an objection to the substance of some moral principles with an objection to moral principles as such. At the same time, this literature has made some valuable contributions to ethics, exploring issues of moral agency and moral development that dominant ethical approaches leave under-theorized. And some care theorists have avoided essentializing gender or romanticizing care and have started to elaborate how a commitment to the moral centrality of care might reshape politics and public life.[41]

What implications do these feminist approaches have for uses of rights? At its most ambitious, care ethics would represent a comprehensive moral alternative, doing away with the need for other values like rights. Among care theorists, Nel Noddings is perhaps the only one who appears to propose a comprehensive care-based ethic.[42] But such a view is untenable, for at least two reasons. First, affirming the moral importance of care in personal relationships does not have self-evident implications for politics. It does not answer hard questions about distributing resources, care and moral attention among and between intimates, fellow citizens, and strangers. Any conceivable society would face such questions, and answering them requires attention to distributive issues involving considerations of justice and rights. Not surprisingly, the fullest attempts by feminist theorists to explore the political implications of an ethic of care involve explicit and unapologetic use of rights.[43] Second, personal relationships themselves can be sites of inequality, exploitation, and abuse. Caring relationships can demean or oppress those cared for, or reduce carers to performers of duties trapped in patterns of chronic self-denial.[44] Hence an ethic of care needs principles about what distinguishes valuable from oppressive forms of care. Theories of care that ignore questions of exploitation and abuse threaten to romanticize the very relationships that feminist proponents of rights sought to criticize in the first place. Dealing with these problems requires ensuring that people are protected from harm and guaranteed the capacity to exercise some control over their lives and to make certain claims on one another – precisely the kind of moral work which rights do.

Most care theorists believe that care should complement or reshape considerations of rights and justice, not supplant them. They affirm a need for more than justice.[45] What might this mean for feminist approaches to rights? First, and most straightforwardly, these arguments stress that rights-talk does not capture the whole of morality. This may seem an obvious point: few rights theorists would actually claim that rights constitute a wholly adequate moral vocabulary. But it is one thing to acknowledge this point and quite another to develop a rich and persuasive account of other moral concepts and values. Thus feminist work elaborating the nature and value of care, trust and attention enriches our understanding of the moral realm.

Second, those who stress the centrality of psychological issues like responsiveness, empathy and perception to an understanding of moral life challenge dominant understandings of the tasks of moral theory. There is a difference, as Lawrence Blum points out, between holding the right principles and having the capacity to perceive others' distress or to recognize a situation as morally salient.[46] Theorists of rights and justice have tended to concentrate on generating correct principles rather than on examining the moral dispositions and capacities people need to sensitively and imaginatively live by those principles.[47] Yet neither inquiry can take the place of the other.

Indeed, work on care and other values may generate insights into the conditions under which rights will be respected. The spread of a human rights culture may depend less on developing people's capacity to discern universal principles and more on what Baier has called a progress of sentiments,[48] on fostering people's sense that the suffering of strangers is a wound to all humanity.[49] In this case work on moral sentiments and moral education, and on values beyond rights, needs to be taken seriously by rights theorists as integral to their own project. Since a focus on moral capacities may enable rights theorists to understand more about how rights as relationships can be established and preserved, combining these approaches represents a fruitful direction for future theoretical work.

Finally, work on care, trust and other values can supplement and enrich rights theory by affecting the substance of rights and of principles of justice. Most contemporary theories of justice continue the centuries-old neglect of basic issues of child-rearing and care for dependents.[50] Some of the most interesting recent feminist work on law, justice, and politics seeks to remedy this neglect by constructing principles of justice and frameworks of rights that take more seriously the facts of human dependency, neediness and vulnerability and hence the moral value and social importance of care.[51]

Feminist work on moral concepts beyond rights helps broaden our understanding of the moral realm and of the tasks of moral theory. This work may also bring important insights to rights theory and feminist politics. But developing these insights requires thinking more creatively about rights rather than abandoning them.

Questioning the Practical Value of Rights

There remains another major feminist objection to rights. Many feminists question the *practical* value of rights, arguing that a politics devoted to securing rights, especially legal rights, fails to enable women to overcome systematic gender inequality. They charge that appeals to rights will not fundamentally change women's lives. In fact, according to stronger versions of the objection, rights approaches are not only useless but may even be detrimental,[52] actually harming women. To focus on rights, therefore, is tantamount to abandoning women.

To abandon someone is to be indifferent to his or her fate, to fail to show concern for how he or she fares. How can a politics based on a concern for someone's rights constitute a failure of concern for that person? In what ways might a feminism centered on demands for women's rights abandon the women it is intended to empower and liberate? The practical objection to rights is complex, reflecting a range of areas and levels of concern. I shall distinguish three ways in which feminists allege that rights fail us in practice: the problem may be *definitional, strategic,* or *substantive.* The first concern arises when rights are defined in ways that prevent women from enjoying or exercising them. The second refers to the tendency of movements for rights to ignore broader strategic issues about how rights can be institutionalized as social practices. And the third contends that a focus on rights can constrain or distort attempts to transform substantive values and aspirations. In practice, definitional, strategic, and substantive concerns are often intertwined, and all three raise questions about the power and limits of the law. But it is helpful to distinguish them because they lead to different sorts of "abandonment" and pose different challenges for feminist rights theory and practice.

Exclusion by Definition: Explicit and Implicit Forms of Gender Discrimination

Focusing on rights can be unhelpful or harmful if rights are defined in ways that leave some people out. The most blatant example of explicit exclusion is the institution of slavery, under which some people are objects of the rights of others, and rights are violated if a slave escapes to his or her freedom. Women have often been explicitly excluded from enjoying rights guaranteed to men. They have, for instance, been denied the right to vote, to hold and inherit property, to have custody of their children, to own property in their own name within marriage, and to enter many professions and occupations. Explicit exclusions like these can only be overcome through struggles to extend rights to those excluded. Under circumstances like these, the value of feminist campaigns for rights appears beyond question. Most feminist rights critics acknowledge this, noting, as Carol Smart does, that there is no reason to visit a late-twentieth-century disillusionment with legal rights upon earlier feminist movements which faced a very different set of circumstances.[53] What most critics do not seem to realize is that many women around the world still face, or until very recently faced, explicit forms of exclusion. For instance, Swiss women were denied suffrage until 1971 and did not get to vote in cantonal elections in Appenzell until 1990. In Morocco, daughters legally inherit half as much as sons and women cannot obtain passports without permission from their husbands or fathers. And Papua New Guinea has no laws against domestic violence, and in parts of the country husbands have the right under customary law to beat their wives if they exhibit willfulness or fail in their duties as wives, mothers, or gardeners.[54] Moreover, many countries that only recently extended rights to women at the statutory or constitutional level have not taken sufficient steps to ensure that women's rights will be enforced by police and judges. Basic struggles for women's legal rights are not a relic of the distant past.

Most feminist concern about exclusionary definitions of rights is directed against rights that exclude women implicitly, not explicitly. Laws and rights formulated in gender-neutral language can still systematically disadvantage women. These disadvantages, if they are serious or pervasive enough, can amount to gender discrimination, threatening women's equal status as employees or citizens.[55] For instance, feminists have denounced medical insurance plans that claim to offer equal coverage for male and female workers but exclude all pregnancy-related costs. Such pregnancy exclusions (in programs that provided benefits for employees undergoing procedures only performed on men, like vasectomies and prostatectomies) were upheld by the United States Supreme Court in the 1970s on the ground that, since not all women are or become pregnant, these programs did not discriminate against women.[56] Feminists have also challenged gender-neutral requirements for jobs, like minimum height rules, which systematically disadvantage women and which either serve no significant job-related purpose, or could be handled in a more gender-inclusive way, for instance by changing equipment to make it suitable for use by shorter people.[57]

Rights and laws can also implicitly exclude women because they are formulated or adjudicated in ways that fail to take the experiences of women into account. For instance, the spousal exclusion in rape law, found in British law and until recently in most US state penal codes,[58] fails to reflect the fact that coercive sex can and does occur within marriage. Spousal exclusion clauses have been rationalized on the ground that marriage constitutes a blanket consent to sexual intimacy. But not only is this reasoning unwarranted, it is a living remnant of the common law view of wives as chattel.[59] Some feminists have argued more generally that rape law, by requiring courts to establish whether or not the victim could be perceived as having consented, ends up interpreting many cases of unwilling submission to rape as consensual sex. Fearful submission, a common reaction to rape, ends up being construed as consent to sex, and the law finds that no rape occurred.[60] Similarly, feminists have argued that the equal force standard restricting the use of force in rightful self-defense to that which is equal to the force employed by one's assailant is based on masculine stereotypes and seriously disadvantages many women, as well as men who are less able to fight than their assailants.[61] And they have charged that the reasonable person standard used in adjudication often ends up being defined in male-biased ways, as for instance when judges conclude that what a female plaintiff experienced as sexual harassment was no more than harmless flirtation.

Many debates have arisen within feminist jurisprudence over how to address the discriminatory effects of such gender-neutral rights and standards. In particular, there is great disagreement among feminists over the advisability of formulating gender-specific rights for women (like maternal rights) or of using a reasonable woman standard, as some courts have done, to guide adjudication of charges of sexual harassment.[62] Proponents of these changes contend they are necessary in order to get judges, lawyers and policymakers to take women's claims seriously. Critics charge that these proposals are wrong in principle, because they vitiate civic equality, or dangerous in practice, because they reinforce oppressive gender stereotypes. These debates raise important and difficult issues about the meaning of equal rights and equal citizenship. But they are not debates over the value of rights-talk: both sides are arguing over how best to define and institutionalize rights in order to move toward gender justice.

Feminist Critiques of Rights-Based Strategies

A second kind of objection to rights-based politics is that it generates ineffective or even counterproductive strategies. This might occur in at least four different ways. First, a feminist politics of rights may ignore the many possible gaps between legal principle and actual practice. For instance, achieving formal equality of rights may have little practical effect because it leaves underlying social inequalities intact. So a rights strategy focused solely on winning formal equality of rights may actually obscure women's continuing subordination by appearing to grant women a dramatic moral victory. This classic critique of equal rights was summarized with elegant irony by Anatole France in his comment that the law, in its egalitarian majesty, forbids rich and poor alike to sleep under bridges.[63] By itself, formal equality of rights may not alter people's circumstances substantially. So, for instance, granting women equal legal rights with men in the labor market will have limited effect if most women continue to be doomed to lower status jobs through a combination of gender inequality within families, unequal access to wealth, education, and other forms of social capital, and the invidious influence of prejudice and harassment.

A gap between legal principle and practice can arise in other ways as well. Procedures for enforcing rights may be excessively costly, ineffective, intimidating, or degrading. Or they may privatize and narrow claims of harm in ways that obscure the larger structural inequalities at the root of the problem.[64] Formal procedures for dealing with rape, gender discrimination, and sexual harassment exhibit many of these features. Conversely, what look like cumbersome administrative procedures sometimes work better than grander-sounding alternatives. For instance, as Kim Scheppele has argued, some Western European legal systems appear to place strong limits on abortion, requiring permission from several doctors before an abortion can be performed. In practice, however, early abortions are fairly easy to obtain. By contrast, the United States has granted constitutional protection for early abortions, but because of state refusal to fund abortions and the intimidating effects of anti-abortion activism on the medical profession, abortions have actually become increasingly difficult to obtain, especially for poor women and women in certain regions.[65] Feminist rights strategies which ignore such gaps between principle and practice can in effect abandon women.

Second, rights strategies may concentrate solely on attaining *ex post facto* redress for violations of rights rather than also focusing on the forms of mobilization required to create conditions for preventing these violations in the first place.[66] The harm has already occurred by the time the rights strategy is available, and successful redress may be so indirect that it is not experienced as empowering by the people who were harmed.

Third, rights strategies can ignore the fact that legal rights may have unintended negative effects. Legal reforms designed to empower women may end up making them more vulnerable to invasive surveillance by state agencies or to administrative or medical treatment that threatens their freedom and dignity.[67]

These three worries about the effectiveness of rights strategies represent valuable warnings against complacency and reminders of the limits of legal reform. They do not, however, demonstrate the futility of feminist efforts to secure rights. In fact, implicit in these criticisms is a commitment to achieving social conditions in which women do have effective, socially guaranteed rights. The main lesson to be drawn is to avoid focusing rights strategies too narrowly. Feminists should not conceive rights simply as commodities the law grants, but as social relationships to be established and secured. Courts and legislatures are necessary but insufficient guarantors of rights; in the end rights can only be secured through collective social and political activity. Hence feminist rights strategies need to take account of a broader range of forms of mobilization required to make rights effective.[68] Initial efforts against sexual harassment, for instance, have understandably focused on establishing new legal definitions, codes and procedures. But women also need to develop a repertoire of less formal individual and collective strategies to confront harassers effectively. Ultimately, the efforts' success will depend on broader processes of social education,[69] and on a shift in cultural norms about the forms *eros* can and should take in relations between co-workers and civic equals.

But while it is important to recognize the limits of legal rights and the potentially negative effects of legal enforcement, the sweeping claim that legal rights do more harm than good is unwarranted. All legal and political action has unintended effects, but these can be positive as well as negative. The history of rights activism abounds with examples of movements which used demands for legal rights as a catalyst for mobilization and social change. Even individual legal defeats need to be viewed in a larger social context. Kathryn Abrams has argued, for instance, that while some courts have made the requirements for a finding of sexual harassment stricter, resulting in highly publicized defeats for individual plaintiffs, the threat of lawsuits has led to a dramatic proliferation of programs to educate managers and employees about sexual harassment. In the long run such programs may do more to achieve respect for women's rights.[70]

A fourth and final worry about rights strategies is that appeals to rights backfire because they give rise to countervailing rights claims.[71] People appeal to a variety of rights, including religious and cultural rights, rights of free speech, and the rights of the unborn, to justify opposition to a range of feminist goals. This is hardly surprising: history abounds with examples of such countervailing rights claims, including those through which women, Blacks, and other subordinated groups invoked rights originally designed to exclude them. A discussion of these different rights controversies is beyond the scope of this essay, but the important point is that they *are* different controversies, which can only be evaluated case by case. The presence of countervailing rights claims does not demonstrate that rights-talk is inherently biased against women, nor does it give feminists a reason to abandon the vocabulary of rights. After all, values other than rights, including duty, virtue, conformity to nature, and many others, can and have been invoked against feminism. Some opposing rights claims represent moral or political positions incompatible with gender justice, and should be rejected by feminists. But others represent genuine moral dilemmas for feminists, or legitimately justify constraints on the pursuit of feminist goals. Feminists should evaluate each conflict on its own terms and strive to resolve or balance such conflicts in ways that strengthen gender equality.

There are many limits to the capacity of legal rights to change the world. And no moral vocabulary, including rights, carries a no-risk guarantee. But law remains a powerful force in shaping social reality. Feminists who dismiss efforts at legal reform because they undermine more radical challenges to male dominance,[72] or who think rights conflicts vitiate the value of all rights strategies, do women a disservice. The point is not to reject rights strategies, but to situate them within broader political and cultural efforts.

Rights and the Substance of Feminist Ideals

While strategic concerns about rights center on how rights may fail to achieve feminist goals, some feminists worry that a politics of rights will impede efforts to *envision* feminist goals. On this view, an excessive focus on rights can constrain or distort the substance of feminist aspirations. I call this final concern about the practical value of rights the substantive objection.

Sometimes people harm themselves in exercising their rights. For instance, women in some wealthy societies exercise control over their bodies by starving themselves to attain a waif-like look. Their choices are heavily influenced, of course, by advertising and popular culture – but this does not change the fact that they are choices. And yet the effects of these choices are often harmful and sometimes deadly. Another example is the widespread voluntary use by women of implants for breast enlargement to "cure" the "problem" which plastic surgeons call "micromastia" (small breast size).[73] Women who opt for breast implants exercise control over their bodies.[74] But the fact that an estimated 1.6 million women in the United States have chosen to enlarge their breasts for cosmetic reasons is an exercise of rights troubling to many feminists.[75]

From a rights perspective, the breast implant issue may appear simple: either women have a moral or legal right to choose breast implants, or they do not. But feminists may want to adopt a different approach, which neither condones nor seeks to prohibit breast implants, but rather criticizes them in their present social and cultural context. In a society with greater gender equality, women and men might choose to have plastic surgery to alter the shape of their body parts to please themselves and their loved ones, just as people now alter their hair styles.[76] What is problematic about current practices of breast enlargement (beyond the health risks these procedures may entail) is what they reveal about women's judgments of self-worth and thereby about the gendered nature of the social bases of self-respect in our society.[77] Perhaps the best feminist response is neither insistence on nor denial of rights, but efforts to change and broaden our culture's images of women's success. An exclusive focus on rights can distort the moral salience of the issue and constrict our moral imagination in responding to it.

Similar arguments can be made about many feminist issues of greater urgency than breast implants. Around the world, gender hierarchy, often combined with hierarchies of class, race, and culture, severely constrains women's possibilities. Struggles to expand and secure women's rights will be critical to any effort to empower women. But feminists also need to strive to broaden women's perceptions of who they can become, to develop values, ideals and narratives that will enable women to resist the forces that constrain and limit their lives. This means articulating new visions of strength and desire and new models of relationship, as well as promoting a richer understanding of the dilemmas and obstacles women face. Constructing feminist visions of new and better possibilities in the lives of both women and men requires acts of moral imagination that rights language by itself cannot capture.

Conclusion

Are rights alchemy or fool's gold? While some feminist worries about the limitations of rights are well founded, they yield no persuasive general challenge to rights. Feminist theorists need to resist the conceptual confusion and political naiveté that underlies the current tendency to dismiss rights or condemn them out of hand. At the same time feminist insights can help us construct better understandings of what rights are, how they work, and what political and cultural strategies are required to secure them.

Equal rights for women represent no magic formula, no instant recipe for a golden age of gender equality. Many hard questions remain about how best to articulate and institutionalize feminist demands for women's moral and social equality. Nevertheless, the rhetoric of rights, and the liberties, immunities, claims and powers rights confer, remain crucial to efforts to protect and empower women and to create and maintain social conditions of gender justice. In challenging the norms and practices of gender hierarchy, feminist theorists tackle questions and tasks that can reshape, and sometimes transcend, the realm of rights. But it is misguided and dangerous for us to turn our backs on rights in the process.

Notes

Earlier versions of this essay were presented at a conference on Feminist Ethics and Social Policy at the University of Pittsburgh, the University of Toronto, the Institute for Advanced Study, the Princeton Center for Human Values, and the National Humanities Center. I am very grateful for the responses I received, particularly from Harlan Beckley, Hilary Bok, David Dyzenhaus, Samuel Fleischacker, Sally Haslanger, Albert Hirschmann, Amy Gutmann, Victoria Kamsler, George Kateb, Joan Scott, Kathryn Sklar, and Joan Tronto. Special thanks to Kent Greenawalt for detailed comments, to Jeff Holzgrefe, Molly Shanley and Michael Walzer for editorial suggestions, and to Matthew Liao for research assistance.

1 Audre Lorde argued that the "master's tools" could not dismantle the "master's house." Yet rights claims have transformed (even if they have not dismantled) many structures of domination. Martha Minow stresses this point in "Interpreting Rights," *Yale Law Journal*, 98 (1987), pp. 1880–1, esp. fn. 76. See Audre Lorde, "The Master's Tools Will Never Dismantle the Master's House," in *This Bridge Called My Back: Writings by Radical Women of Color*, eds Cherríe Moraga and Gloria Anzaldúa (New York: Kitchen Table Press, 1983), pp. 98–101.

2 I borrow the phrase from Henry Steiner, "The Youth of Rights," *Harvard Law Review*, 104, 4 (February 1991), p. 935.

3 Alan Riding, "Women Seize Focus at Rights Forum," *The New York Times* (June 16, 1993), p. A3; Gayle Kirschenbaum, "After Victory, Women's Human Rights Movement Takes Stock," *Ms* 4, 2 (September/October 1993), p. 20; Patrick Tyler, "Forum on Women Agrees on Goals," *The New York Times* (September 15, 1995), pp. A1, A3.

4 Patricia Williams, *The Alchemy of Race and Rights* (Cambridge: Harvard University Press, 1991).

5 There are a few exceptions. Janet Rifkin criticizes the suffragists for perpetuating mystifications which supported the *status quo*. Rifkin, "Toward a Theory of Law and Patriarchy," in D. Kelly Weisberg, *Feminist Legal Theory: Foundations* (Philadelphia: Temple University Press, 1993), p. 413. And Elizabeth Fox-Genovese takes a primarily critical attitude to the achievements of the women's rights movement in *Feminism Without Illusions: A Critique of Individualism* (Durham: University of North Carolina Press, 1991). For a critique of Fox-Genovese, see Marion Smiley, "Is Corporatism the Answer? Fox-Genovese's Feminist Theory," *Law and Social Inquiry*, 18, 1 (Winter 1993), pp. 115–34.

6 Carol Gilligan, *In a Different Voice* (Cambridge: Harvard University Press, 1982); Nel Noddings, *Caring: A Feminine Approach to Ethics* (Berkeley: University of California Press, 1984) and Eva Feder Kittay and Diana Meyer, eds, *Women and Moral Theory* (Totowa, NJ: Rowman and Littlefeld, 1982).

7 Fox-Genovese, *Feminism Without Illusions*; Nancy Hirschmann, *Rethinking Obligation* (Ithaca: Cornell University Press, 1992).

8 Heather Ruth Wishik, "To Question Everything: The Inquiries of Feminist Jurisprudence," *Berkeley Womens Law Journal*, 1, 1 (Fall 1985), pp. 64–77; Catharine MacKinnon, "Feminism, Marxism, Method, and the State: To-

✕   ward Feminist Jurisprudence," *Signs: Journal of Women in Culture and Society,*
      8, 4 (1983); Lucinda Finley, "Breaking Women's Silence in Law," *Notre
      Dame Law Review,* 64, 5 (1989).

  9 Mary Poovey, "The Abortion Question and the Death of Man," in *Feminists
      Theorize the Political,* eds Judith Butler and Joan Scott (New York: Routledge,
      1992) and Wai-chee Dimock, "Rightful Subjectivity," *Yale Journal of Criti-
      cism,* 4, 1 (1990).

 10 Janet Rifkin, "Toward a Theory of Law and Patriarchy," and Diane Polan,
      "Toward a Theory of Law and Patriarchy." Both articles appear in Weisberg,
      ed., *Feminist Legal Theory,* see esp. pp. 413; 424.

 11 Susan Sherwin, *No Longer Patient: Feminist Ethics and Health Care* (Philadel-
      phia: Temple University Press, 1992), p. 140. Sherwin criticizes a focus on
      patients' rights, but also draws an analogy between the status of female
      patients and that of women more generally.

 12 Hirschmann, *Rethinking Obligation,* pp. 232, 286.

 13 Robin Dillon, "Toward a Feminist Conception of Self-Respect," *Hypatia,* 7,
      1 (Winter 1992), p. 57.

 14 Lucinda Finley, "Transcending Equality Theory," in Weisberg, *Feminist Legal
      Theory,* pp. 200–1; Wai-chee Dimock, "Rightful Subjectivity," p. 33.

 15 Simone Weil, "Human Personality," in *The Simone Weil Reader,* ed. George
      Panichas (New York: David McKay, 1977), p. 326. This is also a central
      theme of Fox-Genovese, *Feminism Without Illusions.*

 16 Joel Feinberg, "The Nature and Value of Rights," *Rights, Justice, and the
✕   Bounds of Liberty* (Princeton: Princeton University Press, 1980), p. 151. For
      critiques of Feinberg, see Dillon, "Toward a Feminist Conception of Self-
      Respect" and Dimock, "Rightful Subjectivity."

 17 Suzanne Sherry, "Civic Virtue and the Feminine Voice in Constitutional
      Adjudication," *Virginia Law Review,* 72 (1986).

 18 Dimock, "Rightful Subjectivity," p. 47; Fox-Genovese, *Feminism Without
      Illusions,* p. 32; Ann C. Scales, "The Emergence of Feminist Jurisprudence,"
      in Weisberg, *Feminist Legal Theory: Foundations,* p. 48.

 19 Wesley Newcomb Hohfeld, *Fundamental Legal Conceptions* [1919], ed. W.
      W. Cook (New Haven: Yale University Press, 1923).

 20 For instance, Hohfeld construed liberties very narrowly; on his account I have
      a liberty to do X if others have no right to compel me not to do X. On most
      contemporary views, a liberty right is more robust, since it includes some
      obligation on others not to interfere with exercise of the liberty. My thanks to
      Kent Greenawalt for clarification on this point. Also, because Hohfeld fo-
      cused on established legal rights, he did not consider how rights claims can
      function as demands for social change.

 21 Martha Minow stresses this point in "Interpreting Rights."

 22 Joseph Raz, "Rights-Based Moralities," in *Theories of Rights,* ed. Jeremy
      Waldron (Oxford: Oxford University Press, 1984), p. 182.

 23 This right was formally declared at the recent UN Fourth World Conference
      on Women. Seth Faison, "Women's Meeting Agrees on Right to Say No to
      Sex," *The New York Times* (September 11, 1995), pp. A1, A7.

 24 Marilyn Frye, *The Politics of Reality* (Freedom, California: The Crossing Press,
      1983), pp. 103–4.

 25 Williams, *The Alchemy of Race and Rights,* esp. Ch. 8.

26 Frances Olsen, "Statutory Rape: A Feminist Critique of Rights Analysis," *University of Texas Law Review* (1984), p. 387.

27 Robin West, "Jurisprudence and Gender," in Weisberg, *Feminist Legal Theory: Foundations*, p. 83.

28 Barbara Crossette, "The Second Sex in the Third World," *The New York Times* (September 10, 1995), 4:1.

29 Carole Pateman, "Feminist Critiques of the Public/Private Dichotomy," *The Disorder of Women* (Stanford: Stanford University Press, 1989); Anne Phillips, *Engendering Democracy* (Cambridge: Polity Press, 1991), Ch. 4.

30 Catharine MacKinnon, "Crimes of War, Crimes of Peace," *On Human Rights*, eds S. Shute and S. Hurley, (New York: Basic Books, 1993).

31 Eleanor Roosevelt, cited in Catharine MacKinnon, "Crimes of War, Crimes of Peace," p. 83.

32 Adelaide Villmoare, "Women, Differences, and Rights as Practices," *Law and Society Review*, 25, 2 (1991), pp. 385–410.

33 Gayle Binion, "Human Rights: A Feminist Perspective," *Human Rights Quarterly*, 17, 3 (August 1995), pp. 509–26; Olsen, "The Family and the Market: A Study of Ideology and Legal Reform," *Harvard Law Review*, 96 (1983) and "Statutory Rape"; Minow, *Making All the Difference* (Ithaca: Cornell University Press, 1990) and "Interpreting Rights"; Jennifer Nedelsky, "Reconceiving Rights as Relationships," *Review of Constitutional Studies*, 1, 1 (1993) and Nedelsky and Craig Scott, "Constitutional Dialogue" in *Social Justice and the Constitution*, eds Joel Bakan and David Schneiderman (Ottawa: Carleton University Press, 1992), pp. 59–83; Elizabeth Schneider, "The Dialectic of Rights and Politics," *New York University Law Review*, 61 (1986); Adelaide Villmoare, "Women, Differences, and Rights as Practices"; Patricia Williams, *The Alchemy of Race and Rights*, esp. pp. 164–5.

34 Bernard Williams, *Ethics and the Limits of Philosophy* (Cambridge: Harvard University Press, 1985); Alasdair MacIntyre, *After Virtue* (Notre Dame, IN: University of Notre Dame Press, 1984) and *Whose Justice? Which Rationality?* (Notre Dame, IN: University of Notre Dame Press, 1987).

35 Gilligan, *In a Different Voice*.

36 A useful anthology is Eva Kittay and Diana Meyers, eds, *Women and Moral Theory* (Totowa, NJ: Rowman and Littlefield, 1987). See also Nell Noddings, *Caring: A Feminine Approach to Ethics* (Berkeley: University of California Press, 1984); Joan Tronto, *Moral Boundaries* (New York: Routledge, 1993); Lawrence Blum, *Moral Perception and Particularity* (New York: Cambridge University Press, 1994), Part III. For criticisms of care ethics, see Susan Moller Okin, "Thinking Like a Woman," in *Theoretical Perspectives on Sexual Difference*, ed. Deborah Rhode (New Haven: Yale University Press, 1990), pp. 145–59; the Review Symposium on Noddings' work in *Hypatia*, 5, 1 (Spring 1990), pp. 101–19; Will Kymlicka, *Contemporary Political Philosophy* (Oxford: Clarendon Press, 1990), pp. 262–86; and Katha Pollitt, "Marooned on Gilligan's Island," *The Nation* (December 28, 1992), pp. 799–807.

37 Iris Young, *Justice and the Politics of Difference*, esp. Ch. 4.

38 Kent Greenawalt, *Law and Objectivity* (Oxford: Oxford University Press, 1992), p. 156.

39 Iris Murdoch, *The Sovereignty of Good* (London: Routledge and Kegan Paul,

1970); Sara Ruddick, "Maternal Thinking," *Feminist Studies* (1980), pp. 342–67; Lawrence Blum, *Moral Perception and Particularity*, Ch. 1.

40 Baier, *Moral Prejudices: Essays on Ethics* (Cambridge: Harvard University Press, 1994); *A Progress of Sentiments* (Cambridge: Harvard University Press, 1991); "Hume, the Women's Moral Theorist?" in *Women and Moral Theory*, eds Kittay and Meyers, p. 40.

41 The most sustained example is Joan Tronto, *Moral Boundaries*.

42 In response to criticisms, Noddings has argued that while care may not underlie all of ethics, she remains unsure about exactly what justice contributes. Noddings, "A Response," *Hypatia*, 5, 1 (Spring 1990), pp. 120–6.

43 Tronto, *Moral Boundaries*, pp. 138, 147–53, 166–70, 211 fn. 45.

44 Dimock, "Rightful Subjectivity," p. 32; Jean Grimshaw, *Philosophy and Feminist Thinking* (Minneapolis: University of Minnesota Press, 1986), pp. 251–3; Gilligan, *In a Different Voice*, Chs 5–6.

45 Annette Baier, "The Need for More than Justice," in Marcia Hanen and Kai Nielsen, *Science, Morality and Feminist Theory* (Alberta: University of Calgary Press, 1987), pp. 41–56.

46 Lawrence Blum, *Moral Perception and Particularity*, Ch. 3. See also Barbara Herman, "The Practice of Moral Judgment," *The Journal of Philosophy*, 87, 9 (August 1985), pp. 414–36.

47 Will Kymlicka discusses this issue, though I think he understates its importance to the care–justice debate. Kymlicka, *Contemporary Political Philosophy*, pp. 265–7.

48 Richard Rorty cites Baier on this point in "Human Rights, Rationality, and Sentimentality," in *On Human Rights*, eds S. Shute and S. Hurley (New York: Basic Books, 1993), pp. 128–9.

49 The phrase comes from Nobel laureate Rigoberta Menchu. See Tim Golden, "Guatemala Indian Wins Nobel Peace Prize," *The New York Times* (October 17, 1992), p. A5.

50 Kymlicka, *Contemporary Political Philosophy*, p. 285.

51 Examples include Tronto, *Moral Boundaries*; Susan Moller Okin, *Justice, Gender, and the Family* (New York: Basic Books, 1989), Chs 7–8; Iris Marion Young, "Mothers, Citizenship and Independence," *Ethics*, 105, 3 (1995); Nancy Fraser, *Unruly Practices* (Minneapolis: University of Minnesota, 1989), Chs 7–8 and "After the Family Wage," *Social Justice* (Spring 1994); Minow, *Making all the Difference*.

52 Carol Smart, *Feminism and the Power of Law* (New York: Routledge, 1989), p. 139.

53 Smart, *Feminism and the Power of Law*, p. 139. But Janet Rifkin does criticize suffragists for not challenging the ideology of law. See Rifkin, "Toward a Theory of Law and Patriarchy," p. 413.

54 Regula Stämpfli, "Direct Democracy and Women's Suffrage: Antagonism in Switzerland"; Aicha Afifi and Rajae Msefer, "Women in Morocco: Gender Issues and Politics"; Eileen Wormald, "Rhetoric, Reality and a Dilemma: Women and Politics in New Guinea," all in *Women and Politics Worldwide*, eds Barbara Nelson and Najma Chowdhury (New Haven: Yale University Press, 1994), esp. pp. 567, 467, 476 fn. 10, 697.

55 For a discussion of when disadvantage becomes discrimination, see

Greenawalt, *Law and Objectivity*, pp. 136ff; see also J. Donald Moon, *Constructing Community* (Princeton: Princeton University Press, 1993), Chs 7–8.

56 *Geduldig v. Aiello*, 417 U.S. 484 (1974) and *General Electric Co. v. Gilbert*, 429 U.S. 125 (1976). Controversy over these cases led Congress to pass the Pregnancy Discrimination Act, 42 U.S.C. par. 2000e (k) (1982). For discussion see Part 2 of Weisberg, ed., *Feminist Legal Theory: Foundations.*

57 Minow, *Making all the Difference*, esp. Ch. 3; Greenawalt, *Law and Objectivity*, pp. 136–9.

58 The most recent US Model Penal Code retains the spousal exclusion but recommends a fresh look at its advisability. American Law Institute, *Model Penal Code* (Philadelphia: The Institute, 1985), Art. 213.1 at 274, 341–6. My thanks to Kent Greenawalt for this source.

59 The common law doctrine of marital exception to rape traces to a seventeenth century ruling that "the husband cannot be guilty of rape committed by himself upon his lawful wife, for by their mutual matrimonial consent and contract the wife hath given up her self in this kind unto her husband which she cannot retract." Sir Matthew Hale, *Pleas of the Crown* (London: 1678; Emelyn ed., 1847), pp. 628–9, cited in Rosmarie Tong, *Women, Sex and the Law* (Totowa, NJ: Rowman and Littlefield, 1984), p. 94.

60 Smart, *Feminism and the Power of Law*, pp. 33–4. For how rape laws could be changed, see Jennifer Nedelsky, "The Practical Possibilities of Feminist Theory," *Northwestern University Law Review*, 87, 4 (1993), esp. pp. 1290–4.

61 *State v. Wanrow* 88 Wash. 2d 221, 559 P.2d 548 (1977); Schneider, "The Dialectic of Rights and Politics," pp. 606–8; Greenawalt, *Law and Objectivity*, pp. 136–7.

62 *Ellison v. Brady* 924 F.2d 872 (9th Cir. 1991). For an overview of feminist debates over the reasonable woman standard, see Kathryn Abrams, "The Reasonable Woman: Sense and Sensibility in Sexual Harassment Law," *Dissent*, 421 (Winter 1995), pp. 50–1. See also Nedelsky, "The Practical Possibilities of Feminist Theory" and Drucilla Cornell, "Gender, Sex and Equivalent Rights" in *Feminists Theorize the Political*, ed. Judith Butler and Joan Scott (New York: Routledge, 1992).

63 Anatole France, *Le Lys Rouge* [1894] (NY: French and European Publications, 1964), Ch. 7.

64 Smart, *Feminism and the Power of Law*, p. 145. See also Kristin Bumiller, *The Civil Rights Society: The Social Construction of Victims* (Baltimore: Johns Hopkins, 1988).

65 Kim Lane Scheppele, "Constitutionalizing Abortion," paper presented to the 1992 meeting of the American Political Science Association, Chicago, p. 3.

66 Sharon Marcus, "Fighting Bodies, Fighting Words: A Theory and Politics of Rape Prevention," in Butler and Scott, *Feminists Theorize the Political*, esp. pp. 388, 392.

67 Smart, *Feminism and the Power of Law*, pp. 144, 161–2; Olsen, "Statutory Rape," p. 488.

68 Olsen, "Statutory Rape," p. 488; Schneider, "The Dialectics of Rights and Politics."

69 Abrams, "The Reasonable Woman," esp. pp. 52–4.

70 Kathryn Abrams stressed this point in a lecture at Princeton University, October 1993.

71 Smart, *Feminism and the Power of Law*, p. 145. I am grateful for comments from Sally Haslanger and Harlan Beckley which pushed and helped me to clarify this argument.

72 Diane Polan, "Toward a Theory of Law and Patriarchy," p. 424.

73 Katha Pollitt, "Implants: Truth and Consequences," *The Nation* (March 16, 1992).

74 For a libertarian defense of cosmetic breast implants, see Peter Huber, "A Woman's Right to Choose," *Forbes* (February 17, 1992).

75 As Pollitt notes, "the real breast-implant story . . . isn't about women's bodies; it's about their minds."

76 Surgeons and patients often argue that cosmetic surgery is physically analogous to makeup and psychologically analogous to other mood-boosters, like vacations. See Diana Dull and Candace West, "Accounting for Cosmetic Surgery: The Accomplishment of Gender," *Social Problems*, 38, 1 (February 1991), pp. 54–70.

77 John Rawls argues that the social bases of self-respect represent the most important primary good in *A Theory of Justice* (Cambridge: Harvard University Press, 1971), pp. 62, 178–9, 440–3.

2

Decoding "Dependency": Inscriptions of Power in a Keyword of the US Welfare State

Nancy Fraser and Linda Gordon

Dependency has become a keyword of US politics. Politicians of diverse views regularly criticize what they term *welfare dependency*. Supreme Court Justice Clarence Thomas spoke for many conservatives in 1980 when he vilified his sister: "She gets mad when the mailman is late with her welfare check. That's how dependent she is. What's worse is that now her kids feel entitled to the check, too. They have no motivation for doing better or getting out of that situation."[1] Liberals usually blame the victim less, but they, too, decry welfare dependency. Democratic Senator Daniel P. Moynihan prefigured today's discourse when he began his 1973 book by claiming that "the issue of welfare is the issue of dependency. It is different from poverty. To be poor is an objective condition; to be dependent, a subjective one as well . . . Being poor is often associated with considerable personal qualities; being dependent rarely so. [Dependency] is an incomplete state in life: normal in the child, abnormal in the adult. In a world where completed men and women stand on their own feet, persons who are dependent – as the buried imagery of the word denotes – hang."[2] Today, "policy experts" from both major parties agree "that [welfare] dependency is bad for people, that it undermines their motivation to support themselves, and isolates and stigmatizes welfare recipients in a way that over a long period feeds into and accentuates the underclass mindset and condition."[3]

If we can step back from this discourse, however, we can interrogate some of its underlying presuppositions. Why are debates about poverty and inequality in the United States now being framed in terms of welfare dependency? How did the receipt of public assistance become associated with dependency, and why are the connotations of that word in this context so negative? What are the gender and racial subtexts of this discourse, and what tacit assumptions underlie it?

We propose to shed some light on these issues by examining welfare-related meanings of the word *dependency*.[4] We will analyze *dependency* as a keyword of the US welfare state and reconstruct its genealogy. By charting some major historical shifts in the usage of this term, we will excavate some of the tacit assumptions and connotations that it still carries today but that usually go without saying.

Our approach is inspired in part by the English cultural-materialist critic, Raymond Williams.[5] Following Williams and others, we assume that the terms that are used to describe social life are also active forces shaping it.[6] A crucial element of politics, then, is the struggle to define social reality and to interpret people's inchoate aspirations and needs.[7] Particular words and expressions often become focal in such struggles, functioning as keywords, sites at which the meaning of social experience is negotiated and contested.[8] Keywords typically carry unspoken assumptions and connotations that can powerfully influence the discourses they permeate – in part by constituting a body of doxa, or taken-for-granted commonsense belief that escapes critical scrutiny.[9]

We seek to dispel the doxa surrounding current US discussions of dependency by reconstructing that term's genealogy. Modifying an approach associated with Michel Foucault, we will excavate broad historical shifts in linguistic usage that can rarely be attributed to specific agents.[10] We do not present a causal analysis. Rather, by contrasting present meanings of dependency with past meanings, we aim to defamiliarize taken-for-granted beliefs in order to render them susceptible to critique and to illuminate present-day conflicts.

Our approach differs from Foucault's, however, in two crucial respects: we seek to contextualize discursive shifts in relation to broad institutional and social-structural shifts, and we welcome normative political reflection. Our article is a collaboration between a philosopher and an historian. We combine historical analysis of linguistic and social-structural changes with conceptual analysis of the discursive construction of social problems, and we leaven the mix with a feminist interest in envisioning emancipatory alternatives.

In what follows, then, we provide a genealogy of *dependency*. We sketch the history of this term and explicate the assumptions and connotations it carries today in US debates about welfare – especially assumptions about human nature, gender roles, the causes of poverty, the nature of citizenship, the sources of entitlement, and what counts as work and as a contribution to society. We contend that unreflective uses of this keyword serve to enshrine certain interpretations of social life as authoritative and to delegitimate or obscure others, generally to the advantage of dominant groups in society and to the disadvantage of subordinate ones.

All told, we provide a critique of ideology in the form of a critical political semantics.

Dependency, we argue, is an ideological term. In current US policy discourse it usually refers to the condition of poor women with children who maintain their families with neither a male breadwinner nor an adequate wage and who rely for economic support on a stingy and politically unpopular government program called Aid to Families with Dependent Children (AFDC). Participation in this highly stigmatized program may be demoralizing in many cases, even though it may enable women to leave abusive or unsatisfying relationships without having to give up their children. Still, naming the problems of poor, solo-mother families as *dependency* tends to make them appear to be individual problems, as much moral or psychological as economic. The term carries strong emotive and visual associations and a powerful pejorative charge. In current debates, the expression *welfare dependency* evokes the image of "the welfare mother," often figured as a young, unmarried Black woman (perhaps even a teenager) of uncontrolled sexuality. The power of this image is overdetermined, we contend, since it condenses multiple and often contradictory meanings of dependency. Only by disaggregating those different strands, by unpacking the tacit assumptions and evaluative connotations that underlie them, can we begin to understand, and to dislodge, the force of the stereotype.

Registers of Meaning

In its root meaning, the verb *to depend* refers to a physical relationship in which one thing hangs from another. The more abstract meanings – social, economic, psychological, and political – were originally metaphorical. In current usage, we find four registers in which the meanings of dependency reverberate. The first is an economic register, in which one depends on some other person(s) or institution for subsistence. In a second register, the term denotes a socio-legal status, the lack of a separate legal or public identity, as in the status of married women created by coverture. The third register is political: here dependency means subjection to an external ruling power and may be predicated of a colony or of a subject caste of non-citizen residents. The fourth register we call the moral/ psychological; dependency in this sense is an individual character trait like lack of willpower or excessive emotional neediness.

To be sure, not every use of dependency fits neatly into one and only one of these registers. Still, by distinguishing them analytically we present a matrix on which to plot the historical adventures of the term. In what follows, we shall trace the shift from a patriarchal preindustrial usage in which women, however subordinate, shared a condition of dependency with many men to a modern, industrial, male-supremacist usage that constructed a specifically feminine sense of dependency. That usage is now giving way, we contend, to a postindustrial usage in which growing numbers of relatively prosperous women claim the same kind of independence that men do while a more stigmatized but still feminized sense of dependency attaches to groups considered deviant and superfluous. Not just gender but also racializing practices play a major role in these shifts, as do changes in the organization and meaning of labor.

Preindustrial "Dependency"

In preindustrial English usage, the most common meaning of dependency was subordination. The economic, socio-legal, and political registers were relatively undifferentiated, reflecting the fusion of various forms of hierarchy in state and society, and the moral/psychological use of the term barely existed. The earliest social definition of the verb to depend (on) in the *Oxford English Dictionary* (OED) is "to be connected with in a relation of subordination." A dependent, from at least 1588, was one "who depends on another for support, position, etc.; a retainer, attendant, subordinate, servant." A dependency was either a retinue or body of servants or a foreign territorial possession or colony. This family of terms applied widely in an hierarchical social context in which nearly everyone was subordinate to someone else but did not incur individual stigma thereby.[11]

We can appreciate just how common dependency was in preindustrial society by examining its opposite. The term independence at first applied primarily to aggregate entities, not to individuals; thus in the seventeenth century a nation or a church congregation could be independent. By the eighteenth century, however, an individual could be said to have an independency, meaning an ownership of property, a fortune that made it possible to live without laboring. (This sense of the term, which we would today call economic, survives in our expressions to be independently wealthy and a person of independent means.) To be dependent, in contrast, was to gain one's livelihood by working for someone else. This of course was the condition of most people, of wage laborers as well as serfs and slaves, of most men as well as most women.

Dependency, therefore, was a normal, as opposed to a deviant, condition; a social relation, as opposed to an individual trait. Thus, it did not carry any moral opprobrium. Still, it did mean status inferiority and legal coverture, being a part of a unit headed by someone else who had legal standing. In a world of status hierarchies dominated by great landowners and their retainers, all members of a household other than its "head" were dependents, as were free or servile peasants on an estate. They were, as Peter Laslett put it, "caught up, so to speak, 'subsumed' . . . into the personalities of their fathers and masters."[12]

Dependency also had what we would today call political consequences. While the term did not mean precisely unfree, its context was a social order in which subjection, not citizenship, was the norm. Throughout most of the European development of representative government, independence in the sense of property ownership was a prerequisite for political rights. When dependents began to claim rights and liberty, they perforce became revolutionaries.

Dependency was not then applied uniquely to characterize the relation of a wife to her husband. Women's dependency, like children's, meant being on a lower rung in a long social ladder; their husbands and fathers were above them but below others. For the agrarian majority, moreover, there was no implication of unilateral economic dependency, because women's and children's labor was recognized as essential to the family economy. Women's dependency in preindustrial society was similar in kind to that of subordinate men, only multiplied. But so too were the lives of children, servants, and the elderly overlaid with multiple layers of dependency.

Nevertheless, dependency was not universally approved or uncontested. It was subject, rather, to principled challenges from at least the seventeenth century on, when liberal-individualist political arguments became common. The terms dependence and independence often figured centrally in political debates in this period, as they did in the Putney Debates during the English Civil War. Sometimes they even became key signifiers of social crisis, as in the seventeenth century English controversy about "out-of-doors" servants, hired help who did not reside in the homes of their masters and who were not bound by indentures or similar legal understandings. In the discourse of the time, the anomalous "independence" of these men served as a general figure for social disorder, a lightning rod focusing diffuse cultural anxieties – much as the anomalous "dependence" of "welfare mothers" does today.

Industrial "Dependency": The Worker and his Negatives

With the rise of industrial capitalism, the semantic geography of dependency shifted significantly. What in preindustrial society had been a normal and unstigmatized condition became deviant and stigmatized.

More precisely, certain dependencies became shameful while others were deemed natural and proper. In particular, as eighteenth and nineteenth century political culture intensified gender difference, new, specifically feminine senses of dependency appeared – considered proper for women, but degrading for men. Likewise, emergent racial constructions made some forms of dependency appropriate for the "dark races," but intolerable for "whites." Such differentiated valuations became possible as the term's preindustrial unity fractured. No longer designating only generalized subordination, dependency in the industrial era could be socio-legal or political or economic. With these distinctions came another major semantic shift: now dependency need not always refer to a social relation; it could also designate an individual character trait. Thus, the moral/psychological register was born.

These redefinitions were greatly influenced by Radical Protestantism. It elaborated a new positive image of individual independence and a critique of socio-legal and political dependency. From this perspective, status hierarchies no longer appeared natural or just, and subjection and subsumption were increasingly objectionable. These beliefs informed a variety of radical movements throughout the industrial era, including abolition of slavery, feminism, and labor organizing, with substantial successes. In the nineteenth century these movements abolished slavery and some of the legal disabilities of women. More thorough-going victories were won by white male workers who, in the eighteenth and nineteenth centuries, threw off their socio-legal and political dependency and won civil and electoral rights. In the age of democratic revolutions, the developing new concept of citizenship rested on independence; dependency was deemed antithetical to citizenship.

Changes in the civil and political landscape of dependence and independence were accompanied by even more dramatic changes in the economic register. When white workingmen demanded civil and electoral rights, they claimed to be independent. This entailed reinterpreting the meaning of wage labor so as to divest it of the association with dependency. That in turn required a shift in focus – from the experience or means of labor (for example, ownership of tools or land, control of skills, and the organization of work) to its remuneration and how that was spent. As a result of the struggles of radical workingmen, economic independence came eventually to encompass the ideal of earning a family wage, a wage sufficient to maintain a household and to support a dependent wife and children. Thus, workingmen expanded the meaning of economic independence to include a form of wage labor in addition to property ownership and self-employment.[13]

This shift in the meaning of independence also transformed the meanings of dependency. As wage labor became increasingly normative – and increasingly definitive of independence – it was precisely those excluded from wage labor who appeared to personify dependency. In the new industrial semantics, there emerged three principal icons of dependency, all effectively negatives of the dominant image of "the worker," and each embodying a different aspect of non-independence.

The first icon of industrial dependency was "the pauper," who lived not on wages but on poor relief. In the strenuous new culture of emergent capitalism, the figure of the pauper was like a bad double of the upstanding workingman, threatening the latter should he lag. The image of the pauper was elaborated largely in an emerging new register of dependency discourse – the moral/psychological register. Paupers were not simply poor but degraded, their character corrupted and their will sapped through reliance on charity. Toward the end of the nineteenth century, as hereditarian (eugenic) thought caught on, the pauper's character defects were given a basis in biology. The pauper's dependency was figured as unlike the serf's in that it was unilateral, not reciprocal. To be a pauper was not to be subordinate within a system of productive labor; it was to be outside such a system altogether.

A second icon of industrial dependency was embodied alternately in the figures of "the colonial native" and "the slave." They, of course, were very much inside the economic system, their labor often fundamental to the development of capital and industry. Whereas the pauper personified economic dependency, natives and slaves personified political subjection. Their images as "savage," "childlike," and "submissive" became salient as the old, territorial sense of dependency as a colony became intertwined with a new, racist discourse developed to justify colonialism and slavery.[14] There emerged a drift from an older sense of dependency as a relation of subjection imposed by an imperial power on an indigenous population to a newer sense of dependency as an inherent property or character trait of the people so subjected. In earlier usage, colonials were dependent because they had been conquered; in nineteenth century imperialist culture, they were conquered because they were dependent. In this new conception, it was the intrinsic, essential dependency of natives and slaves that justified their colonization and enslavement. Racialist thought was the linchpin for this reasoning.

Like the pauper, the native and the slave were excluded from wage labor and thus were negatives of the image of the worker. They shared that characteristic, if little else, with the third major icon of dependency in the industrial era: the newly invented figure of "the housewife." As we saw, the independence of the white workingman presupposed the ideal of the family wage, a wage sufficient to maintain a household and to support a non-employed wife and children. Thus, for wage labor to create (white male) independence, (white) female economic dependence was required. (White) women were thus transformed "from partners to parasites."[15] This transformation was by no means universal; since few husbands actually were able to support a family singlehandedly, most families continued to depend on the labor of women and children. Still, several different registers of dependency converged in the figure of the housewife. This figure melded woman's traditional socio-legal and political dependency with her more recent economic dependency in the industrial order. The connotations of female dependency were altered. Although erstwhile dependent white men gained political rights, most white women remained legally and politically dependent. The result was to feminize – and stigmatize – socio-legal and political dependency.

Together, then, a series of new personifications of dependency combined to constitute the underside of the workingman's independence. Henceforth, those who aspired to full membership in society would have to distinguish themselves from the pauper, the native, the slave, and the housewife in order to construct their independence. In a social order in which wage labor was becoming hegemonic, it was possible to encapsulate all these distinctions simultaneously in the ideal of the family wage. On the one hand, and most overtly, the ideal of the family wage premised the white workingman's independence on his wife's subordination and economic dependence. But on the other hand, it simultaneously contrasted with counterimages of dependent men – first with degraded male paupers on poor relief and later with racist stereotypes of Negro men unable to dominate Negro women. The family wage, therefore, was a vehicle for elaborating meanings of dependence and independence that were deeply inflected by gender, race, and class.

In this new industrial semantics, white workingmen appeared to be economically independent, but their independence was largely illusory and ideological. Since few actually earned enough to support a family singlehandedly, most depended in fact – if not in word – on their wives' and children's contributions. Equally important, dominant understandings of wage labor in capitalism denied workers' dependence on their employers, thereby veiling their status as subordinates in a unit headed by someone else. Thus, hierarchy that had been relatively explicit and visible in the peasant–landlord relation was mystified in the relationship of factory operative to factory owner. There was a sense, then, in which the economic dependency of the white workingman was spirited away through linguistic sleight of hand – somewhat like reducing the number of poor people by lowering the official poverty demarcating line.

By definition, then, economic inequality among white men no longer created dependency. But non-economic hierarchy among white men was considered unacceptable in the United States. Thus, dependency was redefined to refer exclusively to those non-economic relations of subordination deemed suitable only for people of color and for white women. Whereas all relations of subordination had previously counted as dependency relations, now capital–labor relations were exempted. Socio-legal and political hierarchy appeared to diverge from economic hierarchy, and only the former seemed incompatible with hegemonic views of society. It seemed to follow, moreover, that were socio-legal dependency and political dependency ever to be formally abolished, no social-structural dependency would remain. Any dependency that did persist could only be moral or psychological.

The Rise of American Welfare "Dependency": 1890–1945

Informed by these general features of industrial-era semantics, a distinctive welfare-related use of dependency developed in the United States. Originating in the late nineteenth century discourse of pauperism, modified in the Progressive Era and stabilized in the period of the New Deal, this use of the term was fundamentally ambiguous, slipping easily, and repeatedly, from an economic meaning to a moral/psychological meaning.

As we saw, the most general definition of economic dependency in this era was simply non-wage-earning. By the end of the nineteenth century, however, that definition had divided into two: a "good" household dependency, predicated of children's and wives' relation to the male breadwinner, and an increasingly "bad" (or at least dubious) charity dependency, predicated of recipients of relief. Both senses had as their reference point the ideal of the family wage, and both were eventually incorporated into the discourse of the national state. The good, household sense was elaborated via the census and by the Internal Revenue Service, which installed the category of dependent as the norm for wives.[16] The already problematic charity sense became even more pejorative with the development of public assistance. Such assistance became increasingly stigmatized, and it was harder and harder to rely on relief without being branded a pauper.

Ironically, reformers in the 1890s introduced the word dependent into relief discourse as a substitute for pauper precisely in order to destigmatize the receipt of help. They first applied the word to children, the paradigmatic "innocent" victims of poverty.[17] Then, in the early twentieth century, Progressive-era reformers began to apply the term to adults, again to rid them of stigma. Only after World War II did dependent become the hegemonic word for a recipient of aid.[18]

The attempt to get rid of stigma by replacing pauperism with dependency failed. Talk about economic dependency repeatedly slid into condemnation of moral/psychological dependency. Even during the Depression of the 1930s, experts worried that receipt of relief would create "habits of dependence" or, as one charity leader put it, "a belligerent dependency, an attitude of having a right and title to relief."[19] Many needy people accepted public aid only after much hesitation and with great shame, so strong was the stigma of dependency.[20]

Most important, the New Deal intensified the dishonor of receiving help by consolidating a two-track welfare system. First-track programs like unemployment and old age insurance offered aid as an entitlement, without stigma or supervision and hence without dependency. Such programs were deliberately designed to foster the myth that beneficiaries merely got back what they put in. They constructed an honorable status for recipients; today no one calls these programs "welfare." Intended to replace temporarily the white workingman's family wage, first-track programs excluded most minorities and white women. In contrast, second-track public assistance programs, among which Aid to Dependent Children (ADC), later Aid to Families with Dependent Children (AFDC), became the biggest and most well known, continued the private charity tradition of searching out the deserving few among the many chiselers. Funded from general tax revenues instead of from earmarked wage deductions, these programs created the appearance that claimants were getting something for nothing.[21] They established entirely different conditions for receiving aid: means-testing; morals-testing; moral supervision; home visits; extremely low stipends – in short, they humiliated, infantilized, and thus created the "welfare dependency" they feared.[22]

The racial and sexual exclusions of the first-track programs were not accidental. They were designed to win the support of Southern legislators who wanted to keep Blacks dependent in another sense, namely, on low wages or sharecropping.[23] Equally deliberate was the construction of the differential in legitimacy between the two tracks of the welfare system.[24] Most Americans today still distinguish between "welfare" and "nonwelfare" forms of public provision and see only the former as creating dependency. The assumptions underlying these distinctions, however, had to be constructed politically. Old people became privileged (non-welfare) recipients only through decades of militant organization and lobbying. All programs of public provision, whether they are called welfare or not, shore up some dependencies and discourage others. Social Security subverted adults' sense of responsibility for their parents, for example. Public assistance programs, by contrast, aimed to buttress the dependence of minorities on low-wage labor, of wives on husbands, of children on their parents.

The conditions of second-track assistance made recipients view their dependence on public assistance as inferior to the supposed independence of wage labor.[25] Yet the designers of ADC did not initially intend to drive white solo mothers into paid employment. Rather, they wanted to protect the norm of the family wage by making dependence on a male breadwinner continue to seem preferable to dependence on the state.[26] ADC occupied the strategic semantic space where the good, household sense of dependency and the bad, relief sense of dependency intersected. It enforced at once the positive connotations of the first and the negative connotations of the second.

Thus, the poor solo mother was enshrined as the quintessential welfare dependent. That designation has thus become significant not only for what it includes, but also for what it excludes and occludes. Although it appears to mean relying on the government for economic support, not all recipients of public funds are equally considered dependent. Hardly anyone today calls recipients of Social Security retirement insurance dependents. Similarly, persons receiving unemployment insurance, agricultural loans, and home mortgage assistance are excluded from that categorization, as indeed are defense contractors and the beneficiaries of corporate bailouts and regressive taxation.

Postindustrial Society and the Disappearance of "Good" Dependency

With the transition to a postindustrial phase of capitalism, the semantic map of dependency is being redrawn yet again. Whereas industrial usage had cast some forms of dependency as natural and proper, postindustrial usage figures all forms as avoidable and blameworthy; and it focuses even more intensely on the traits of individuals. One major influence here is the formal abolition of much of the gender- and race-based legal and political dependency that was endemic to industrial society. Housewives, paupers, natives, and the descendants of slaves are no longer formally excluded from most civil and political rights; neither their subsumption nor their subjection is viewed as legitimate. Thus, major forms of dependency deemed proper in industrial usage are now considered objectionable, and postindustrial uses of the term carry a stronger negative charge.

A second major shift in the geography of postindustrial dependency is affecting the economic register. This is the decentering of the ideal of the family wage, which had been the gravitational center of industrial usage. The relative deindustrialization of the United States is restructuring the political economy, making the single-earner family far less viable. The loss of higher paid "male" manufacturing jobs and the massive entry of women into low-wage service work is meanwhile altering the gender composition of employment.[27] At the same time, divorce is common and, thanks in large part to the feminist and gay and lesbian liberation movements, changing gender norms are helping to proliferate new family forms, making the male breadwinner/female homemaker model less attractive to many.[28] It no longer goes without saying that a woman should rely on a man for economic support, nor that mothers should not also be "workers." Thus, another major form of dependency that was positively inflected in industrial semantics has become contested if not simply negative.

The combined result of these developments is to increase the stigma of dependency. With all legal and political dependency now illegitimate, and with wives' economic dependency now contested, there is no longer any self-evidently "good" adult dependency in postindustrial society. Rather, all dependency is suspect, and independence is enjoined upon everyone. Independence, however, remains identified with wage labor. Everyone is expected to "work" and to be "self-supporting." Any adult not perceived as a worker shoulders a heavier burden of self-justification.

With the formal dismantling of coverture and Jim Crow, it has become possible to claim that equality of opportunity exists and that individual merit determines outcomes. With capitalist economic dependency already abolished by definition, and with legal and political dependency now abolished by law, postindustrial society appears to some conservatives and liberals to have eliminated every social-structural basis of dependency. Whatever dependency remains, therefore, can be interpreted as the fault of individuals.

Welfare Dependency as Postindustrial Pathology

The worsening connotations of welfare dependency have been nourished by several streams from outside the field of welfare. New postindustrial medical and psychological discourses have associated dependency with pathology. Social scientists began in the 1980s to write about chemical, alcohol, and drug dependency, all euphemisms for addiction.[29] Because welfare claimants are often – falsely – assumed to be addicts, the pathological connotations of drug dependency tend also to infect welfare dependency, increasing stigmatization.

A second important postindustrial current is the rise of new psychological meanings of dependency with very strong feminine associations. In the 1950s, social workers influenced by psychiatry began to diagnose dependence as a form of immaturity common among women, particularly among solo mothers (who were often, of course, welfare claimants). The problem was that women were supposed to be just dependent enough, and it was easy to tip over into excess in either direction. The norm, moreover, was racially marked, as white women were usually portrayed as erring on the side of excessive dependence, while Black women were typically charged with excessive independence.

Psychologized dependency became the target of some of the earliest second-wave feminism. Betty Friedan's 1963 classic, *The Feminine Mystique* (New York: Norton), provided a phenomenological account of the housewife's psychological dependency and drew from it a political critique of her social subordination. More recently, however, a burgeoning cultural-feminist, postfeminist, and antifeminist self-help and pop-psychology literature has obfuscated the link between the psychological and the political. In Colette Dowling's 1981 book, *The Cinderella Complex* (New York: Summit Books), women's dependency was hypostatized as a depth-psychological gender structure: "women's hidden fear of independence" or the "wish to be saved." The late 1980s saw a spate of books about "co-dependency," a supposedly prototypically female syndrome of supporting or "enabling" the dependency of someone else. In a metaphor that reflects the drug hysteria of the period, dependency here, too, is an addiction. Apparently, even if a woman manages herself to escape her gender's predilection to dependency, she is still liable to incur the blame for facilitating the dependency of her husband or children.[30] This completes the vicious circle: the increased stigmatizing of dependency in the culture at large has also deepened contempt for those who care for dependents.

The 1980s saw a cultural panic about dependency. In 1980, the American Psychiatric Association codified "Dependent Personality Disorder" (DPD) as an official psychopathology. According to the 1987 edition of the *Diagnostic and Statistical Manual of Mental Disorders* (DSM-III-R), "the essential feature of this disorder is a pervasive pattern of dependent and submissive behavior beginning by early childhood . . . People with this disorder are unable to make everyday decisions without an excessive amount of advice and reassurance from others, and will even allow others to make most of their important decisions . . . The disorder is apparently common and is diagnosed more frequently in females."[31]

The codification of DPD as an official psychopathology represents a new stage in the history of the moral/psychological register. Here the social relations of dependency disappear entirely into the personality of the dependent. Overt moralism also disappears in the apparently neutral, scientific, medicalized formulation. Thus, although the defining traits of the dependent personality match point for point the traits traditionally ascribed to housewives, paupers, natives, and slaves, all links to subordination have vanished. The only remaining trace of those themes is the flat, categorical, and uninterpreted observation that DPD is "diagnosed more frequently in females."

If psychological discourse has further feminized and individualized dependency, other postindustrial developments have further racialized it. The increased stigmatization of welfare dependency followed a general increase in public provision in the United States, the removal of some discriminatory practices that had previously excluded minority women from participation in AFDC, especially in the South, and the transfer of many white women to first-track programs as social-insurance coverage expanded. By the 1970s the figure of the Black solo mother had come to epitomize welfare dependency. As a result, the new discourse about welfare draws on older symbolic currents that linked dependency with racist ideologies.

The ground was laid by a long, somewhat contradictory stream of discourse about "the Black family," in which African-American gender and kinship relations were measured against white middle class norms and deemed pathological. One supposedly pathological element was "the excessive independence" of Black women, an ideologically distorted allusion to long traditions of wage work, educational achievement, and community activism. The 1960s and 1970s discourse about poverty recapitulated traditions of misogyny towards African-American women; in Daniel Moynihan's diagnosis, for example, "matriarchal" families had "emasculated" Black men and created a "culture of poverty" based on a "tangle of [family] pathology."[32] This discourse placed Black AFDC claimants in a double-bind: they were pathologically independent with respect to men and pathologically dependent with respect to government.

By the 1980s, however, the racial imagery of dependency had shifted. The Black welfare mother that haunted the white imagination ceased to be the powerful matriarch. Now the pre-eminent stereotype is the unmarried teenage mother caught in the "welfare trap" and rendered drone-like and passive. This new icon of welfare dependency is younger and weaker than the matriarch. She is often evoked in the phrase "children having children," which can express feminist sympathy or antifeminist contempt, Black appeals for parental control or white-racist eugenic anxieties.

Many of these postindustrial discourses coalesced in the early 1990s. Then-Vice President Dan Quayle brought together the pathologized, feminized and racialized currents in his comment on the May 1992 Los Angeles riot: "Our inner cities are filled with children having children . . . with people who are dependent on drugs and on the narcotic of welfare."[33]

Thus postindustrial culture has called up a new personification of dependency: the Black, unmarried, teenaged, welfare-dependent mother. This image has usurped the symbolic space previously occupied by the housewife, the pauper, the native, and the slave, while absorbing and condensing their connotations. Black, female, a pauper, not a worker, a housewife and mother, yet practically a child herself – the new stereotype partakes of virtually every quality that has been coded historically as antithetical to independence. Condensing multiple, often contradictory meanings of dependency, it is a powerful ideological trope that simultaneously organizes diffuse cultural anxieties and dissimulates their social bases.

Postindustrial Policy and the Politics of Dependency

Contemporary policy discourse about welfare dependency is thoroughly inflected by these assumptions. It divides into two major streams. The first continues the rhetoric of pauperism and the culture of poverty. It is used in both conservative and liberal, victim-blaming and non-victim-blaming ways, depending on the causal structure of the argument. The contention is that poor, dependent people have something more than lack of money wrong with them. Conservatives, such as George Gilder and Lawrence Mead, argue that welfare causes moral/psychological dependency.[34] Liberals, such as William Julius Wilson and Christopher Jencks, blame social and economic influences, but agree that claimants' culture and behavior are problematic.[35]

A second stream of thought begins from neoclassical economic premises. It assumes a "rational man" facing choices in which welfare and work are both options. For these policy analysts, the moral/psychological meanings of dependency are present but uninterrogated, assumed to be undesirable. Liberals of this school, such as many of the social scientists associated with the Institute for Research on Poverty at the University of Wisconsin, grant that welfare inevitably has some bad, dependency-creating effects, but claim that these are outweighed by other, good effects like improved conditions for children, increased societal stability, and relief of suffering. Conservatives of this school, such as Charles Murray, disagree.[36] The two camps argue above all about the question of incentives.

Do AFDC stipends encourage women to have more out-of-wedlock children? Do they discourage them from accepting jobs? Can reducing or withholding stipends serve as a stick to encourage recipients to stay in school, keep their children in school, get married?

Certainly, there are real and significant differences here, but there are also important similarities. Liberals and conservatives of both schools rarely situate the notion of dependency in its historical or economic context; nor do they interrogate its presuppositions. Neither group questions the assumption that independence is an unmitigated good nor its identification with wage labor. Many poverty and welfare analysts equivocate between an official position that dependency is a value-neutral term for receipt of (or need for) welfare and a usage that makes it a synonym for pauperism.

These assumptions permeate the public sphere. In the current discussion of welfare dependency, it is increasingly claimed that "welfare mothers ought to work," a usage that tacitly defines work as wage-earning and child-raising as nonwork. Here we run up against contradictions in the discourse of dependency: when the subject under consideration is teenage pregnancy, these mothers are cast as children; when the subject is welfare, they become adults who should be self-supporting.

None of the negative imagery about welfare dependency has gone uncontested, of course. Much of it was directly challenged in the mid-1960s by an organization of women welfare claimants, the National Welfare Rights Organization. NWRO women cast their relation with the welfare system as active rather than passive, a matter of claiming rights rather than receiving charity. They also insisted that their domestic labor was socially necessary and praiseworthy. Their perspective helped reconstruct the arguments for welfare, spurring poverty lawyers and radical intellectuals to develop a legal and political-theoretical basis for welfare as an entitlement and right. Edward Sparer, a legal strategist for the welfare rights movement, challenged the usual understanding of dependency: "The charge of antiwelfare politicians is that welfare makes the recipient 'dependent.' What this means is that the recipient depends on the welfare check for his [sic] material subsistence rather than upon some other source . . . whether that is good or bad depends on whether a better source of income is available . . . The real problem . . . is something entirely different. The recipient and the applicant traditionally have been dependent on the whim of the caseworker."[37] The cure for welfare dependency, then, was welfare rights. Had the NWRO not been greatly weakened by the late 1970s, the revived discourse of pauperism in the 1980s could not have become hegemonic.

Even in the absence of a powerful National Welfare Rights Organization, many AFDC recipients maintained their own oppositional interpretation of welfare dependency. In their view, it is a social condition, not a psychological state, hence what a leftwing English dictionary of social welfare calls enforced dependency, "the creation of a dependent class" as a result of "enforced reliance . . . for necessary psychological or material resources."[38]

Meanwhile, during the period in which NWRO activism was at its height, New Left revisionist historians developed an interpretation of the welfare state as an apparatus of social control. They argued that what apologists portrayed as helping practices were actually modes of domination that created enforced dependency.[39] Another challenge to mainstream uses of dependency arose from a New Left school of international political economy. The context was the realization, after the first heady days of postwar decolonization, that politically independent former colonies remained economically dependent. In dependency theory, radical theorists of "underdevelopment" used the concept of dependency to analyze the global neocolonial economic order from an anti-racist and anti-imperialist perspective. In so doing, they resurrected the old preindustrial meaning of dependency as a subjected territory, seeking thereby to divest the term of its newer moral/psychological accretions and to retrieve the occluded dimensions of subjection and subordination.

What all these oppositional discourses share is a rejection of the dominant emphasis on dependency as an individual trait. They seek to shift the focus back to the social relations of subordination. But they do not have much impact on mainstream talk about welfare in the United States today. On the contrary, with economic dependency now a synonym for poverty, and with moral/psychological dependency now a personality disorder, talk of dependency as a social relation of subordination has become increasingly rare. Power and domination tend to disappear.[40]

Conclusion

Dependency, once a general-purpose term for all social relations of subordination, is now differentiated into several analytically distinct registers. In the economic register, its meaning has shifted from gaining one's livelihood by working for someone else to relying for support on charity or welfare; wage labor now confers independence. In the socio-legal register, the meaning of dependency as subsumption is unchanged, but its scope of reference and connotations have altered: once a socially approved majority condition, it first became a group-based status deemed proper for some classes of persons but not others and then shifted again to designate (except in the case of children) an anomalous, highly stigmatized status of deviant and incompetent individuals. Likewise, in the political register, dependency's meaning as subjection to an external governing power has remained relatively constant, but its evaluative connotations worsened as individual political rights and national sovereignty became normative. Meanwhile, with the emergence of a newer moral/psychological register, properties once ascribed to social relations came to be posited instead as inherent character traits of individuals or groups, and the connotations here, too, have worsened. This last register now claims an increasingly large proportion of the discourse, as if the social relations of dependency were being absorbed into personality. Symptomatically, erstwhile relational understandings have been hypostatized in a veritable portrait gallery of dependent personalities: first, housewives, paupers, natives, and slaves; then poor, solo, Black teenage mothers.

These shifts in the semantics of dependency reflect some major sociohistorical developments. One is the progressive differentiation of the official economy – that which is counted in the GDP – as a seemingly autonomous system that dominates social life. Before the rise of capitalism, any particular dependency was knotted into a net of dependencies, which constituted a single, continuous fabric of social hierarchies. Although women were subordinated and their labor often controlled by others, their labor was visible, understood, and formally valued. With the emergence of religious and secular individualism, on the one hand, and of industrial capitalism, on the other, a sharp, new dichotomy was constructed in which economic dependence and economic independence were opposed to one another. A crucial corollary of this dependence/ independence dichotomy, and of the hegemony of wage labor in general, was the occlusion and devaluation of women's unwaged domestic and parenting labor.

The genealogy of dependency also expresses the modern emphasis on individual personality. Fear of dependency, both explicit and implicit, posits an ideal, independent personality in contrast to which those considered dependent are deviant. This contrast bears traces of a sexual division of labor that assigns men primary responsibility as providers or breadwinners and women primary responsibility as caretakers and nurturers and then treats the derivative personality patterns as fundamental. It is as if male breadwinners absorbed into their personalities the independence associated with their ideologically interpreted economic role, whereas the persons of female nurturers became saturated with the dependency of those for whom they care. The opposition between the independent personality and the dependent personality maps onto a whole series of hierarchical oppositions and dichotomies that are central in modern culture: masculine/feminine, public/private, economy/family, work/care, success/love, individual/community, and competitive/self-sacrificing.

A genealogy cannot tell us how to respond politically to today's discourse about welfare dependency. It does suggest, however, the limits of any response that presupposes rather than challenges the definition of the problem that is implicit in that expression. An adequate response would need to question our received valuations and definitions of dependence and independence in order to allow new, emancipatory social visions to emerge. Some contemporary welfare-rights activists adopt this strategy, continuing the NWRO tradition. Pat Gowens, for example, elaborates a feminist reinterpretation of dependency: "The vast majority of mothers of all classes and all educational levels 'depends' on another income. It may come from child support . . . or from a husband who earns $20,000 while she averages $7,000. But 'dependence' more accurately defines dads who count on women's unwaged labor to raise children and care for the home. Surely, 'dependence' doesn't define the single mom who does it all: child-rearing, homemaking, and bringing in the money (one way or another). When care-giving is valued and paid, when dependence is not a dirty word, and interdependence is the norm – only then will we make a dent in poverty."[41]

Notes

A longer version of this article has been published in *Signs: Journal of Women in Culture and Society* 19, 2 (Winter 1994), pp. 309–36, under the title "A Genealogy of *Dependency*: Tracing a Keyword of the US Welfare System." Nancy Fraser is grateful for research support from the Center for Urban Affairs, Northwestern University; the Newberry Library/National Endowment for the Humanities; and the American Council of Learned Societies. Linda Gordon thanks the University of Wisconsin Graduate School, Vilas Trust, and the Institute for Research on Poverty. We both thank the Rockefeller Foundation Research and Study Center, Bellagio, Italy. We are also grateful for helpful comments from Lisa Brush, Robert Entman, Joel Handler, Dirk Hartog, Barbara Hobson, Allen Hunter, Eva Kittay, Felicia Kornbluh, Jenny Mansbridge, Linda Nicholson, Erik Wright, Eli Zaretsky, and the *Signs* reviewers and editors.

1 Quoted in Karen Tumulty, *Los Angeles Times* (July 5, 1991), p. A4.
2 Daniel P. Moynihan, *The Politics of a Guaranteed Income: The Nixon Administration and the Family Assistance Plan* (New York: Random House, 1973), p. 17.
3 Richard P. Nathan, "The Underclass – Will It Always Be With Us?" Unpublished paper quoted by William Julius Wilson, "Social Policy and Minority Groups: What Might Have Been and What Might We See in the Future," in *Divided Opportunities: Minorities, Poverty, and Social Policy*, eds Gary D. Sandefur and Marta Tienda (New York: Plenum Press, 1986), p. 248.

4 Another part of the story, of course, concerns the word *welfare,* but that is the subject for another essay. Here we note only that US usage is unlike that of most other North American and European countries, which use *welfare* (or its equivalent) broadly and nonpejoratively to encompass the whole range of public services, including universalist programs like health and education, through which membership in society is enacted. In the US, in contrast, the term *welfare* is reserved for programs targeted for poor people, and it carries strong negative connotations. In this essay, our focus is US political culture and thus North American English usage. Our findings concerning *dependency* should be of more general interest, however, as some other languages have similar meanings embedded in analogous words. In this essay we have of necessity used British sources for the early stages of our genealogy, which spans the sixteenth and seventeenth centuries. We assume that these meanings of *dependency* were brought to "the New World" and were formative for the early stages of US political culture.

5 Raymond Williams, *Keywords: A Vocabulary of Culture and Society* (Oxford: Oxford University Press, 1976).

6 This stress on the performative, as opposed to the representational, dimension of language is a hallmark of the pragmatic tradition in the philosophy of language. It has been fruitfully adapted for socio-cultural analysis by several writers in addition to Williams. See, for example, Pierre Bourdieu, *Outline of a Theory of Practice* (Cambridge: Cambridge University Press, 1977); *In Other Words,* trans. Matthew Adamson (Oxford: Polity Press, 1990); and *The Logic of Practice,* trans. Richard Nice (Stanford: Stanford University Press, 1990). Also, Nancy Fraser, *Unruly Practices: Power, Discourse and Gender in Contemporary Social Theory* (Minneapolis: University of Minnesota Press, 1989); "Structuralism or Pragmatics? On Discourse Theory and Feminist Politics," in Fraser, *Justice Interruptus: Critical Reflections on the "Postsocialist" Condition* (Routledge, 1997); and "Pragmatism, Feminism, and the Linguistic Turn," in Benhabib, Butler, Cornell, and Fraser, *Feminist Contentions: A Philosophical Exchange* (New York: Routledge, 1994). See, in addition, Judith Butler, *Gender Trouble: Feminism and the Subversion of Identity* (New York: Routledge, 1990); and Joan Wallach Scott, *Gender and the Politics of History* (New York: Columbia University Press, 1988).

7 Nancy Fraser, "Struggle Over Needs: Outline of a Socialist-Feminist Critical Theory of Late-Capitalist Political Culture," in Fraser, *Unruly Practices.*

8 Williams, *Keywords.*

9 Pierre Bourdieu, *Outline of a Theory of Practice.*

10 Michel Foucault, "Nietzsche, Genealogy, History," in *The Foucault Reader,* ed. Paul Rabinow (New York: Pantheon, 1984).

11 Joan R. Gundersen, "Independence, Citizenship, and the American Revolution," *Signs: Journal of Women in Culture and Society,* 13, 1 (1987), pp. 59–77.

12 Peter Laslett, *The World We Have Lost: England Before the Industrial Age* (New York: Charles Scribner, 1971), p. 21.

13 One might say that this redefinition foregrounded wage labor as a new form of property, namely, property in one's own labor power. This conception was premised on what C. B. Macpherson called "possessive individualism," the assumption of an individual's property in his (sic) own person. (See

Macpherson, *The Political Theory of Possessive Individualism: Hobbes to Locke* [Oxford: Oxford University Press, 1962].) Leading to the construction of wages as an entitlement, this approach was overwhelmingly male. Allen Hunter (personal communication) describes it as a loss of systemic critique, a sense of independence gained by narrowing the focus to the individual worker and leaving behind aspirations for collective independence from capital.

14 The evolution of the term *native* neatly encapsulates this process. Its original meaning in English, dating from about 1450, was tied to dependency: "one born in bondage; a born thrall," but without racial meaning. Two centuries later it carried the additional meaning of colored or Black [OED].

15 Hilary Land, "The Family Wage," *Feminist Review*, 6 (1980), pp. 55–77, p. 57. Jeanne Boydston, *Home and Work: Housework, Wages, and the Ideology of Labor in the Early Republic* (New York: Oxford, 1991).

16 Nancy Folbre, "The Unproductive Housewife: Her Evolution in Nineteenth-century Economic Thought," *Signs: Journal of Women in Culture and Society*, 16, 3 (1991), pp. 463–84.

17 Amos Griswold Warner, *American Charities and Social Work* (New York: Thomas Y. Crowell, 1894 through 1930). Edith Abbott and Sophonisba P. Breckinridge, *The Administration of the Aid-to-Mothers Law in Illinois* (Washington: US Children's Bureau, Publication no. 82, 1921), p. 7. National Conference of Charities and Correction, Proceedings (1890s through 1920s).

18 Studies of welfare done in the 1940s still used the word *dependents* only in the sense of those supported by family heads. See, e.g., Josephine Chapin Brown, *Public Relief 1929–1939* (New York: Henry Holt, 1940); Frank J. Bruno, *Trends in Social Work* (New York: Columbia University Press, 1948); and Donald S. Howard, *The WPA and Federal Relief Policy* (New York: Russell Sage, 1943).

19 Lilian Brandt, *An Impressionistic View of the Winter of 1930–31 in New York City* (New York: Welfare Council of New York City, 1932), pp. 23–4. Gertrude Vaile, untitled essay in *College Women and the Social Sciences*, ed. Herbert Elmer Mills (New York: John Day, 1934), p. 26. Mary L. Gibbons, "Family Life Today and Tomorrow," *Proceedings*, National Conference of Catholic Charities 19 (1933), pp. 133–68.

20 E. Wight Bakke, *Citizens Without Work: A Study of the Effects of Unemployment Upon Workers' Social Relations and Practices* (New Haven: Yale University Press, 1940) and *The Unemployed Worker: A Study of the Task of Making a Living Without a Job* (New Haven: Yale University Press, 1940).

21 Nancy Fraser and Linda Gordon, "Contract Versus Charity: Why Is There No Social Citizenship in the United States?" *Socialist Review*, 22, 3 (1992), pp. 45–68.

22 Nancy Fraser, "Women, Welfare, and the Politics of Need Interpretation," in *Unruly Practices*. Also Linda Gordon, "The New Feminist Scholarship on the Welfare State" and Barbara J. Nelson, "The Origins of the Two-Channel Welfare State: Workmen's Compensation and Mothers' Aid," both in *Women, the State, and Welfare*, ed. Linda Gordon (Madison: University of Wisconsin Press, 1990).

23 Jill Quadagno, "From Old-Age Assistance to Supplemental Social Security Income: The Political Economy of Relief in the South, 1935–1972." In *The Politics of Social Policy in the United States*, ed. Margaret Weir, Ann Shola Orloff, and Theda Skocpol (Princeton: Princeton University Press, 1988).

24 The Social Security Board propagandized for Social Security Old Age Insurance (the program today called just "Social Security") precisely because, at first, it did not seem more earned or more dignified than public assistance. To make Social Security more acceptable, the Board worked to stigmatize public assistance, even pressuring states to keep stipends low. See Jerry R. Cates, *Insuring Inequality: Administrative Leadership in Social Security, 1935–54* (Ann Arbor: University of Michigan Press, 1983).

25 Jacqueline Pope, *Biting the Hand that Feeds Them: Organizing Women on Welfare at the Grass Roots Level* (New York: Praeger, 1989), pp. 73, 144. Guida West, *The National Welfare Rights Movement: The Social Protest of Poor Women* (New York: Praeger, 1981). Milwaukee County Welfare Rights Organization, *Welfare Mothers Speak Out* (New York: Norton, 1972).

26 Linda Gordon, "Social Insurance and Public Assistance: The Influence of Gender in Welfare Thought in the United States, 1890–1935," *American Historical Review*, 97, 1 (1992), pp. 19–54.

27 Joan Smith, "The Paradox of Women's Poverty: Wage-earning Women and Economic Transformation," *Signs: Journal of Women in Culture and Society*, 10, 2 (1984), pp. 291–310.

28 Judith Stacey, "Sexism By a Subtler Name? Postindustrial Conditions and Postfeminist Consciousness in the Silicon Valley," *Socialist Review*, 96 (1987), pp. 7–28 and *Brave New Families: Stories of Domestic Upheaval in Late Twentieth Century America* (New York: Basic Books, 1990). Kath Weston, *Families We Choose: Lesbians, Gays, Kinship* (New York: Columbia University Press, 1991).

29 For example, M. Haynes, "Pharmacist Involvement in a Chemical-Dependency Rehabilitation Program," *American Journal of Hospital Pharmacy*, 45, 10 (1988), pp. 2099–101.

30 Virginia Sapiro, "The Gender Basis of American Social Policy," in *Women, the State, and Welfare*, ed. Gordon.

31 American Psychiatric Association, *Diagnostic and Statistical Manual of Mental Disorders*, 3rd edition revised (Washington DC: American Psychiatric Association, 1987), pp. 353–4.

32 Lee Rainwater and William L. Yancey, *The Moynihan Report and the Politics of Controversy* (Cambridge, MA: The MIT Press, 1967).

33 Dan Quayle, "Excerpts From Vice President's Speech on Cities and Poverty," *The New York Times*, May 20, 1992, p. A11.

34 George Gilder, *Wealth and Poverty* (New York: Basic Books, 1981). Lawrence Mead, *Beyond Entitlement: The Social Obligations of Citizenship* (New York: The Free Press, 1986).

35 William Julius Wilson, *The Truly Disadvantaged: The Inner City, the Underclass, and Public Policy* (Chicago: The University of Chicago Press, 1987). Christopher Jencks, *Rethinking Social Policy: Race, Poverty, and the Underclass* (Cambridge, MA: Harvard University Press, 1992).

36 Charles Murray, *Losing Ground: American Social Policy, 1950–1980* (New York: Basic Books, 1984).

37 Edward V. Sparer, "The Right to Welfare," in *The Rights of Americans: What They Are – What They Should Be*, ed. Norman Dorsen (New York: Pantheon, 1970), p. 71.

38 Noel and Rita Timms, *Dictionary of Social Welfare* (London: Routledge & Kegan Paul, 1982), pp. 55–6.

39 Although the New Left critique bore some resemblance to the NWRO critique, the historians of social control told their story mainly from the perspective of the "helpers" and so occluded the agency of actual or potential welfare claimants in articulating needs, demanding rights, and making claims. See Gordon, "The New Feminist Scholarship on the Welfare State," op. cit. On needs claims, see Fraser, "Struggle Over Needs," and Nelson, "The Origins of the Two-Channel Welfare State."

40 For an argument that Clinton's recent neoliberal discourse continues to individualize dependency, see Fraser, "Clintonism, Welfare and the Antisocial Wage: The Emergence of a Neoliberal Political Imaginary," *Rethinking Marxism*, 6, 1 (1993), pp. 1–15.

41 Pat Gowens, "Welfare, Learnfare – Unfair! A Letter to My Governor," *Ms.* (September–October, 1991), pp. 90–1.

3

Towards a Feminist Vision of Citizenship: Rethinking the Implications of Dignity, Political Participation, and Nationality

Uma Narayan

Introduction

From Aristotle's idea of citizenship as a status belonging to those who engaged in the activities of political and civic self-government and hence only to free males, to the French Revolution of 1789, "when even women succeeded in claiming address as *citoyenne*,"[1] the term "citizenship" has connoted respect, dignity, status-equality, self-government and the rights associated with these values. In his 1949 essay, "Citizenship and Social Class,"[2] T.H. Marshall delineated three stages of citizenship that focused, respectively, on rights to individual freedom and justice, rights to the exercise of political power, and finally rights to basic forms of economic security and to a share in the "full social heritage." Citizenship has also been a key term in numerous feminist political struggles, from women's suffrage to current conflicts about welfare rights. As Fraser and Gordon put it, "It is a weighty, monumental, humanist word."[3]

I take citizenship in its most general sense to refer to the relationships that those who inhabit a nation have to the state, and to the various aspects of collective national life. In this essay I shall explore three contexts in which the term has been deployed, and attempt to set out the ways in which each is relevant to a feminist rethinking of citizenship. In the first section, I explore the notion of citizenship as a status that connotes social standing and dignity, and argue against the view that important aspects of social standing and dignity should be grounded in an individual's "contributions" to national life. In the second section, I consider the idea of citizenship as active participation in civic and political life and examine the social implications of taking political participation seriously. I argue that a feminist vision of equal representation and substantive equal citizenship for women and members of other marginalized groups needs to focus not only on promoting their *political* participation and representation, but on their access to and voice within a variety of public institutions within which interests are articulated and promoted. In the final section, I look at the idea of citizenship-as-nationality and examine how many of the criteria and procedures that govern the acquisition of citizenship as nationality discriminate against women who are non-citizens. I argue that we need to extend the scope of our political concerns to those who are not citizens of the state within which they live, and suggest that concerns articulated in the name of citizenship should often be broadly construed to include all those who are ongoing members of the national community.

Although the term "citizenship" has often been used in struggles to secure greater dignity and participation for members of marginalized groups, it has often *simultaneously functioned* to justify the exclusion of other members of the national community, a tendency clearly illustrated by the historical struggles over suffrage. Since "citizenship" has tended to be a central notion in defining those whose interests count, its capacity to exclude others makes it of interest to feminists, since those excluded from its scope have often been women. Feminist usages of the term have however often replicated the problem by focusing on the interests of relatively privileged women, such as middle-class white women in the US context. A feminist rethinking of citizenship which is concerned with attending to the interests of underprivileged women must be sensitive to the ways in which our use of categories such as "citizen-national" or "citizen-worker" might function to marginalize and exclude women who are non-nationals or non-workers from the theoretical considerations and practical concerns of our politics. This essay attempts to be attentive to both these facets of inclusion and exclusion embedded in our uses of the term "citizenship," and to rethink the implications of social standing, political participation and national membership, each of which has strong connections to "citizenship," in ways that are adequately inclusive with respect to contemporary feminist political contexts. My analysis of social standing and dignity, political participation and nationality as facets of citizenship is intended to apply to a number of national contexts, although many of the examples I use in my discussion pertain to the United States.

Citizenship as Social Standing and Dignity

In many national contexts, to be a citizen was to have a type of public or civic standing denied to non-citizens. Judith Shklar points out that the notion of citizenship as "social standing" has been an important notion in the American political context, and she argues that "the two great emblems of public standing, the vote and the opportunity to earn" have been central to the American idea of citizenship. Shklar contends that voting and earning were not merely *instrumentally* valued (as means to promote one's interests and to make money), but were "marks of civic dignity" whereby people who lacked them felt "dishonored, not just powerless and poor."[4] From the start, citizenship as social standing was defined in contrast to those who were excluded from this status and Shklar argues that "The value of citizenship was derived primarily from its denial to slaves, to some white men, and to all women."[5] Shklar concludes "This vision of economic independence, of self-directed 'earning' as the ethical basis of democratic citizenship has retained its powerful appeal. We are citizens only if we 'earn.'"[6]

The work of slaves, and women's domestic work and childcare activity were forms of labor that did not "earn," and both male and female slaves as well as all other women were excluded from the vote. Even the waged labor of working-class women was not taken to constitute them as "free laborers" entitled to the vote. Today, there still continues to be a disjunction for many groups between what Shklar calls the "two emblems" of public standing. For example, waged work does *not* guarantee many immigrant laborers the rights to represent their interests, a concern I shall return to later. In this section, I wish to argue that the social standing of citizens should neither be grounded in their ability to *earn* nor depend on their ability to "contribute" to national life, even if the scope of "contributions" is widened to include activities other than paid labor. I shall also argue that the state's obligation to provide basic welfare rights should be seen as vitally connected to preserving the dignity and social standing of *all* those who are part of the national community.

There are problematic implications to regarding waged work as an "emblem" of citizenship and social standing. The intimate bond between earning and citizenship helps explain middle-class feminist concerns at being excluded from the world of paid work. It also helps to explain the importance that issues such as affirmative action, comparable worth, and harassment at the workplace have had in recent feminist agendas. The emphasis on equalizing work-related opportunities for women and members of other marginalized groups is undoubtedly urgent since their lack of equal access to well-paid and prestigious occupations has been central to their status as second-class citizens. However, I would argue that, when pursuing these legitimate agendas, we need to be careful not to reinforce the assumption that engaging in waged work is a *necessary condition* for individuals to deserve the social standing and to warrant the rights and dignity associated with citizenship.

There are several good feminist reasons to be critical of the tendency to assign paid work such an overwhelmingly important status in political thought. The primacy accorded *waged* work has helped reinforce the relative unimportance of the *unwaged* work, of the domestic labor and the care of dependents predominantly performed by women. In many countries, feminists have had more success in equalizing women's opportunities for waged work than in conferring dignity on housework and the care of dependents. Women who enter waged work in contexts where men systematically fail to shoulder an equitable share of household and care-giving tasks, and where social and institutional policies are not designed to render these tasks compatible with full-time waged work, end up with the unsatisfying options of part-time work or of attempting in exhaustion to struggle with these varied and conflicting demands.[7]

One way to counter the privileged position of waged work as an emblem of the social standing of citizens would be to insist that the work of having and raising children is itself an important contribution to national life, entitling those who do this work to the rights, dignity and standing of citizenship. The efforts of US feminists to argue for this position, in the context of struggles for women's welfare rights in the 1920s, illuminate both the benefits and the limitations of this approach. Countering prevalent masculine visions of republican citizenship that tied the dignity of citizenship not only to waged work, but to military service, voting, or serving on juries (all activities that excluded women), the feminists of the 1920s insisted on seeing the raising of children, or future citizens, as itself an activity of citizenship. In this view, the domestic sphere contained "the nurseries of the state."[8] The ensuing argument for welfare rights for women took the form of insisting that "If producing citizens to the State be the greatest service a woman citizen can perform, the State will ultimately recognize the right of the woman to protection during her time of service."[9] More recently, Carol Pateman has argued for a "sexually differentiated" conception of citizenship that would give motherhood and women's capacity to create life political relevance for defining citizenship.[10]

However, I believe there are serious problems with attempts to characterize the work of raising children as a "citizenship activity" that should ground the dignity and rights of citizens. First, characterizing childcare as the "rearing of future citizens" opens the door to severe state monitoring and regulation of this activity. The state could then justify linking its provision of welfare for children to ensuring that they are raised in a manner befitting "future citizens," a tendency at work in current proposals to withhold welfare entitlements for children born out of wedlock. Second, the view that raising children is a "service to the State" is likely to run up against claims that the state does not want this service from citizens who clearly lack independent resources for raising children, which could be used to justify current proposals for punitive measures against women who have children while on welfare. These problems make me hesitant about characterizing raising children as "citizenship activity" and make me sympathetic to Chantal Mouffe's view that our conception of citizenship should be remedied not by making sexual difference politically relevant but by making it "effectively nonpertinent."[11]

I have an additional reason for resisting the view that motherhood should be regarded as a "citizenship activity" that grounds women's rights to welfare. While such a grounding challenges the privileged link between waged labor and the social standing of citizens, it fails to challenge the assumption that welfare rights should be grounded in an individual's "contributions" to national life. I believe feminist interpretations of the idea of citizenship as social standing need to resist locating the dignity and worth of individuals in their capacities to be *contributors* to national life, and to insist that dignity, worth and social standing matter to all who are *participants* in national life, that is, *who are part of the national community*, independently of how they *contribute* to it. I am afraid that even broad conceptions of "citizenship contribution" will tend to exclude and marginalize groups of individuals in the national community who are unable to render those contributions. For instance, adding raising children to the list of things that count as "citizenship contributions," along with paid labor and soldiering, still leaves as problematic the welfare rights of those who may temporarily or permanently lack the capacities to make any of these contributions.

Further, if we endorse views of welfare rights as tied to "contributions," we risk subscribing to the problematic idea of "free and equal persons" that remains central to mainstream political theories whose visions of justice exclude "the fact of human dependency needs and its corollary, a just social organization capable of meeting dependency needs."[12] The exclusion of dependency relations from the "circumstances of justice" has deep roots in a picture of the sort of individual who warranted the dignity of citizenship. T.H. Marshall points out that the eighteenth-century idea of citizenship meant free status and the rights attached to that status, such as the right to own property, make valid contracts, the liberty of one's person, and eventually, the rights to freedom of speech, thought and religious faith.[13] These rights attached to citizens of "civil society," who were "free, rational men," who could contract freely with one another, represent their own interests and contribute to society.

Social movements that attempted to secure these civil and political rights for members of excluded groups, such as slaves, or white women, understandably made their case on the grounds that members of these excluded groups possessed the rationality, and the related capacities for self-representation, self-government and social contribution, that warranted their possession of these rights. However, such political rhetoric reinforces the notion that the rights and status of citizenship properly belong only to those who are "fully cooperating members of society," making those who temporarily or permanently lack these capacities, and who are dependent on other individuals or social institutions, ineligible for claims to the respect and dignity accorded to citizens. The adverse effects of this dominant view of the "autonomous, rational, self-governing" citizen are most clearly felt in our prevalent attitudes towards social provision such as welfare. As Fraser and Gordon succinctly put it, "Receipt of welfare is usually considered grounds for disrespect, a threat to, rather than a realization of, citizenship."[14]

A feminist vision of citizenship needs to be critical of theories that have located individual dignity and worth in capacities to be "autonomous, self-governing and self-supporting," a view which suggests that the only rights such citizens need are "negative rights," rights to freedom from intrusion and interference that protect these self-governing capacities, at the cost of ignoring the importance of "positive rights" to the provision of the basic means of subsistence required for dignity and standing in a society. A feminist conception of the dignity and worth of all citizens needs to conceptualize rights differently, so as to ground *both positive and negative rights as crucial components of human dignity.* How might this proceed?

If rights are understood as instruments for *preserving basic social dignity for all individuals,* we can avoid a bifurcated theory of rights that sees "negative rights" as grounded in "human capacities for self-government" and "positive rights" as *separately grounded* in a vision of "human needs." Meaningful exercise of one's capacities as well as the adequate satisfaction of one's needs are *both* vital components of one's social dignity and standing in national life. Lack of protection for individuals' important negative or positive rights is tantamount to declaring that the fate, flourishing and future of those individuals do not matter, or are of no concern, to the rest of society. To be treated as an entity whose vital interests do not matter to society is to be reduced to the status of a creature who is accorded no dignity. Those interests encompass both the freedom to set one's own projects and to act, which requires negative rights, and the freedom from want that is deeply corrosive of dignity, which requires positive rights.

I believe that the central concept needed to ground both negative and positive rights as central to citizenship is not that of "capacities to be self-governing" but the rather different concepts of "human vulnerabilities" and "human dignity." Human dignity is at risk when humans are left without protection for important vulnerabilities. Human dignity is at risk when humans are rendered vulnerable to intrusions on their capacities for self-government and autonomy, and to a lack of *adequate means* for the satisfaction of basic needs. Rights can then be seen as social means to *minimize such vulnerabilities*, as attempts to ensure a minimum amount of *social dignity* to all members of society – a conceptual vision that helps to see an underlying unity behind the roles of negative and positive rights.

I am suggesting both that the concept of individual worth should be distinguished from an individual's *instrumental* value to society qua "contributor," and that it be understood as compatible with forms of dependency on the state or on other individuals that promote or protect individual well-being. Individuals have dignity and worth when their basic interests and flourishing are treated as matters of social concern and regard in their own right. This social concern is concretely manifested in the range of negative and positive rights accorded to the individual. Although the term "dignity" has roots in rights discourse, I believe that the notion of human dignity needs to be loosened from its grounding in individual capacities to be self-governing and to partially be perceived as a consequence of the *social recognition* of the value of each human life. Resituating the idea of dignity and worth in social concern and regard for basic interests would, I think, make for a more adequate rights theory.

While both negative and positive rights are *enabling conditions* for individual autonomy and for individual participation in social affairs and contributions to national life, and are partly to be valued for this reason, I am opposed to "contractual" models of rights that tend to make particular sorts of "contributions" *preconditions* for the possession of rights. Further, I would like to widen the individualistic focus characteristic of rights ethics, by stressing that it is not only individual dignity and suffering that are at stake in social protection for rights, but also a social and political vision of the democratic polity, a vision of the sort of shared public values and national community that should inspire allegiance and pride among its citizens. Welfare rights should not be grounded in what individuals "contribute" to society, not only because this is likely to exclude many who need assistance, but also because we need to shift part of our sense of pride and self-worth from our individual capacities for being "autonomous contributors," *to our belonging to a society that is responsive to the social dignity and worth of all who are members of its national community, independent of their contributions.*

Thus, in the context of the current welfare rights debate in the United States, my analysis implies that regardless of whether we think welfare recipients should be *encouraged* to enter the labor force, we need to resist the view that individuals' "contributions" to the workforce should be a *precondition* for entitlements to welfare. Feminist concerns with women's status as citizens have revealed that one deeply gendered facet of that concept lies in its ties to "contribution" either in the form of paid work or soldiering. However, I believe that expanding the idea of "citizen contribution" to include raising children is not the solution to creating a concept of citizenship that is more inclusive of women. I am arguing that feminists need to challenge the view that "contributions" are the proper basis for having one's basic dignity and worth guaranteed qua member of the national community, even as we acknowledge that the state policies should enable a variety of forms of participation from its members, an issue I turn to in the next section.

Citizenship as Political Participation

In this section, I would like to explore the idea of engaged participation in political activity as an important facet of what it means to be a citizen. I shall primarily discuss the views of three important feminists who have considered the links between citizenship and political participation, Mary Dietz, Anne Phillips, and Iris Young. The importance of citizenship as active political participation has been most forcefully developed by the tradition of civic republicanism. The civic republican tradition has had a mixed reception among feminists. Some feminists have criticized aspects of the civic republican tradition for its "masculine" values of heroism and military glory, and its disdain for the domestic and the private.[15] Others, such as Dietz, find civic republican critiques of the pressure group politics of liberal democracy appealing, and endorse the idea that citizens must learn to transcend their local interests and limited perspectives to address the wider concerns of the polity as a whole.

This leads to a debate between two different feminist accounts of how one's specific interests or group identity might relate to one's political activity qua citizen. Feminists inspired by aspects of civic republican ideals stress that democratic political activity has the power to "transform the individual as teacher, trader, corporate executive . . . friend or mother into a special sort of political being, a citizen among other citizens."[16] Mary Dietz suggests that when we enter the arena of political dialogue as citizens, we transcend our particular identities and assume the status of "equals who render judgment on matters of shared importance, deliberate

over issues of common concern and act in concert with each other."[17] On
the other hand, Iris Young finds this ideal of citizenship problematic,
arguing that the insistence that citizens should leave behind particular
affiliations and experiences reinforces privilege because "the perspectives
and interests of the privileged will tend to dominate this unified public."[18]

I too have reservations about Dietz's picture of political activity. I would
not restrict the notion of "political activity" to a dialogue among members
"of a shared community where we acknowledge others as being of equal
account" since this has the unsettling effect of excluding from the domain
of "political activity" a huge array of modern political struggles – struggles
for the abolition of slavery, for suffrage, for national independence –
which were precisely struggles to be recognized *as* valued members of the
"shared community" and *as* those who were of "equal account." The ideal
of political activity as a dialogue among those of equal account is one that
only begins to make some sense in the aftermath of these struggles for
political inclusion. This makes me sympathetic to Young's recognition
that members of marginalized groups in contemporary liberal democracies
continue to face barriers to equal representation of their concerns and
hence to constituting those who are of equal account. And, as I shall argue
in the next section, the struggle to extend the horizons of the "shared
community" to include the concerns of resident non-citizens remains an
ongoing challenge.

I am sympathetic to Young's recognition that the formal political
equality conferred by the vote has not resulted in *substantive political
equality* for all. The concerns of members of marginalized groups still tend
to be underrepresented in political discourse; very few members of
marginalized groups tend to be present among the body of "representatives" elected to political office, and they face a variety of obstacles to
sustained engagement in political activity. Both the arenas of representative and of participatory democracy seem, in different ways, to impede
attention to the concerns and viewpoints of members of these groups,
making the problem of how to ensure more adequate representation in the
political arena of continuing concern.[19]

On this question, there are again differences among feminists. Young's
primary concern is with securing political representation for the interests
of oppressed groups. She proposes public funding to promote the
self-organization of oppressed groups, requirements that policymakers
take into account the proposals that emanate from such groups, and a veto
power for these groups with regard to policy proposals that most directly
affect them.[20] Phillips has reservations about Young's proposals for group
representation, citing worries such as "the difficult problems of group
closure (people coming to define themselves politically through what is

only one frozen single aspect of their lives); the question of who is to legislate on which groups qualify for additional group representation; and the almost insuperable obstacles to establishing what any group wants."[21] I share Phillips's reservations. I am concerned that public funding for the self-organization of oppressed groups might lead to state surveillance and control of the activities of these groups. Any serious consideration of the fact that oppressed groups are themselves internally heterogeneous with respect to identities, interests and political perspectives leads to worries about the problematic results of taking the policy proposals put forward by the leadership of these groups as definitive of the interests of *all* members of the group. For instance, state funding for the representation of ethnic immigrant minorities might well result in their "representation" by a politically conservative male leadership.[22] I think that while Young's *analysis* acknowledges the internal heterogeneity of groups, her *proposals* run the risk of treating "oppressed groups" as totalized unities, where all members are assumed to share common interests and policy perspectives simply by virtue of their being "oppressed."

While Young's proposals are problematic, it is clear that feminists need to share her concern about the fact that women, members of ethnic minorities, and working-class people are disproportionately absent from the body of elected representatives in liberal democracies as we know them, and from many areas of active political participation. What might be some alternatives to Young's proposals? I would distinguish between two problems that often seem to get conflated in discussions of the representation of marginalized groups. The first problem is that of promoting the presence of women, racial minorities and working-class people among *the body of office-holders and elected representatives*, and the second is that of promoting *greater active political participation* among members of marginalized groups. The first problem requires us to explore ways of reducing obstacles to standing for office and winning office. Reducing the degree to which being wealthy, or having the backing of the wealthy, affects one's abilities to run for office, and encouraging political parties to diversify their candidates for political office are both, I would argue, partial solutions to this problem. The problem of "authority," where those who are not "mainstream citizens" are stereotypically perceived to be lacking in the competence and authority valued in elected officials, is more difficult to overcome in the short run. In the long run, part of what it will take to reduce these stereotypes is a greater distribution of members of marginalized groups in other arenas of achievement and authority – in the world of remunerative work, and in appointed (as opposed to elected) positions of public office.

The second problem, that of encouraging the active political participation of members of marginalized groups, requires attention to large-scale social and institutional factors that impede such participation. If we endorse civic republicanism's emphasis on the importance of political activity, we need to link it with attempts to undo the social structures and arrangements that hinder such participation. Political theory should more often ask itself the question "What would a society that really valued the political participation of all segments of its members look like?" A number of broad answers suggest themselves. Such a society would have to be concerned with reducing the sorts of large disparities of wealth and power that facilitate some and obstruct others from having a say in the political domain. Such a society would have to be concerned with reducing institutional and social barriers that impede the entry of certain groups of people into educational and professional contexts, contexts where encounters with those "different from ourselves" can enrich our political understandings. Such a state would be committed to ensuring a quality education for all its members, seeing education as an important asset to informed political participation by its citizens. Such a state would work to provide institutionalized ways of caring for dependents, so that care-giving tasks do not chronically deprive caregivers of the time or energy required for political participation.

I am arguing that a variety of policies that work to reduce disparities, ensure equal access to the workplace, provide quality education and affordable childcare might be grounded not only in terms of their value to the particular lives of *individual citizens,* but also in terms of their *enabling a variety of forms of citizen participation in national political life.* Such provisions and policies need to be understood in part as *social preconditions for the possibility of politically active citizens* who are vital to the political health of liberal democratic societies. Feminists need to insist on the connections between issues of decent education, reproductive rights, affordable childcare and equal access to the workplace and our collective social need to promote the active political participation of all citizens. Many of the negative and positive rights I discussed in the previous section not only serve to protect individual dignity and to constitute a decent polity, but also serve to promote the shared social good of active civic and political participation.

This brings me to a different but related question. Feminists have struggled with the question of what is to "count" as the political activity of citizens. On the *broadest* view, political activity might be seen as encompassing all areas marked by negotiations over power. On this view, a woman's individual struggle to renegotiate gender roles and domestic chores with her partner, or employees working to foster more equitable policies within a particular institution, would be political activity just as much as attending a town meeting or taking part in political discourse over matters of national concern. On a *narrower* reading of political activity, only the latter would qualify as political activity. Anne Phillips supports the latter view, saying:

> The implication . . . is that we would be acting as citizens if we campaigned in public for men to take full share in household tasks; we would not be acting as citizens when we sort out the division of labor inside our own home. In the older language of democratizing everyday life, each of these was equally "political." In the new language of citizenship, only the one that takes place in a public arena can seriously contend for the name. Again, the point is not that we should stop arguing about who does the housework, just that citizenship acts on a different terrain.[23]

Phillips goes on to say that she finds this conclusion "perfectly acceptable, as long as it is not used to disparage the more private work of transforming personal relations."[24] While I am sympathetic to Phillips's desire not to *conflate* these activities, while valuing both of them, I want to stress more strongly the *connections* between these two sorts of activities. If the political activity of citizenship involves understanding the different perspectives and concerns of other citizens, while attempting to convey our own problems and perspectives to them, then debates and struggles within the family, or in the classroom or workplace seem to have a crucial part to play in shaping the understandings that citizens carry into more formal political activity. Negotiations with a partner over domestic chores, dealing with co-workers' struggles to balance work and family responsibilities, and learning about these issues in the classroom are all ways in which citizens might become aware of the political importance of the issue of affordable childcare, an awareness they may carry into the realm of public political activity.

I want to insist that citizens do not only encounter the problems, concerns and perspectives of those "different from themselves" at town meetings or during elections but in a wide variety of more everyday encounters. A society that values participation in political activity must not only ensure that political activity in the most public sense is easier for most citizens, but also must strive to ensure that places such as classrooms, campuses and workplaces foster the entry and participation of a wide range of individuals, who can encounter and learn from each other in these contexts in politically important ways. The barriers to inclusion that still operate in many professional and institutional contexts are not only objectionable in that members of marginalized groups are denied full access to a range of important and enriching life-opportunities, but also because they narrow the kinds of encounters and relationships many of us might have with a range of fellow members of the national community.

Political participation has been a key activity associated with citizenship, enabling members of the national community to have knowledge of and a say in matters of public importance. While I share the feminist concern to promote political participation among women and other marginalized groups, I believe that this concern should extend beyond issues of greater representation for women and other marginalized groups among elected representatives and encouraging their presence in participatory political forums such as town meetings. I believe we should see a variety of policies – to reduce huge disparities of wealth, to ensure equal access to the workplace, to provide quality education and affordable childcare – as connected to enabling public participation in areas of national life that are importantly connected to the articulation and representation of the interests of members of marginalized groups of citizens. I believe we should see arenas such as workplaces and classrooms as areas in which we may transcend our local and parochial perspectives by encountering and learning from members of the national community different from ourselves. While we should not lose our concern with greater representation and participation for members of marginalized groups in *explicitly political* domains and processes, I believe we need to attend to the fact that the presence of members of these groups in *a wide variety of public institutions* is also crucial to promoting public articulation of and awareness of their interests as serious concerns for the national community. In short, I wish to argue that a feminist vision of substantive equal citizenship for women and members of other marginalized groups – equality of social standing and having an equal say in matters of public concern – needs to focus not only on issues of political participation and representation but on promoting access to a wide range of public institutions in order to give marginalized groups visibility and voice.

Citizenship as Nationality

The connections between citizenship and nationality raise a number of issues pertinent to feminist inquiry. Judith Shklar usefully defines citizenship-as-nationality as "the legal recognition, both domestic and international, that a person is a member, native-born or naturalized, of a state."[25] Shklar's definition covers both individuals whose membership amounts to being "subjects" of a particular nation state and those who enjoy the *political rights* that connote "full membership" in a given state. Many groups who were "subjects" of nation states were historically denied

feminist doubts about the value of rights talk:

1) care plus/instead of rts
2) too abstract/conflictual   Kiss 2
3) obscures male dominance
4) reinforces the status quo.

As Kiss argues, 'feminists doubts about rights reveal 'some valuable insights and promising directions of research and political action'

3 lessons to draw from the strengths + weaknesses of feminist critiques of rights.   K3

<u>Bo</u>undary <u>criti</u>que — need for boundaries

<u>Care, trust + other values</u> rts talk does not capture the whole of morality

<u>Practical value</u>: rts fail to help <u>women</u>

- <u>definition</u>

     they NB when do help.

- strategy

Rts as trumps — sometimes appropriate.

the political rights of citizenship such as the vote and had to engage in political struggles to transform themselves from "mere subjects" to "political citizens" of their nation.

Mainstream political theory has tended to focus almost exclusively on relationships between citizens and the state, failing to consider questions about obligations modern states may owe to non-citizens. John Rawls, for instance, restricts his theory of justice to "the basic structure of society . . . conceived as a closed system isolated from other societies."[26] Questions of distributive justice, in this view seem to arise only among those who are already full members of the national community. Any political theory that restricts the scope of principles of justice to "full-fledged" members, or considers societies as closed systems, is clearly inadequate to a world in which national boundaries are increasingly porous, and where membership in national life is frequently a matter of degrees. Many countries have substantial numbers of immigrants who are legally part of its ongoing workforce but who are not eligible for citizenship and lack political, social and civil rights as non-citizens. Michael Walzer aptly compares the situation of several European states that have "guest workers," with rights of residence tied to their remaining employed, but who have no possibility of acquiring citizenship, to a "family with live-in servants."[27] Walzer points out that guest workers are often prevented from bringing dependents with them, housed in sex-segregated barracks, and forced to leave during recessions. Moreover, "civil liberties of speech, assembly and association – otherwise strongly defended – are commonly denied to them."[28]

Feminist thinking about citizenship risks replicating the limitations of mainstream political theory if it only concerns itself with the extensions of legal and political rights to those who are *already* citizens of particular nation states. It must also attend to the fact that even within liberal democratic states, lack of citizenship-as-nationality is a source of special vulnerability and marginalization for many groups of people. The scope of feminist political concerns must extend beyond struggles to promote equality and full citizenship to all citizens to concern itself with the well-being of large groups of people who are *non-citizens in the nations in which they live*. Feminists need to attend, theoretically and practically, to the fact that "immigrants, refugees, exiles, guestworkers and other moving groups and persons constitute an essential feature of the world, and appear to affect the politics of and between nations to a hitherto unprecedented degree."[29] In addition, feminist attention to the problems of non-citizens needs to specifically attend to the often gender-specific problems that affect *non-citizen women*.

One reason feminist concern with non-citizens is urgent is because possession of citizenship is often the *precondition* for other civil, political and welfare rights. Since immigrant groups often constitute racially or ethnically distinctive populations that are targets of hostility and discrimination, the lack of entitlement to civil, political and welfare rights compounds their vulnerabilities. Immigrant women and their dependent children are particularly vulnerable if denied rights to welfare and medical care, since they often disproportionately lack the linguistic and educational skills required for employment, and because their status as immigrant women confines them to the least lucrative and protected segments of the labor force. Thus, current attacks on welfare rights in the United States not only pose a threat to the dignity and survival of poor citizen women, but threaten non-citizen women who face the additional burden of substantial anti-immigrant sentiments.

Citizenship-as-nationality is also pertinent to feminist concerns because the legal *criteria* that determine who is eligible to have, acquire or retain this identity have often been problematic along dimensions of race, national origin, and gender. Often, women automatically lost their citzenship-as-nationality when they married foreign nationals, and could not confer their nationality on their children or spouse, while men who married foreign nationals retained their own citizenship and could confer it on their wives and children.[30] The United States had immigration laws that banned the conferral of citizenship on several groups of Asian immigrants until 1946, and set up ethnically restrictive quotas based on the national origins of immigrants that lasted until 1965.[31] Racist and ethnocentric views of national identity, based on mythic views of "bloodties" or "common culture" have often been rationales for such exclusionary policies.[32]

Citizenship-as-nationality has also been problematic in terms of the *legal procedures* that have governed its acquisition, procedures that have often disproportionately affected immigrant women seeking naturalization. An example is provided by the US Cable Act of 1922 which sought to establish citizenship independent of marital status, in a manner that was both progressive and problematic. It was progressive insofar as US women would no longer lose their citizenship if they married a foreign national. It was problematic in that it subjected an immigrant woman, whose citizenship previously followed on her husband's naturalization, to difficult and burdensome "naturalization exams" that tested her knowledge of history, government and the legal system, and which made it virtually impossible for many immigrant women to secure citizenship. These exams were difficult enough for many immigrant men, but were greater obstacles to immigrant women who tended to lack the education and access to the information required by these exams.[33] A contemporary example of rules governing citizenship acquisition that disadvantage immigrant women is found in US immigration regulations that make it virtually impossible for battered women who are foreign nationals married to US citizens to leave their abusive marriages without facing the threat of deportation.[34] Both criteria and procedures that regulate the acquisition of citizenship are hence an important area for ongoing feminist scrutiny.

Feminist concern with non-citizens needs to cover not only procedures and criteria for acquiring citizenship but also those regulating refugee status. Large numbers of people are rendered "stateless" as a result of war and civil conflicts and end up as "refugee populations" within other nation states. The creation of vulnerable "stateless persons" must be recognized as a chronic outcome of contemporary wars and civil unrest, and protection of their basic human rights needs to be of concern at national and international levels. Stateless refugee women are often inadequately served by refugee policies. For example, criteria for political asylum often require proof that one has *personally* engaged in political activity that makes one a target of political repression in one's country. However, women are often subject to torture and political intimidation because they are family members of politically active *men*. In addition, refugee policies that give significant weight to applicants' education and employment experience discriminate against women who are refugees from countries where women's education and employment may be limited.[35] Striving to make criteria for political asylum sensitive to such gendered vulnerabilities on the part of refugee women remains important.

Feminist engagement with issues of citizenship has largely tended to focus either on women being rendered "second-class citizens" in virtue of their lacking the full complement of the rights included in citizenship, or on how the attributes, values and practices that defined full membership of the political community implicitly or explicitly privileged men.[36] Feminist literature on citizenship seems less attuned to the fact that the category of citizenship can function to marginalize and occlude the interests and problems faced by non-citizen residents. Our concerns that *second-class citizenship* remains a fact of life for many fellow-citizens must hence extend to deal with the fact that *second-class membership* in national life remains the lot of many non-citizens, immigrant women in particular. Feminist politics needs to widen its concerns for the rights of women who are fellow-citizens, to include the rights and interests of non-citizens. We need, for instance, to oppose policies designed to *permanently* bar long-term inhabitants from legal citizenship, to support interim means of representation for those who are non-citizens, and to recognize and protect the distinct interests and vulnerabilities of women and children among the non-citizen population.

Conclusion

I referred at the start of this essay to the fact that, historically, the concept of citizenship has had a Janus-faced quality. On the one hand, the term has had a significant role in struggles to secure greater dignity, rights and participation for members of marginalized groups; on the other hand, it has often *simultaneously functioned* to justify the exclusion of other members of the national community. Feminist deployments of the term citizenship risk replicating this historical problem, unless they attend to the fact that using "citizenship" as a term that grounds political claims might at times be problematic in a world where many nations increasingly contain large numbers of people who participate in its national life, but who are non-citizens. A feminist commitment to paying serious attention to the problems of women who are additionally marginalized by factors such as race, class, or sexual orientation entails a concern for the problems of non-citizen women, many of whom also suffer from the effects of poverty and racism.

Citizenship has always been about membership, participation and belonging as well as about respect, dignity, status-equality, and a variety of rights. In a world increasingly traversed by global migrations, the language of citizenship must become rich enough to extend to all inhabitants of a nation, making a person's sustained residence within a country, rather than legal citizenship of that country, the fundamental basis for a variety of rights, and for the status of being a member of its collective national life. While it would be utopian to expect to completely dismantle the distinction between citizens and non-citizens, feminists need to argue for a variety of policies that would "close the gap" between the entitlements and rights of citizens and those of non-citizen residents. There are difficult public policy questions regarding the criteria that should be used to determine which non-citizens will count as "members" of the national community, questions that are beyond the scope of this essay. However, feminists need to be attentive to these questions and concerned that these criteria are adequately attentive to the predicaments of non-citizen women.

Political theory, both mainstream and feminist, needs to reflect seriously about how the terms of our political visions and political struggles might be affected if we routinely kept non-citizens in mind. Where particular issues substantially affect the fates of non-citizens, we need to enrich the idea of citizenship so as to make clear we are talking about matters concerning what states might owe *all* their ongoing members. We need to ensure that the terms in which we cast our demands and ground our claims on a variety of issues do not unreflectively exclude from their scope either groups of fellow citizens or non-citizen members of the national community whose interests are at stake. For example, as I argued in the first section, we need to ground our arguments for state provision of welfare rights in a way that excludes neither "non-contributors" nor non-citizens, if we care about belonging to a polity that is responsive to the dignity and worth of all its members. The fact that many non-citizen residents end up becoming citizens, and are parents of children born within the national territory who qualify for citizenship, must also inform our vision of the national polity within which we are citizens. An implication of my discussion of the value of political participation to the health of liberal democratic societies is that immigrants and their children should have access to state-funded education, not only because it is crucial to their economic survival, but because we could otherwise risk the creation of a class of *future citizens* who would be unable to engage in informed political participation.

I believe citizenship should primarily function as a term that reminds us that we are not merely private individuals but participants in a shared national life, members who have a collective as well as individual stake in the decency and humaneness of our policies and public arrangements, and responsibilities to call for and support such arrangements. It should function to remind us that there is "a reciprocal relationship between the citizen community and the individual citizen's rights"[37] – where such rights are seen to require guarantee by the political culture and public institutions of the community and where such institutions and culture are seen to require thoughtful participation and active commitment by individual members of the community. In recalling to us the need to think about the public values that we as citizens ought to expect of public institutions and arrangements, the language of citizenship opens up the difficult question of how one can give an account of such values that is compatible with tolerance for a variety of choices of good lives. We need a vision of shared values that ought to inform our public arrangements that neither treats the good life as entirely a private concern of private individuals, nor is so "thick" as to unjustifiably privilege certain ways of life over others. I believe that a public commitment to the value of the dignity and worth of all members, to the value of political participation of all members as crucial to the health of a liberal democratic society, are instances of such values that are crucial to our thinking about citizenship, values that we all ought to expect of our social and political arrangements, but are nevertheless compatible with tolerance for a plurality of good lives.

Notes

1 Nancy Fraser and Linda Gordon, "Contract versus Charity: Why is there no Social Citizenship in the United States?," *Socialist Review*, 22, 3 (July/September 1992), p. 45.
2 T.H. Marshall, "Citizenship and Social Class," in *Class, Citizenship and Social Development: Essays by T.H. Marshall*, ed. Seymour Martin Lipsett (Chicago: University of Chicago Press, 1964).
3 Fraser and Gordon, "Contract versus Charity," p. 45.
4 Judith Shklar, *American Citizenship: The Quest for Inclusion* (Cambridge, MA: Harvard University Press, 1991), p. 6.
5 Shklar, *American Citizenship: The Quest for Inclusion*, pp. 16–17.
6 Shklar, *American Citizenship: The Quest for Inclusion*, p. 17.
7 See Mona Harrington, *Women Lawyers: Rewriting the Rules* (New York: Knopf, 1994).
8 Gwendolyn Mink, "The Lady and the Tramp: Gender, Race and the Origins of the American Welfare State," in *Women, the State and Welfare*, ed. Linda Gordon (Madison, WI: The University of Wisconsin Press, 1990), p. 97.
9 Mink, "The Lady and the Tramp," p. 98.
10 Carol Pateman, "Feminism and Participatory Democracy: Some Reflections on Sexual Difference and Citizenship," unpublished paper presented to the American Philosophical Association, May 1986. Cited in Chantal Mouffe, "Feminism, Citizenship and Radical Democratic Politics," in *Feminists Theorize the Political*, eds Judith Butler and Joan W. Scott (New York: Routledge, 1992), fn 8.
11 Mouffe, "Feminism, Citizenship and Radical Democratic Politics," p. 376.
12 Eva Feder Kittay, "Human Dependency and Rawlsian Equality," draft 1995, p. 13.
13 Marshall, "Citizenship and Social Class," p. 78.
14 Fraser and Gordon, "Contract versus Charity," p. 45.
15 See Hanna Fenichel Pitkin, *Fortune is a Woman: Gender and Politics in the Thought of Nicholas Machiavelli* (Berkeley: University of California Press, 1984), p. 5.
16 Mary Dietz, "Citizenship With A Feminist Face: The Problem of Maternal Thinking," *Political Theory*, 13, 1 (1985), p. 14.
17 Dietz, "Citizenship With A Feminist Face," p. 28.
18 Iris Young, "Polity and Group Difference: A Critique of the Ideal of Universal Citizenship," *Ethics*, 99 (January 1989), p. 257.
19 See Anne Phillips, *Engendering Democracy* (Cambridge: Polity Press and University Park, PA: Pennsylvania State University Press, 1991).
20 Young, "Polity and Group Difference," p. 259.
21 Anne Phillips, *Democracy and Difference* (University Park, PA: The Pennsylvania State University Press, 1993), p. 116.

22 See Jeffrey Weeks, "The Value of Difference," in *Identity: Community, Culture and Difference*, ed. Jonathan Rutherford (London: Lawrence and Wishart, 1990), p. 94.

23 Phillips, *Democracy and Difference*, p. 86.

24 Ibid.

25 Shklar, *American Citizenship: The Quest for Inclusion*, p. 4.

26 John Rawls, *A Theory of Justice* (Cambridge: Harvard University Press, 1971), p. 8.

27 Michael Walzer, *Spheres of Justice* (New York: Basic Books Inc., 1983), p. 52.

28 Walzer, *Spheres of Justice*, p. 57.

29 Arjun Appadurai, "Disjuncture and Difference in the Global Cultural Economy," *Theory, Culture and Society*, 7 (1990), p. 297.

30 Wendy Sarvasy, "Beyond the Difference versus Equality Policy Debate: Citizenship and the Quest for a Feminist Welfare State," *Signs: Journal of Women in Culture and Society* (Winter 1992), p. 351.

31 Rogers M. Smith, "The 'American Creed' and American Identity: The Limits of Liberal Citizenship in the United States," *The Western Political Quarterly*, 41, 2 (1988), p. 245.

32 Smith, "The 'American Creed' and American Identity," p. 244.

33 See Sarvasy, "Beyond the Difference versus Equality Policy Debate."

34 See Michelle Anderson, "License to Abuse: The impact of conditional status on female immigrants," *Yale Law Journal*, 102, 6 (1993), pp. 1401–30; and Uma Narayan, " 'Male-Order' Brides: Immigrant Women, Domestic Violence and Immigration Law," *Hypatia*, 10, 1 (Winter 1995).

35 See Donald Galloway, "Strangers and Members: Equality in an Immigration Setting," *Canadian Journal of Law and Jurisprudence*, VII, 1 (January 1994), p. 169.

36 See Kathleen B. Jones, "Citizenship in a Woman-Friendly Polity," *Signs: Journal of Women in Culture and Society*, 15, 4 (July 1990). Jones begins her review essay on feminist literature on citizenship with these two themes. There is no indication in the review of feminist concerns with how the category of citizenship can eclipse the interests of women who are non-citizen residents.

37 Anna Yeatman, "Beyond Natural Right: The Conditions for Universal Citizenship," in *Postmodern Revisioning of the Political* (New York: Routlege, 1994), p. 58.

4

The Jurispolitics of Privacy

Anita L. Allen

Introduction

In the American context, liberty is the central political value of "libertar-ians" and some "conservatives"; equality the central political value of "liberals"; and community the central value of "communitarians." Privacy, by contrast, is no one's central political value. Still, privacy is widely valued. As the jurispolitical portrait of privacy presented here will show, the freestanding privacy rights found in American law originated both in the traditional political assumption that women appropriately occupy subordinate domestic roles in a well-ordered society, *and* in the progressive assumption that men and women ought to be equals at home and in the world. The result is a jurisprudence of privacy whose implications for women are ambiguous.

For more than two decades, privacy has been widely associated with liberal and feminist political activism on behalf of birth control and abortion rights. But while some feminists have been vocal proponents of the legal tool of "privacy" rights to secure certain kinds of control over reproductive activity, many others have been among the harshest critics of privacy as a political ideal. Feminist lawyers and philosophers have raised serious doubts about the ability of legal privacy rights to help women control reproduction, in a world in which men still dominate women's sexuality and poor women are unable to purchase reproductive services to which they have a constitutional right. Feminist lawyers have argued that privacy's conceptual emphasis on isolation and independence fails to resonate with the many women whose lives are structured around inti-macy and care. In sum, feminist critiques contend that privacy rights have uncertain practical value for women, are dangerous, and are misleading.

One response to feminist critiques would be to reject the idea of "privacy rights" categorically. The problem with this response is that it ignores the ubiquity of the privacy concept in contemporary morality and social policy, the rhetorical power of privacy discourse in the political realm, and the expansive role of privacy concepts in legal precedents. A better response would be to accept continued reliance on the discourse of "privacy rights" in law and practical politics, hoping to win and preserve incremental improvements in the quality of life for women. Common among legal feminists, this second response embraces privacy rights as a strategy, while eschewing privacy as a progressive principle within political theory, presumably in favor of egalitarian and communitarian principles. The result is a Janus-faced stance toward privacy rights, approval as a matter of practice, disapproval as a matter of theory.

A Janus-faced, realpolitik-driven stance toward privacy is the very least one can justify. I would argue that privacy has been and can continue to be a useful conceptual tool for women in both constitutional and civil (tort) law. Rather than giving up on privacy as either a theoretical concept or practical tool, feminists need to challenge problematic understandings of privacy as well as struggle against material conditions that prevent many women from enjoying rights of privacy.

Viewed as an abstract political concept, privacy signifies boundaries of inclusion and exclusion. First, it signifies boundaries of inclusion and exclusion separating citizens from government; separating, that is, "private" individuals and institutions from the "public" authority exercised by government employees, agents, and agencies. Second, privacy signifies boundaries of inclusion and exclusion separating citizen from citizen. I will explore the gendered ways in which the legal concept of privacy has been constructed in citizen-to-government and citizen-to-citizen contexts. In the citizen-to-government context, I will examine the usefulness of the constitutional right to privacy, especially in abortion law, and argue that constitutional privacy remains a useful concept for feminism. In the citizen-to-citizen context, I will set out how problematic ideas about women's roles, modesty, and shame shaped the evolution of the common law privacy torts. I will argue that, despite its origins, the privacy tort can be useful for addressing some present-day feminist concerns, including sexual harassment.

The Citizen-to-Government Dimension

The story of the role of women's concerns in the development of a freestanding constitutional right to privacy – a largely citizen-to-government domain – is familiar. The right to privacy was the product of decades of political and legal efforts in the state of Connecticut and elsewhere in the United States to invalidate laws criminalizing contraception. The constitutional right to privacy was conceived by family planning activists and lawyers as a conservative-sounding device to secure a radical outcome – the legalization of birth control. The legalization of birth control was seen as a way to help women, especially poor women, achieve control over their lives. Tellingly, the political strategies lawyers originally adopted to win the privacy right in the courts included de-emphasizing women as independent actors and emphasizing either the socially sacred private marital relationship or the esteemed private physician/patient relationship.

In 1965, in *Griswold v. Connecticut*,[1] the Supreme Court held that married couples have a right to use birth control because of a general "right to privacy" found in the "penumbra" of the Constitution. Soon thereafter, the Court held in *Eisenstadt v. Baird*[2] that unmarried persons have a right to use birth control. The creation of a right to privacy in *Griswold* and *Eisenstadt* spawned a much broader notion of a constitutional right to private decision-making regarding sexuality, marriage, health-care, and families. In 1973 in *Roe v. Wade*,[3] the Court described the right to abortion as a fundamental constitutional right of all women. Although the Supreme Court has moved away from the idea of a *fundamental* privacy right, the controversial idea of a right to privacy as flowing from the Fourteenth Amendment's promise of liberty lives on in constitutional law concerning abortion.

Many theorists insist that the whole idea of "decisional" privacy rights established by *Griswold* is a mistake.[4] They raise several arguments. First, they argue that as an aspect of liberty, freedom or autonomy, decisional privacy stands apart from paradigmatic forms of privacy, such as seclusion, solitude, and anonymity. Second, they contend that people lose their ability to treat privacy and liberty as distinct concepts if we speak of "decisional" privacy.

Defenders of the decisional usage of "privacy" insist that such arguments against decisional privacy are mistaken. They counter that although decisional privacy denotes aspects of liberty, freedom, and autonomy, it denotes aspects of these that are closely connected to a central facet of the concept of privacy, to deeply felt conceptions of a *private life beyond legitimate social control*.[5] This is a notion of privacy that is understood and valued by large segments of the American public, including both men and women, for whom excluding others from "personal" decision-making is an important aspect of privacy.

The current practice of referring to freedom from interference with personal life as "privacy" recalls the ancient distinction between private and public spheres. Greek thought distinguished the "public" sphere of the *polis*, or city-state, from the "private" sphere of the *oikos*, or household. Roman law similarly distinguished *res publicae*, concerns of the community, from *res privatae*, concerns of individuals and families. The public realm was the sector in which select men – free men with property whose economic virtue had earned them citizenship and the right to participate in collective governance – could flourish. By contrast, the private realm was the sector of mundane economic and biologic necessity. Wives, children, and slaves populated the private economic sphere, living as subordinates and ancillaries to autonomous male caretakers.

Modern liberal thought seems to have inherited the classical premise that social life should be organized into public and private realms.[6] It also inherited the premise that the private sphere is properly constituted by the home, the family, and intimate association. However, while classical thought tolerated the private and celebrated the public, modern liberal thought often reflects an opposing tendency to celebrate the private as an essential domain for the expression and cultivation of personal identity, freedom, and responsibility. Modern liberal thought often regards state intervention and regulation in the public domain as necessary for collective welfare, but conceives of the private domain as one where state intervention is an inappropriate intrusion upon individual decisions and relationships. The political concept of a limited, tolerant government – elaborated by John Locke and Thomas Jefferson, as a requirement of natural rights, and by Adam Smith and John Stuart Mill as a requirement of utility – entails a non-governmental, private sphere of autonomous individuals, families, and voluntary associations.

While mainstream liberal political theory often speaks of public and private spheres as if they were fixed natural categories, feminist political theory rejects this way of understanding the distinction between private and public domains. Feminist privacy theorists often emphasize that the public and the private are not fixed metaphysical realities, but represent often contested and shifting demarcations, where the line between these spheres reflects contingent understandings of how, as a matter of policy, we believe power ought to be allocated among individuals, social units, and government. The realm of privacy at any given time is a result of public political debates and legal decision-making, that normatively construct certain areas of individual life, decisions and association as matters to be protected from state intrusion.

There has been considerable debate about whether constitutional privacy is a useful basis for protecting women's reproductive rights, in areas such as abortion. Many prominent mainstream legal scholars are prepared to abandon privacy-based arguments for women's reproductive autonomy in favor of arguments based on liberty and equality.[7]

Some of the impetus for abandoning privacy jurisprudence comes from the belief that it is confusing to talk about privacy, if what one means by it is not "limited access" but decisional "autonomy" or "liberty." Moreover, many lawyers and politicians believe the Supreme Court has talked about privacy in confusing ways. They are correct. Early reproductive rights cases reflected a degree of confusion. The precise relationship presumed to exist between decisional privacy and conventional privacy was not clear in *Griswold* and *Roe*. In *Griswold* Justice Douglas seemed to conflate physical privacy and decisional privacy when he raised the issue of enforcement of criminal contraception laws by the state entering the bedrooms of married couples.[8] Justice Blackmun in *Roe* seemed to conflate physical privacy with decisional privacy rights when he said that a "pregnant woman cannot be isolated [from the fetus] in her pregnancy." The issue in *Roe* was not whether women could be "isolated" from (physically inaccessible to) their fetuses, but how the law would allocate decisional prerogatives among women, medical professionals and government.

The Supreme Court has long remedied the simplistic, impartial and confused understandings of privacy reflected in the earliest reproductive rights cases. In 1986, in *Thornburgh v. American College of Obstetricians and Gynecologists*, Blackmun cleared up the confusion by explaining that the "privacy" of the Fourteenth Amendment abortion cases is the claim to be "beyond the reach of government" when making certain personal and intimate decisions affecting sex, reproduction, marriage, and family life.[9] At the same time, Justice Blackmun expressly recognized that, in the context of abortion, conventional forms of privacy, such as anonymity and confidentiality in recordkeeping and reporting, are key ancillaries for safeguarding decisional privacy.[10] After *Thornburgh*, abortion law cases reviewing the constitutionality of spousal and parental notification and consent requirements have raised anonymity, secrecy, confidentiality, and other information access concerns without appearing to confuse or conflate physical or informational with decisional privacy concerns.[11] Indeed, the body of constitutional abortion law up to and including *Planned Parenthood v. Casey* in 1992 reflects a solid understanding of the semantics of "privacy." It acknowledges decisional ("autonomy") and non-decisional ("inaccessibility") uses of privacy and appreciates that confidentiality and anonymity are needed to protect independent abortion decision and action. Today, constitutional abortion law reflects no special or hopeless confusion about the definition of the word "privacy."

A number of feminist legal theorists who advocate strong abortion rights also favor constitutional alternatives to the doctrine of privacy-related liberty. They view privacy law as distorting the truths of women's lives and impeding women's equality. Catherine MacKinnon has famously assaulted privacy jurisprudence in abortion law, arguing that "the doctrine of privacy has become the triumph of the state's abdication of women in the name of freedom and self-determination."[12] MacKinnon argues that privacy law and other "legal attempts to advance women"[13] wrongly treat women "as if women were citizens – as if the doctrine was not gendered to women's disadvantage, as if the legal system had no sex, as if women were gender-neutral persons temporarily trapped by law in female bodies."[14] Echoing many of MacKinnon's key concerns, Joan Williams' skepticism about arguments premised on "choice," "liberty," and "privacy" stems from a perception that women seeking abortion do not feel especially free and do not have a number of realistic, attractive alternatives. In general, privacy's "[c]hoice rhetoric is not appropriate where patterns of individual behavior follow largely unacknowledged gender norms that operate to disempower women."[15] Ruth Colker argues that the privacy-related liberty doctrine relies on the false ontological assumption of the existence of an autonomous sphere of women and fetuses dwelling together beyond public life.[16]

In sum, some feminist objections to privacy as a basis for women's reproductive rights rest on the view that privacy jurisprudence not only fails to attend to the fact that many women lack the power to make effective use of these rights, but also works to reinforce the view that the state has no obligation to ensure that women have the resources necessary for the effective enjoyment of rights in such "private" areas. I agree that men and women are not equal, that reproductive privacy law did not make them equal. But I disagree with the strong tendency among feminists to broadly condemn privacy jurisprudence, as if the good it does every day in the United States means nothing at all. It may be true that reproductive privacy did not dramatically alter the lives of upper middle-class women, who always had access to birth control and abortion, even when it was illegal. If these women viewed reproductive privacy as a major key to a subordination-free world of golden opportunity, they were bound to be disappointed. I suspect reproductive privacy has done more relative good for low income people than middle and upper income people, despite the irony that, as discussed below, middle-class white feminists invoke the plight of the poor to show that privacy jurisprudence has utterly failed. It has not utterly failed, and far from it. Many poor men and women benefit tangibly from privacy-based reproductive rights. For example, in 1995 the clinics of Planned Parenthood of Metropolitan Washington saw 10,000 patients, mostly poor African Americans and Hispanics. Without *Griswold* and *Roe*, many fewer such clinics probably would exist. The difficult lives of the adults, teenagers and communities these clinics serve would be even more difficult.

Still, feminists have pointed out that women in traditional heterosexual relationships cannot use privacy rights fully to their advantage because they lack resources needed to make their personal preferences effective and that poor women cannot use privacy rights fully to their advantage, because they often cannot afford the contraception and abortions to which they have a nominal right. Many prominent legal feminists blame the refusal of the United States Supreme Court to compel state and federal government to pay for the abortions of poor women otherwise eligible for welfare on the supposed inherent limitations of a privacy-based constitutional abortion jurisprudence. They agree that once abortion is characterized as a private matter, it is easy to conclude that abortion should be privately financed and that the public sector should not be required to foot the bill. Thus, another impetus for moving away from privacy jurisprudence rests on the belief that government-funded abortion services for the poor have been denied *because of* the implications of privacy. This criticism of privacy jurisprudence is problematic for a number of reasons. First, taken to its logical conclusion, it implies that liberal values, in principle, rule out all public programs. Although extreme libertarians have taken this view, more moderate and nuanced liberal political theories that value limited government do not proscribe all forms of public assistance. Relevantly, other "liberal" Western nations have sought in practice to balance independence from government interference with reliance on government aid needed to make meaningful independence possible.

While liberals often explain privacy rights as negative liberties, as freedom from government involvement, feminists often give privacy an affirmative twist, arguing that privacy rights can mandate government involvement where, without it, material needs render privacy rights ineffective. A number of feminist legal theorists have suggested that American constitutionalism could accommodate affirmative understandings of privacy-related liberty that are broad enough to support public abortion funding. For example, responding critically to the abortion funding cases, Rachael Pine and Sylvia Law argue that a "feminist concept of reproductive freedom" must encompass the proposition that "government has the obligation to insure that people can make reproductive decisions freely."[17] Reacting to *Rust v. Sullivan*,[18] Dorothy Roberts describes a "liberation theory" version of constitutional liberty that would "recognize the importance of information for self-determination" and therefore "place an affirmative obligation on the government to provide [abortion] information to people who are dependent on government funds."[19] Those who say privatizing abortion access conceptually rules out public subsidies needlessly abdicate privacy theory to its least progressive interpreters.

Blaming privacy jurisprudence for the funding decisions implies that these decisions would have stood a chance of coming out differently had *Roe* been decided on equal protection grounds. There are many reasons to doubt that the funding cases would have come out differently if *Roe* had been expressly defended under equal protection principles.[20] For present purposes, suffice it to say that the logic of equal protection in American constitutional law has rarely demanded that the poor be given the resources needed to make them the substantive equals of other citizens. Equality is open in US jurisprudence to thin "equal opportunity" rather than thick "equality of results" interpretations. The court could have acknowledged the goal of abolishing discriminatory abortion laws, while ruling that the Constitution's Equal Protection Clause does not require government abortion subsidies. Privacy was given a safe unprogressive spin, and equality would have been too. The middle-aged and elderly white, affluent majority on the court between 1965 and 1995 could hardly have been expected to read any political ideal as having radical distributive consequences.

The Citizen-to-Citizen Dimension

Women's significant role in developing the right to privacy tort is less well known than women's role in the development of the constitutional right to privacy. But it is hardly less of a story.[21] While a freestanding constitutional privacy right emerged in the third quarter of the twentieth century as a product of liberal and radical concerns about women's health and social equality, the freestanding common law privacy right emerged in the late nineteenth century, a product of traditional ideals of women as modest and secluded. Today, the common law and statutes of most states permit civil suits for "invasion of privacy." At least four categories of offensive conduct qualify for compensation under the states' "right to privacy" rubrics: intrusion into seclusion, embarrassing publications of private facts, publications that place a person in a false light, and commercial appropriation of a person's name, likeness, or identity.

Conflicts involving women's unique roles and capacities have contributed to the growth of the privacy tort. Heralded as the first American privacy decision, the 1881 case of *DeMay v. Roberts* reveals the extent to which some Americans valued female modesty.[22] In *DeMay*, the Roberts, a poor married couple, sued a physician who delivered their baby in their home in the presence of an "unprofessional young unmarried man."[23] Some time after the delivery, the Roberts discovered that the physician's companion had not been a medical practitioner. They sued for deceit, assault, and, although it was not yet a formal cause of action, invasion of privacy.

An appeals court affirmed a jury award for Mrs. Roberts' "shame and mortification," asserting that "[i]t would be shocking to our sense of right, justice and propriety to doubt . . . that . . . the law would afford an ample remedy."[24] A dark, stormy night, combined with his own illness and fatigue, led the physician to make his house call with the help of someone to carry his bags and lantern. Because of heavy rain, both the doctor and his aide remained with the Roberts in their tiny house throughout Mrs. Roberts' protracted labor. The court's decision in favor of the Roberts implied that exigent circumstances do not excuse an invasion of privacy accomplished through "deceit." The court thought it deceitful of the physician to fail to explain that the man he introduced to the Roberts as a "friend" was not a medical student or doctor.

The court's reasoning reflects assumptions that a wife's feminine modesty and her husband's prerogatives require strenuous legal protection. The judge's repetition of the adjectives "unprofessional," "unmarried," and "young" in his written opinion suggests that liability could have been avoided by the companionship of an old, married, professional man. In that instance, the affront to the husband's household authority and the woman's presumed modesty would have been less severe. A *young unmarried* man is a potential seducer; a old married man is not. Today it is often said that dignity and individuality are the moral values privacy rights promote. A hundred and thirty years ago, respect for the dignity of women included respect for their modesty. Of course, the notion of female individuality was all but foreign to the period.

In 1890, Samuel D. Warren and Louis D. Brandeis published "The Right to Privacy."[25] This high-toned law review article argued for express recognition of a new common law right, a right of privacy, protecting "inviolate personality," the "sacred precincts of private and domestic life," and the "robustness of thought and delicacy of feeling" in society.[26] As conceived by Warren and Brandeis and initially applied by the courts, the "right to privacy" bore the mark of an era of male hegemony. Warren and Brandeis argued that every man (*sic*) needs a place of solitude, a retreat from the "intensity and complexity of life,"[27] a sanctuary beyond the reach of scurrilous journalism, curiosity-seekers, gossips, and the "prurient" interests of the "indolent" public. They argued that just as, for example, physical injuries to body and property are compensable, injuries to personality arising by virtue of acts "overstepping . . . the obvious bounds of propriety and of decency"[28] should be compensable.

Praised for its role in helping courts to recognize that privacy is an aspect of human dignity, the Warren and Brandeis article has also been criticized as petty, duplicative, and an unconstitutional limitation on freedom of speech. As feminists must emphasize, the article uncritically glorified domestic life, completely ignoring the burdens of domesticity that fall disproportionately on women.

Warren and Brandeis related the "inevitable," progressive development of the rights in civilized society from limited rights of non-interference with body and property to expanded rights of non-interference with "family relations."[29] To argue that the law had already begun to make progress in the direction of recognizing the compensability of offenses to our spiritual natures, they cited a line of cases in which parents and husbands were held to have had rights of recovery against male seducers. Their recognition of an historical "regard for human emotions"[30] was based on cases in which remedies were granted for the alienation of a wife's affections and for shame caused by a daughter's seduction. Under the English law fiction of *per quod servitium amisit,* parents could maintain an action for the loss of a minor daughter's "services" caused by unwed pregnancy.

Women came into play in the Warren and Brandeis article as seduced wives and daughters; but they also appeared through the colorful image of an actress "caught on the stage by a camera."[31] Warren and Brandeis cited with approval the 1890 case of *Manola v. Stevens & Meyers,* in which an actress, who was surreptitiously photographed by her employer while dressed in tights, successfully enjoined the publication of the photograph. The New York court granted Marion Manola an *ex parte* injunction to restrain the publication of the publicity photograph, "owing to her modesty."[32] Manola had openly performed before public audiences in tights. Still, Warren and Brandeis had no problem assimilating Manola's case to their argument. The *Manola* case was a clear example of judicial protection of inviolate personality and delicate feeling injured by unwanted publicity. The case was particularly strong for their purposes because it involved the courts going so far as to protect from further degradation the residual modesty of a theatrical woman who had behaved immodestly in public in the first place.

In the case of *Roberson v. Rochester Folding Box Company,*[33] the New York Court of Appeals seemed more concerned with the orderly growth of the law than conventional modesty. In *Roberson,* the defendant manufactured and distributed 25,000 copies of an advertisement for flour, each one bearing a likeness of an attractive young woman named Roberson. The unauthorized prints were displayed in stores, saloons, warehouses, and other public areas. Roberson went to court complaining of the humiliation and severe nervous shock. Her request for an injunction and damages was granted by the lower court on the ground that publication and circulation of her likeness for profit violated her right to privacy[34] and her property right in the use of her likeness.[35] Although an intermediate court affirmed the judgment, the New York Court of Appeals reversed it. The court mentioned the Warren and Brandeis article but concluded that the "so-called 'right of privacy'" had not as yet found a place "in our jurisprudence."[36] Roberson lost her case in the Court of Appeals, but the standard of female modesty prevailed in the court of popular opinion. The *Roberson* decision was roundly criticized. A year after the decision, the New York legislature enacted a narrowly drawn privacy statute providing a remedy in cases where the name or picture of a person has been appropriated for commercial advertising purposes.[37] In *Kunz v. Allen,*[38] a woman who had been shopping in a dry-goods store was filmed by the owners without her knowledge or consent. The merchants used this film with her "face, form, and garments" to advertise their business in a local theater, causing the plaintiff to become "the common talk of the people in the community."[39] It was said that people thought "that she had for hire permitted her picture to be taken and used as a public advertisement."[40] She brought suit for damages for invasion of privacy, but the case was dismissed for failure to show actual damages. On appeal, the court reversed the adverse judgment, contending that if a person's picture were allowed to be used without her consent for advertising purposes, it could be used and exhibited anywhere: "It may be posted upon the walls of private dwellings or upon the streets. It may ornament the bar of the saloon keeper, or decorate the walls of a brothel."[41] Because of these lurking dangers, the court agreed that no man or woman should be subject to such use of his or her face and features and recognized a valid claim for invasion of privacy.

Similarly, in *Graham v. Baltimore Post Company*, a judge held that a woman has a claim for the unauthorized publication of her picture in a newspaper advertisement.[42] The judge emphasized the plaintiff's gender in rationalizing his decision: "the same act that might well be a violation of the right of privacy, as applied to a woman, might be dismissed, with legal indifference, as applied to a man."[43] He also suggested that the social standing of a female plaintiff and the media organ would be relevant to her privacy claim, writing that "[a] debutante's picture published . . . in the social section of a respectable Sunday supplement, or in certain magazines . . . might be unauthorized, but at the same time be unobjectionable when weighed by accepted standards of propriety."[44]

Later courts and judges would often follow suit, sometimes treating interference with female modesty as the paradigm privacy invasion.[45] Some courts would explicitly acknowledge that the sex of the plaintiff is relevant to liability in privacy cases.[46] Plainly, concern for the boundaries of women's privacy has played a significant role in establishing and shaping legal precedent for the right to privacy tort. Cases involving characteristically female experiences, such as childbirth[47] and objectification of beauty,[48] have contributed to shaping doctrine, clarifying the meaning of legal privacy.

The early history of the privacy tort – mired as it was in paternalism and out-moded conventions of female modesty and seclusion – seems to justify feminist rejection of privacy as a practical political value. However, with respect to women, the privacy tort has not functioned solely to affirm entitlement to domestic seclusion and modesty. Sometimes it has functioned ambiguously, as in the case of attempts to sue for the publication of rape victims' identities. In the 1970s and 1980s, some people read the call for legal bans on rape-victim publicity as upholding traditional concepts: "good" women are sexually modest and need special legal protection from the social consequences of an especially shameful crime.[49] Others read such bans progressively, arguing they would free women from stereotyping and media exploitation: women should be able to control their lives and reputations, with the help of laws that prevent the experience of rape from becoming the exclusive framework for a woman's subsequent social and professional exchanges.

In the 1980s some litigants, lawyers, and judges put the privacy doctrines in tort law to untraditional uses. Litigants have marshalled the privacy tort as a weapon to fight wrongs that include sexual harassment in the workplace. An outstanding example of the privacy concept functioning in tort law to a woman's benefit was a 1983 Alabama case, *Phillips v. Smalley Maintenance Services, Inc.*[50] In *Phillips* a woman brought suit after being fired for refusing to perform oral sex at the request of her male boss. The Alabama Supreme Court held that sexually explicit questions and demands for oral sex are actionable as a tortious invasion of privacy. Viewed as an employment case consistent with the goals of equal employment for women, *Phillips* set a precedent that could help women negotiate the politics of the workplace, keeping their jobs rather than (solely) their modesty. Perhaps because Title VII of the Civil Rights Act and the Equal Protection Clause of the Fourteenth Amendment provide more encompassing frameworks for attacking worker discrimination, the full potential of the privacy tort as a weapon against sexual harassment in the workplace remains unexploited.

Tort law has helped to vindicate some of women's many interests in informational privacy and confidentiality. In one case a poor woman brought an action for invasion of privacy after the embarrassing details of her sad life, which she had narrated to welfare authorities in order to qualify for benefits, wound up in the newspaper.[51] In another case, a woman sued a physician for invasion of privacy, after he gave her name to a daughter she had secretly placed for adoption many years before. The Oregon Supreme Court judge who heard the case on appeal thought breach of "confidence" (rather than "privacy") was centrally at issue, but agreed with the plaintiff that a physician who reveals information in sealed adoption records is civilly liable.[52]

Today, the "right to privacy" tort, along with the closely related "publicity" and "breach of confidentiality" torts, often serves women well. The growing recognition that failure to respect women's legitimate expectations of physical and informational privacy is grounds for litigation may help to deter offensive conduct in the future. Where offenses occur, women plaintiffs are empowered to seek monetary damages and other appropriate remedies. One could cite any number of cases in which privacy doctrines have been utilized by female plaintiffs to good effect. Still, no privacy case involving a woman has done for any area of tort law what *Griswold* and *Roe* did for reproductive law. The useful life of the "right to privacy" in tort law is close to its beginning.

Conclusion

Deep normative controversies surround aspirations for privacy. These controversies concern the drawing of physical, informational, and decisional boundaries between citizens and government, and among citizens. To convert an abstract value like privacy into a practical reality is inevitably to confront the controversies both of political theory and the politics of the moment. Poor people and homosexuals have found the politics of privacy extremely difficult to translate into legal rights. Middle-class heterosexual women have found it easier.

In the United States, the translation of the political ideal of privacy into a practical legal right has been, overtly at times and subtly at others, a highly gendered politics. How much and what kinds of privacy does a woman need to pursue her interests, fulfill her responsibilities, and maintain her human dignity? American law's answers to this question have, historically, reflected contradictory subordinating and liberating impulses. Against the background of a divided history, feminists today understandably disagree about whether privacy is a worthy political ideal, usefully embodied in law.

I would argue that privacy deserves a place in the pantheon of core political values recognized by political theories sensitive to feminist concerns. As the privacy doctrines of tort law implicitly recognize, men and women typically utilize privacy for essential work, recreation, and rest. Privacy helps to equip us for responsible social participation. As the privacy doctrines of constitutional law recognize, the power to make decisions about sex, marriage, and procreation circumscribes the reach of government in ways that enhance personal freedom and foster the spirit of toleration. Women have won important gains under the banner of constitutional privacy. The "right to privacy" in matters of reproduction has meant fewer interrupted educations and careers. It has meant a reduced mortality rate from botched abortions. These are important gains. Opportunities for privacy and private choice enrich women's lives.

Notes

1 *Griswold v. Connecticut*, 381 U.S. 479 (1965).
2 *Eisenstadt v. Baird*, 405 U.S. 438 (1972).
3 *Roe v. Wade*, 410 U.S. 113 (1973).
4 See, e.g., Ruth Gavison, "Privacy and the Limits of Law," *Yale Law Journal*, 89 (1980), pp. 421–71.
5 See, e.g., Judith W. DeCew, "Defending the 'Private' in Constitutional Privacy," *Journal of Value Inquiry*, 21 (1987), pp. 171–87.
6 See Hannah Arendt, *The Human Condition* (Chicago: University of Chicago Press, 1958), pp. 38–78; Jurgen Habermas, *The Structural Transformation of the Public Sphere: An Inquiry Into a Category of Bourgeois Society* (Thomas Burger and Frederick Lawrence trans., Cambridge, MA: MIT Press, 1989), pp. 3–4.
7 I discuss the views of a number of such scholars in Anita L. Allen, "The Proposed Equal Protection Fix for Abortion Law: Reflections on Citizenship, Gender, and the Constitution," *Harvard Journal of Law and Public Policy*, 18 (1995), pp. 419–55. In my book *Uneasy Access: Privacy for Women in a Free Society* (Totowa, NJ: Rowan and Littlefield, 1987), I respond broadly to assault on privacy.
8 *Griswold v. Connecticut*, 381 U.S. 479, 485–6 (1965) (Douglas, J.).
9 *Thornburgh v. American College of Obstetricians and Gynecologists*, 476 U.S. at 747, 771, 772 (1986) (Blackmun, J.).
10 *Thornburgh v. American College of Obstetricians and Gynecologists*, 476 U.S. at 765–7 (1986) (Blackmun, J.). The court held that "[t]he decision to terminate a pregnancy is an intensely private one that must be protected in a way that assures anonymity."
11 See, e.g., *Planned Parenthood v. Casey*, 112 Sup.Ct. 2791 (1992); *Rust v. Sullivan*, 500 U.S. 173 (1991); *Hodgson v. Minnesota*, 497 U.S. 417 (1990).
12 See Catharine A. MacKinnon, "Privacy v. Equality: Beyond *Roe v. Wade*," *Feminism Unmodified: Discourses on Life and Law* (Cambridge: Harvard University Press, 1987), pp. 93–102; Catharine A. MacKinnon, "Reflections on Sex Equality Under Law," *Yale Law Journal*, 100 (1991), pp. 1281–328, 1311.
13 MacKinnon, "Reflections," p. 1286.
14 Ibid.
15 Joan Williams, "Gender Wars: Selfless Women in the Republic of Choice," *New York University Law Review*, 66 (1991), pp. 1559–634, 1633.
16 Ruth Colker, *Abortion and Dialogue: Pro-Choice, Pro-Life, and American Law* (Bloomington: Indiana University Press, 1992), p. 86; Ruth Colker, "Femi-

nism, Theology, and Abortion: Toward Love, Compassion, and Wisdom," *California Law Review,* 77 (1989), pp. 1011–75, 1050.

17 Rachael N. Pine and Sylvia A. Law, "Envisioning a Future for Reproductive Liberty: Strategies for Making the Rights Real," *Harvard Civil Rights-Civil Liberties Law Review,* 27 (1992), pp. 407–63, 421 and notes 53–4.

18 *Rust v. Sullivan,* 500 U.S. 173 (1991).

19 Dorothy E. Roberts, "*Rust v. Sullivan* and the Control of Knowledge," *George Washington Law Review,* 61 (1993), pp. 587–656, 640.

20 See Anita L. Allen, "The Proposed Equal Protection Fix for Abortion Law: Reflections on Citizenship, Gender, and the Constitution," *Harvard Journal of Law and Public Policy,* 18 (1995), pp. 419–55, 438–55.

21 We attempt to tell the whole story, abbreviated here, in Anita L. Allen and Erin Mack, "How Privacy Got Its Gender," *Northern Illinois University Law Review,* 10 (1990) pp. 441–78.

22 *DeMay v. Roberts,* 9 N.W. 146 (Mich. 1881).

23 *DeMay v. Roberts,* 9 N.W. at 148.

24 *DeMay v. Roberts,* 9 N.W. at 148–9.

25 Samuel D. Warren and Louis D. Brandeis, "The Right to Privacy," *Harvard Law Review,* 4 (1890), pp. 193–220.

26 Warren and Brandeis, "The Right to Privacy," pp. 205, 195–6.

27 Warren and Brandeis, "The Right to Privacy," p. 196.

28 Warren and Brandeis, "The Right to Privacy," p. 196.

29 Warren and Brandeis, "The Right to Privacy," pp. 194, 195.

30 Warren and Brandeis, "The Right to Privacy," p. 194.

31 Warren and Brandeis, "The Right to Privacy," p. 195. See also, *New York Times,* June 15, 18, and 21 (1890), as cited in Warren and Brandeis, p. 195, note 7.

32 *New York Times,* June 15, 18, and 21 (1890), as cited in Warren and Brandeis, "The Right to Privacy," p. 195, note 7.

33 *Roberson v. Rochester Folding Box Company,* 65 N.Y.S. 1109 (1900), aff'd 71 N.Y.S. 876 (A.D. 1901), rev'd 64 N.E. 442 (N.Y. 1902). Cf. *Pavesich v. New England Life Insurance Company,* 50 S.E. 68 (Ga. 1905); the court held that a male plaintiff has a privacy right in a case against a defendant who appropriated his photographic image.

34 "Privacy is regarded as a product of civilization . . . , [which] implies an improved and progressive condition of the people in cultivated manners and customs with well-defined and respected domestic relations. The privacy of the home in every civilized country is regarded as sacred, and when it is invaded it tends to destroy domestic and individual happiness. It seems to me, therefore, that the extension and development of the law so as to protect the right of privacy should keep abreast with the advancement of civilization." *Roberson v. Rochester Folding Box Company,* 65 N.Y.S. 1109, 1111 (1900).

35 "Every woman has a right to keep her face concealed from the observation of the public. Her face is her own private property." *Roberson v. Rochester Folding Box Company,* 65 N.Y.S. at 1111.

36 *Roberson v. Rochester Folding Box Company,* 64 N.E. 442, 447 (N.Y. 1902).

37 Civil Rights Law, Laws of 1903, Ch. 132, Sec. 2, p. 308.

38 *Kunz v. Allen,* 172 P. 532 (Kan. 1918).

39 *Kunz v. Allen,* 172 P. at 532.

40 *Kunz v. Allen,* 172 P. at 532.

41 *Kunz v. Allen,* 172 P. at 533, quoting *Pavesich v. New England Life Insurance Company,* 50 S.E. 68, 80 (Ga. 1905).

42 *Graham v. Baltimore Post Company* (Balt. Super. Ct. 1932), reported in "The Right to Privacy," *Kentucky Law Journal,* 22 (1933), pp. 108–21.

43 "The Right to Privacy," p. 116.

44 Ibid.

45 See *Bennett v. Norban,* 151 A.2d 476, 479 (Pa. 1959). The court argued that "if a *modest* young girl should be set upon by a dozen ruffians who did not touch her but by threats compelled her to undress, give them her clothes, and flee naked through the streets, it could not be doubted that her privacy had been invaded as well as her clothes stolen." [emphasis added].

46 *Barber v. Time, Inc.,* 159 S.W.2d 291, 294 (Mo. 1942).

47 *DeMay v. Roberts,* 9 N.W. 146 (Mich. 1881).

48 *Roberson v. Rochester Folding Box Company,* 65 N.Y.S. 1109, aff'd 71 N.Y.S. 876 (A.D. 1901), rev'd 64 N.E. 442 (N.Y. 1902).

49 *Hubbard v. Journal Publishing Company,* 368 P.2d 147 (N.M. 1962); *Cox Broadcasting Corporation v. Cohn,* 420 U.S. 469 (1975); *Florida Star v. B.J.F.,* 491 U.S. 524 (1989).

50 *Phillips v. Smalley Maintenance Services, Inc.,* 435 So.2d 705 (Ala. 1983).

51 *Harris v. Easton Publishing Company,* 483 A.2d. 1377 (Pa. 1984).

52 *Humphers v. First Interstate Bank of Oregon,* 696 P.2d 527, 533 (Or. 1985).

5

Revisioning the Family:
Relational Rights and Responsibilities

Martha Minow and Mary Lyndon Shanley

Few social institutions have figured more prominently in the political debates of the 1990s than "the family." Some commentators saw the disintegration of traditional family life in such sociological trends as extra-marital cohabitation (of both heterosexual and same-sex couples), out-of-wedlock births to single mothers as well as unwed couples, and rising divorce rates. Others saw new freedom in these trends and welcomed the diversity of family forms. And while people argued about whether such changes constituted a radical break with the past or were better understood as following along a continuum that combined continuity and alteration, it was clear that social mores and practices, new developments in repro-ductive technologies, and shifting macroeconomic factors changed expec-tations and behaviors of family members.

Complementing studies of changing social behavior, political and legal theorists struggled to develop conceptualizations of "family" that would clarify issues such as what factors make someone a member of a legal family, the extent of responsibilities of family members for one another, the nature of sexual equality within the family, and the proper boundary of familial privacy. These theoretical concerns arose not only from changes in social behavior, but also from the gradual erosion over the course of the nineteenth and twentieth centuries of the legal understanding of the family as a natural, prepolitical, hierarchical, indissoluble, and private association made up of a heterosexual couple and their biological children. The collapse of the common law paradigm of the patriarchal family has left political and legal theory with a plethora of competing accounts about the nature of family relationships and of the family's relation to the state. This chapter examines what we see as the principles that should guide thinking about families in liberal society and help shape a family policy and law that respects sexual equality and diversity of family forms, takes seriously the responsibilities generated by family relationships, and recog-nizes the role of the larger society in sustaining viable and vibrant families.

Two prominent approaches to conceptualizing family relationships and family law – one contractual,[1] the other communitarian[2] – have arisen in the wake of the collapse of the common law paradigm. Each of these seems to us inadequate because neither fully encompasses either the significant tension that exists between the individual per se and the relationships of which he or she is a part, or that between regarding the family as a private association or as a creature of state action. In distinction to these approaches, we propose grounding family policy and law in an understanding of family as a nexus of what we call "relational rights and responsibilities." The notion of relational rights and responsibilities builds on rights-based approaches to legal and political theory. However, it rejects purely individualistic and contractual models of such rights and emphasizes that any claim arising out of family membership – for example, a right to custody or visitation – must be legally construed in a manner that is sensitive to the inequalities, dependencies, and competing interests that arise from the web of family relationships.[3] At the same time, it does not subordinate the rights and interests of individuals and minority groups to the reinforcement of predominant community values and standards.

Even as we present the considerations that lead us to espouse such an approach, however, we are aware that what the rights and responsibilities of family members are, and who should be counted as a member of a family, are hotly contested issues. We believe that an adequate conceptualization of what constitutes a "family," as well as just family policies, regulations, and benefits, will require a further democratization of political and legal decision-making. Individuals with different reference points (for example of race, sex, religion, national origin, sexual orientation, and class) must present their interests and values in forums where those views will be given serious consideration. The reshaping of family law and public policy, then, will require both our best thinking about family life and a serious democratization of political and legal discussion and decision-making.

Changes in Family Life and Law from the Nineteenth Century to the Mid-Twentieth Century

Although there have always been significant differences among liberal political theorists concerning the nature of the family and its relation to civil society, certain general features of liberal theory's understanding of proper family relationships and of the relation between the family and the state infused works of liberal political theorists and lawyers from the seventeenth century through the nineteenth.[4] The family was a natural and therefore a "private" association, consisting of a male, a female, and their biological children. In this family the husband/father exercised authority over his wife and children (and in many instances his servants, tenants, and slaves), was responsible for the economic support of members of the household, and represented them in the public sphere. The mother/ wife was responsible for managing household life and expenditures, seeing to the physical care of household residents, and providing emotional support and nurture to family members. The responsibility for both the moral education and the economic support of children fell to their parents (but servants, tenants, and slaves did not have claims for such support and education).

This depiction of the family as a natural association that gave authority over children to their parents and over servants to the head-of-household was deeply gendered: the husband had authority over the wife, and the father was the head-of-household. Liberal theory also assumed that there was a clear division between the private realm of the family, created by nature through human sexual mating and reproduction, and the public realm of politics, created by convention through the social contract. Hence at one and the same time liberalism assumed that government authority and law properly regulated public, but not private, matters, and that the representative of the household in the public realm – the citizen – was male.[5]

There were, of course, always disjunctions between the picture of family in political theory and law and the actual lives of families. In the United States, domestic relations law until the mid-nineteenth century did not encompass the family life of slaves, who instead were governed by slave codes and property laws.[6] Children born out of wedlock, widows, and abandoned wives and their children as well as those who explicitly rejected conventional family life and instead pursued solitary or communal households also fell outside the legal norms of the patriarchal family in nineteenth-century US law.[7]

The disjunction between the picture of the family in political theory and law and many people's lived or desired experiences increased from the mid-nineteenth century to our own day.[8] Abolitionist efforts before the Civil War brought the experiences of slaves into debates over political rights; both experience in abolition activities and rhetorical analogies between slavery and marriage enabled white women reformers to seek changes in the legal status of married women and to seek direct political participation through the vote.[9] In both respects the women's rights reformers rejected the picture of the wife's legal personality as subsumed in the husband's and sought to secure her independent rights to hold property, enter into contracts, and express political preferences. Notions of romantic love and the propriety of individual choice of marriage partner led to the view that if marriage was created by the consent of the parties to live in a certain way, and if one of them violated that agreement, then their union could be dissolved.[10] The growing acceptance of formal legal adoption from the mid-nineteenth century on reflected the notion that binding relationships between parent and child could be created by volition and consent as well as by biology, although adoption did try to mirror the "natural family" through efforts to match race and religion and to seal from view the adoptee's family of origin.[11]

Legal and political reforms responded to changing work patterns, tides of immigration, and continuing racial tensions throughout the first half of the twentieth century. As unmarried women and immigrant women sought waged work in rapidly urbanizing and industrial America, their activities challenged the seeming inevitability of the male-headed household, as did the volunteer projects of more privileged women. Anti-racism efforts first against lynching and then against racial segregation laid the foundations for challenges to antimiscegenation laws and race-matching in adoption by the middle of the twentieth century. Migrations from rural to urban areas and from the South to the North, along with continuing immigration, produced diverse communities and extensive personal experiences with change. World War II drew many women into traditionally male employment roles and also gave many African-American and other minority men experiences serving the country that contrasted sharply with their continuing treatment as second-class citizens at home. By mid-century, the Black civil rights movement and the women's liberation movement insisted that the law reflect the collapse of ascriptive status and redefine the meaning of "equality" with respect to both race and sex.

The "second wave" of feminism underscored the depth of challenge to the conception of the male-headed nuclear family as "natural." The power of husbands over wives was no longer treated as natural, and patriarchal control increasingly faced serious challenges in both public and private settings. Egalitarian notions also affected popular and legal views of children. In place of earlier practices that treated children as analogous to property controlled by parents, laws and judicial decisions restricted the power of parents over children in areas such as child labor, extended a certain set of fundamental liberties to children, and invited children's views in matters such as custody following divorce.

Cumulatively, these developments have a common theme: political theorists could no longer view the family as a prepolitical entity, and legal theorists faced complicated judgments over the extent to which families were private and immune from the intervention of the state. The various conceptualizations of family underlying many of the debates on family policy and law reflect the complexity of human aspirations that include the desire to enjoy both autonomy and interrelationship, to savor both independence and intimacy. But while the challenge to the notion that the family is a natural and private association of a heterosexual couple and their biological children has been widespread, scholarship did not arrive at consensus on any alternative legal understanding of "family." Three legal approaches have attempted to deal with these complexities of family life and family law during the past 25 years – contractarian, communitarian and rights-based; we examine each in turn and show why we consider the last, when formulated to take account of family relationships, the most promising foundation for a theory of family law.

Contract-based Theories of Family: The Primacy of Individual Volition

Ever since Sir Henry Maine characterized the development of modern law as a movement from status to contract, these concepts have been juxtaposed as competing bases for legal regimes: one must choose between ascriptive roles and obligations on the one hand, or freely chosen roles and obligations on the other. Hence proponents of a contractual ordering of family life point out the consistency between their views and one of the deepest aspirations of liberal society: the right of individuals to have their freedom limited only by self-assumed obligations.

Given the burdens that ascriptive notions about women's "nature" and proper roles have placed on women seeking equality in both the family and public life, it is not surprising that some feminists see contract as an instrument to provide women greater freedom, self-determination, and equality without subjecting either women or men to traditional sex roles.[12] Unlike traditional marriage law's assumptions about the sexual division of labor in both household and larger society, contractual ordering could allow spouses to decide for themselves how to order their personal as well as their financial relationship during their marriage and in the event of divorce.

Contracts could also provide for pluralism and a diversity in family life impossible to achieve under a uniform domestic relations law. If marriage were regulated by contract, for example, there would seem to be no reason why two individuals of the same sex should be prohibited from entering such a contract. Arguing both for contractual ordering and for legal recognition of same-sex marriage, Lenore Weitzman asserts that "there is a serious question as to whether the state has any legitimate interest interfering with contracts regarding non-commercial sexual relations between consenting adults," although she acknowledges that legal recognition of same-sex marriages might be hampered by the fact that homosexual relations are "still prohibited by the criminal codes of most states."[13] Marjorie Shultz finds that the repeated refusals by the states to formalize unions of same-sex couples by legal marriage "reflect a hesitancy to pursue fully the implications of pluralism and privacy. Where diverse individual outcomes are valued and pluralism is necessary, some form of private ordering of conduct and values is the appropriate regulatory structure."[14] The point of marriage is to create clear expectations and binding obligations to promote stable interpersonal relationships. It is reasonable to ask the state to enforce agreements that would underpin the material aspects of such relationships, but it is not a legitimate concern of the state who may marry whom, or how spouses should order the personal and material aspects of their relationship.

Proponents of contractual ordering of reproduction see it, like contract marriage, as a way of breaking down gender stereotypes and increasing the scope of human choice in establishing families. Contracts could facilitate diverse ways of bringing children into a family, including children born through contract pregnancies ("surrogate mother" arrangements) and through sperm donation from known donors; such arrangements might help gay and lesbian couples, and single persons, become parents; make possible a genetic relationship between at least one parent and the child; and stipulate in advance of conception the degree of contact, if any, to be had between the "surrogate" or sperm donor and the child.[15] Contracts might be used to regulate the degree of contact between biological parent(s) and offspring in open adoptions; in some accounts, contracts could make adoption a market transaction.[16] Some feminists welcome contract pregnancy as a way to illustrate that childbearing and child-rearing are quite distinct human functions and that child-rearing need not be and should not be assigned exclusively to the woman who bears the child (or to women rather than men, for that matter). From this perspective, contract pregnancy seems to expand choice for both the woman who bears the child and for the commissioning parent(s). Carmel Shalev argues that one aspect of autonomy is "the deliberate exercise of choice with respect to the individual's reproductive capacity," and that pregnancy contracts should be strictly enforced out of respect for women's decision-making capacity.[17]

While private ordering has liberating aspects, it also entails more worrisome implications. The assumption that bargains will be freely struck masks configurations of social power that provide the backdrop to any contracts. Generations of labor leaders have pointed out the fallacy of assuming that workers and employers are equal bargaining agents. With

respect to the marriage contract, one of John Stuart Mill's great insights in
The Subjection of Women was his observation that the decision to marry for
the vast majority of women could scarcely be called "free." Given women's
low wages, scarcity of jobs, and lack of opportunity for higher or even
secondary education, marriage was for them a "Hobson's choice," that or
none.[18] Even the "I do" of someone very much in love and desirous of
marriage does not in-and-of-itself guarantee freedom. With respect to
contract pregnancy, the notion that the "labor" of pregnancy and childbirth can be sold like any other bodily labor sweeps away "any intrinsic
relation between the female owner, her body, and reproductive capacities."[19] As Carole Pateman points out, this objectification of women's
bodies and reproductive labor could be more alienating than liberating,
while to extol the "freedom" of a woman who agrees to bear a child
because she needs the money ignores the restraints or compulsions of
economic necessity.

As contract provides no guarantee of freedom to those entering marriage
or pregnancy contracts, it similarly offers no guarantee of an equal relationship between the parties to the contract. Leaving decisions about property
distribution to contracts between the marriage partners does not insure
that such agreements will be more fair than statutory stipulations regarding
equitable distribution. Similarly, descriptions of contract pregnancy as
nothing more than womb rental in a supposedly neutral market masks the
profoundly gendered nature of the structures that surround such transactions. Contractual ordering does not alter those background economic and
social conditions that create relationships of domination and subordination between men and women as well as between rich and poor.

Contractual ordering also fails to deal with the fact that certain dependencies that develop in intimate relationships cannot be adequately addressed by contract. Persons who may be considered independent actors at
the time a contract is signed make whole series of decisions – not only
career decisions but other life choices as well – the consequences of which
can neither be anticipated nor allocated between the parties when they
occur. "Surrogate" mothers who attempt to revoke their agreements often
describe the emergence of an unanticipated sense of relationship that
emerged unbidden during the course of pregnancy. To speak of the
"freedom" of the contracting woman as residing in her intention as an
"autonomous" agent misunderstands the relationship between woman and
fetus, and the influence of that relationship on the woman's sense of
herself.[20]

The model of the individual on which proposals for contracts-in-lieu-
of-marriage and pregnancy contracts rest – that of a self-possessing individual linked to others only by agreement – fails to do justice to the

complex interdependencies involved in family relations and child rearing. Proposals to replace family law by private ordering reflect the serious limitations of a version of liberalism that understands freedom as the ability to determine and pursue one's goals without interference from government or other individuals, and obligation as arising only from specific acts of the will. It also does away with any recognition of a public interest in the ordering of family relationships. Contractual ordering regards individuals as what Hegel called "immediate self-subsistent persons," abstracted from their social relationships.[21] The bases of marriage, reproductive activity, and family life thus become indistinguishable from those of civic and economic association. From this perspective, as Carole Pateman has pointed out, "Marriage and the family are . . . treated as if they were an extension of civil society and so constituted by, and their relationships exhausted by, contract."[22] Contractual ordering is not so much a movement away from status as its negation or mirror image: "The undifferentiated social bonds of a hierarchy of ascription are replaced by the undifferentiated, universal bond of contract."[23]

In its capacity to replace the outmoded, hegemonic, and frequently oppressive understandings of gender norms of traditional statutory and common law rules infusing family law, contract seems a tool of liberation to many advocates of gender equality and pluralism of family forms. But this tool is too crude to deal with the complex relationships of family life. Although persons may freely decide to marry, marriage itself is a social practice; stipulations governing the rights and responsibilities of spouses and parents reflect shared understandings of propriety and fairness which may be subject to debate, but should not be set aside by idiosyncratic agreements. Too often other people are deeply affected by the contracts over whose terms they have no say. Rejecting the contractarians' notion of marriage as a partnership to be shaped by the wills of the parties, genetic material and babies as marketable resources, and gestation as comparable to any other waged labor, other legal and political theorists emphasize the influence of community and the socially constructed nature of both families and their individual members.

Community-based Theories of Family: The Importance of Social Norms and Traditions of the Good

Unlike contract-based theorists, who leave family definition and responsibilities to the private ordering of individuals, community-based theorists regard families as expressions of personal and social relationships larger than individuals and not resting primarily on agreement.[24] Community-based theorists reject the picture of the self adopted by contractarians, who start with the autonomous individual and neglect both the context of larger social relationships and "communal notions of equity and responsibility" in relationships.[25] These theorists all emphasize that families are not simply private associations but also crucial institutions that help compose civil society and the polity.

Some community-based theorists turn to traditional sources to articulate the content of social norms and the shape of relationships endorsed by the community.[26] Others stress a commitment by the society to pursue the common good rather than a regime of entirely private, individual choices.[27] Some expressly embrace the title "communitarian" in search of public values larger than the preferences of individuals and more than a mere aggregation of those preferences.[28] They value civil society and criticize liberalism's tendency to ignore or reject history, tradition, or collective decisions about the good life.

Community-based theorists stress that no person becomes autonomous without first going through an extended period of dependency. "Selves" are formed through the intense relationships of infancy and childhood. Community-based theorists also remind us that individuals are shaped by membership in particular ethnic, regional, and religious communities whose values may depart from the values of society's majority. Where contract-based theories would urge freedom for individuals to embrace their own values under a state neutral about all values except individuals' freedom to contract, community-based theories regard it as neither possible nor desirable "that the state should refrain from coercive public judgments about what constitutes the good life for individuals."[29] William Galston rejects the assumption that the only political alternatives are private individual choice and repressive state-imposed norms. There is, he argues, "a third way: a nonneutral, substantive liberalism committed to its own distinctive conception of the good, broadly (though not boundlessly) respectful of diversity, and supported by its own canon of the virtues," including tolerance, the work ethic, and the "disposition and the capacity to engage in public discourse."[30]

Many feminists endorse at least parts of the community-based critiques of contractarian versions of liberal individualism. They agree with the critique of autonomous individualism that neglects or distorts how human identities are formed; they add that this picture is deeply gendered in both imagining a male self and neglecting historically female work in nurturing children and dependents.[31] In a moving essay on family life Jean Elshtain points out the way in which the notion of the autonomous individual has not only denied the importance of community but has also denigrated women's traditional sphere of activity and ignored the contribution "women's work" has made to sustaining both families and civil society. Any viable human community, she notes, must include persons "devoted to the protection of vulnerable human life. That, historically, has been the mission of women. The pity is not that women reflect an ethic of social responsibility but that the public world has, for the most part, repudiated such an ethic."[32]

Feminist community-based theorists agree that political life should hold more than the fulfillment of ends chosen independently by individuals,[33] and that more than calculated self-interest can and should bind together the political community.[34] But while they join other communitarians in the critique of marriage as merely a contract, they are skeptical about turning to traditional articulations of shared norms about how spouses and parents should act toward one another as a basis for understanding spousal responsibilities. These shared norms have been too thoroughly permeated by gender inequality to act as a model for contemporary marriage law. In such discussions, feminists no less than other community-based theorists face difficult disagreements about which norms and values the community should endorse and law should enforce.

Once the topic for debate is the content of values deserving public endorsement and enforcement, disagreements can grow intense even among people who share a critique of the excesses of individualism. Elshtain, for example, argues not only that "the family is a prerequisite for any form of social life" but also that "a particular ideal of the family is imperative to create a more humane society."[35] Much contemporary debate over families involves disagreements about what precisely the terms of that particular ideal should be, and whose intimate relationships should be excluded from public support or even punished.

Consider the question whether same-sex couples should be allowed to marry. Community-based theorists join in agreeing that this is not a question to be left to the parties themselves, as contractarians would have it. Nor do community-based theorists ask, as rights-based theorists do, whether individuals regardless of sexual orientation should enjoy a right against state control over intimate relationships. Community-based theorists instead view questions such as same-sex marriage as questions for the community to decide, based on tradition, normative theories of the good, or other collective judgments. The result is considerable disagreement.

Jean Elshtain opposes gay and lesbian marriage. She argues that maintaining marriage as a heterosexual union crucially emphasizes the link between sexual expression and procreative activity. The commitments entailed in marriage stand, and should stand, in contrast to unrestrained, public, and commercial sex and the ethos of the "'wanting' self" so familiar in the world of contract. Although not all families will raise children, "the symbolism of marriage–family as social regenesis is fused in our centuries-old experience with marriage ritual, regulation, and persistence." Because there is great social value in preserving the family as an institution "framed within a horizon of intergenerationality," Elshtain is willing to privilege "a restrictive ideal of sexual and intimate relations."[36] She would not leave same-sex couples unprotected; she favors ordinances that allow unmarried couples to register as domestic partners and to assume mutual financial responsibility for each other and receive recognition as a couple for certain purposes such as certain insurance and housing. She would, nonetheless, restrict marriage itself to heterosexual couples in order to emphasize that "marriage is not, and never has been, primarily about two people . . . [but] about the possibility of generativity."[37]

In contrast, other community-based theorists argue in favor of legalizing marriage for same-sex couples. Doing so, they argue, would express the value to society of stable, committed adult relationships, particularly where children are involved. Michael Sandel argues that legal recognition of same-sex marriage would reaffirm the state's interest in protecting the social institution of marriage. Homosexual marriage would reinvigorate "failing public norms of monogamy, loyalty, and mutual care." It would "cultivat[e] the disposition to cooperation rather than competition without which democratic community is unthinkable."[38] Milton Regan favors legalizing gay and lesbian marriage because doing so would recognize "the role of marriage in promoting a relational sense of identity," that is, it would emphasize society's commitment to a non-contractarian view of commitment and responsibility.[39] Theorists with this perspective would endorse the substantive ends of intimate relationships rather than merely a right of choice in intimate settings.

The arguments on both sides refer to values, traditions, and substantive ends, many of which overlap and converge; nothing internal to this debate can resolve it. Community-based theorists invite such debates given their commitment to the substantive good. They further present conflicts over how to ground the values that should prevail and even how to justify critiques of the excesses of individualism. Some, such as Glendon, would combat excessive individualism by norms of individual responsibility and state obligation to protect families.[40] Others, such as Galston, pursue community-based norms from a functional or instrumental perspective; social power should be deployed to reduce divorce, for example, in order to lessen the chances that children of divorce fail to grow into independent and contributing members of the society, economic community, and polity.[41] Still others focus on the need to revitalize traditions such as the centrality of status.[42]

Having embraced as a political task the substantive choices about familics and intimate roles and duties, community-based theorists have to confront deep divisions about policy choices and the values implicated by them. The community-based theories proceed with the view that one way of life is to be preferred or some are to be disfavored. Not only does this run counter to the liberty and tolerance usually advocated in pluralist societies, it also invites potentially unresolvable and intense conflicts about what should and should not be preferred, and may exacerbate social and political divisions along religious and cultural lines. Religious and cultural views and practices vary regarding what kind of family form is desirable, who is a good parent, what range of choice should be granted over reproduction and to whom, and what duties adult children owe their parents. The community-based theories lack the easy accommodation for pluralism afforded by contract-based theories that leave many such matters to private agreement. We think that they also lack a similar accommodation for pluralism afforded by rights-based theories that endorse individual freedoms.

The vision of individual freedoms and equality in a rights-based approach to family law, we believe, presents the possibility of recognizing the importance of family privacy and diversity without relying on private ordering or community traditions to preserve those values. Such an approach also recognizes the political and negotiated nature of social norms and values, including many rights. One problem with "rights-talk" applied to family policy and law has been the tendency to see familial rights as protections for individual freedom, rather than as rights that create, foster, and protect valued relationships. Because they deal with persons in relationship, they must take account of inequalities and dependencies among family members. It is impossible to have an adequate account of certain rights pertaining to family relationships – such as the right to divorce; maternal and paternal rights; rights to custody, visitation, and child support – without paying adequate attention to these various normative dimensions of family relationships. We believe that a theory of relational rights and responsibilities offers a promising avenue for a new foundation for conceptualizing "families" and formulating family policy and law.

Rights-based Theories of Family: The Tension Between Individualism and Family Relationship

Community-based theories seem to invite disputes over what kinds of families and family values society should endorse (whereas contract-based approaches seem to promote pluralism of family forms and intimate choices) yet they may fail to protect individuals against oppressive bargains and ongoing patterns of social inequality. Advocates of rights-based approaches to family law seem to hope that they will be able to promote pluralism while also putting forward as societal values certain basic freedoms guaranteed to each individual. These rights-based approaches are rooted both in classical liberalism and in US constitutionalism.

Extending individual rights to the realm of families is a relatively new phenomenon: prior to the mid-twentieth century, the Supreme Court seldom confronted disputes claiming constitutionally protected rights associated with family formation or dissolution, definitions of kinship or affiliation, and obligations of care and support based on family ties. Instead, those matters remained subject to state regulation, and often the states in turn relied on traditions, religious or otherwise. The states did define terms for family formation and dissolution but also tended to exempt families from otherwise prevailing rules of contract, tort, and criminal law. In these respects, US courts followed a tradition of non-interference in family lives, at least when that tradition coincided with state purposes and values. The states did require parents to comply with compulsory school laws for their children, and often scrutinized the living conditions, household composition, and child-rearing practices of poor, immigrant, African-American, and Native American families, which at times led to the removal of children from their family homes.

In the mid-twentieth century, litigation involving various "rights" of family members began to impart a federal, constitutional dimension to family law. The Supreme Court pronounced constitutional bases for a right to marry (*Loving v. Virginia* 1967); the right to procreate (*Skinner v. Oklahoma* 1942; *Griswold v. Connecticut* 1965); the right not to procreate (*Griswold v. Connecticut* 1965; *Eisenstadt v. Baird* 1972; *Roe v. Wade* 1973); the right to retain or establish parental ties (*Stanley v. Illinois* 1972; *Caban v. Mohammed* 1979). The Court rejected claims for a right to engage in consensual homosexual activity (*Bowers v. Hardwick* 1986), and restricted claims of parental status outside of marriage (*Lehr v. Robertson* 1983; *Michael H. v. Gerald D.* 1989). The Court also recognized as worthy of constitutional protection certain claims of parental decision-making power (*Wisconsin v. Yoder* 1972; *Parham v. J.R.* 1979) and family privacy (*Moore v. City of East Cleveland* 1977).

Two fundamental conceptions of rights undergird these decisions. The first views the family as a unitary entity, entitled to protection from state scrutiny or interference; the second locates rights in distinct individuals who should be guarded from state obstruction in intimate choices and behaviors.[43] Both approaches offer a critical purchase on otherwise prevailing governmental actions, but the second in particular begins to challenge legal assumptions about proper family relationships. Elizabeth Schneider has documented efforts to marshal individual rights against assault by spouses, and against the screen of family privacy that had shielded such practices from arrest, prosecution, and punishment.[44] Nan Hunter, Sylvia Law, and more recently William Eskridge have asserted individual rights to marry that should extend to couples of the same sex, not only to recognize gay and lesbian rights but also to combat gender hierarchies that harm women even in heterosexual marriages.[45] Nancy Polikoff argues that courts should recognize that both partners in a lesbian couple should have parental rights with regard to children living in their household.[46] Despite this widespread invocation of rights, commentators do not always agree about what rights are relevant and which should prevail in any particular case. Earl Maltz, for example, does not think that there is a constitutional protection for same-sex marriage.[47] John Robertson advocates recognition of a right to use medical technology and to purchase genetic and gestational services from others.[48] In contrast, Margaret Jane Radin invokes "the right of inalienability" to empower individuals to resist the incursions of the market especially in the context of genetic material and "surrogate," or contract mother arrangements.[49]

The most pronounced conflict, however, pits the vision of individuals enjoying rights against the picture of the family as a unitary entity entitled to rights against state intrusion. Many of the asserted individual rights specifically prevail upon the state to pry behind closed doors of family homes either to protect individuals from harm or to enable them to alter the otherwise prevailing pattern of relationships. Thus, the right to be free from abuse in marriage brings the state into the household by justifying actual police investigations and more basically by instituting a norm of mutual respect between spouses. The right to choose contraception or abortion enables not just a couple but an individual to make choices without the interference of others, including the intimate partner.

Another approach to the critique of the family as a unitary entity has emerged from feminist engagement with the work of John Rawls. Although Rawls notably neglects the internal ordering of families, his work has strengthened the intellectual resources for rights-based theories. *A Theory of Justice* develops a strong foundation for notions of individual rights even when they challenge traditions and conventions. Rawls's work has also led to debates about what the rights pertaining to family members might be, and whether a rights-based discourse is, in the end, adequate for a political or legal theory of the family. Notably, Susan Okin criticizes Rawls for failing to take gender seriously in formulating the principles of justice and for failing to carry these principles fully into the context of families.[50] Attacking the common law notion that the family is a unitary entity that should be shielded from the state's prying eye, Okin argues that the traditional liberal defense of family privacy has made it difficult to

recognize the gender inequality that permeates social and legal arrangements affecting women's lives in both families and civil society. Okin
maintains further that when Rawls identifies "the monogamous family" as
one of the major social institutions that is to be guided by his two
principles of justice, he fails to acknowledge that most families violate the
principle of equal liberty and the principle that any inequalities should
work to the benefit of the least well-off. No one uncertain about what sex
he or she will have, Okin argues, would accept the prevailing gender
structures of society and the family as just.

This argument by Okin makes tremendous strides toward a theory of
justice addressing families. It demands that such a theory explore the ways
that gender-based practices affect the distribution of power and goods
both in families and in larger social institutions, and in the interaction
between both realms. Similarly, Okin opens the way toward consideration
of state recognition for relationships between same-sex couples as part of
a larger effort to eliminate the significance of gender roles.[51]

Eva Kittay, like Okin, criticizes aspects of Rawls' view of families, in
particular his assumption that heads-of-households can be understood as
mutually disinterested decision-makers except regarding intergenerational
ties. Missing from Rawls's depiction of family life is attention to those
relationships of care-giving and dependency that exist not simply between
generations, but among those living at the same time. Dependency may
arise from youth or age, disability or illness, or mutual reliance; neither
dependent people nor those who care for them conform to Rawls' model
of the self-sufficient, "disinterested," autonomous individual.[52]

In this respect, Kittay criticizes the understanding of liberal rights that
neglects the significance of care and relationships of care to both a theory
of justice and an ideal way of life. Kittay joins others such as Annette Baier,
Carol Gilligan, Virginia Held, Sara Ruddick and Joan Tronto who regard
it as a moral imperative that all people should benefit from conditions for
continuous care and connection.[53] An ethic of care that values the efforts
of continuous attention and help must find a place in any adequate
account of family lives and in any just family law. The work of theorists
who explore an ethic of care tends to expose a conceptual limitation in
rights, conventionally conceived, as a basis of thinking about families:
whether assigned to individuals or to families as entities, rights may fail to
highlight, protect, or define relationships of moral connection. Yet many
rights associated with family life – the rights to marry, divorce, procreate,
receive child support – involve not individuals per se but the claims,
responsibilities, and boundaries of particular human relationships. Defining such rights requires articulation of the moral predicates and scope of
such relationships.[54]

We agree with these feminist critics of rights theory that a political theory inattentive to relationships of care and connection between and among people cannot adequately address many themes and issues facing families. Many community-based theories share with the feminist theories of care a rejection of the model of the self-sufficient and self-interested individual. However, in their rejection of that model, community-based theorists critical of the liberal tradition often do not distinguish contractarian from rights-based approaches in political theory and law. But these approaches are distinguishable. Contractarian views acknowledge human relationships but treat them all as chosen and susceptible to market or market-like bargains. Little scope for public articulation of values persists in a contract-based regime beyond preservation of the institution of contract and perhaps rejection of extreme bargains. Rights-based views instead require public articulation of the kinds of freedoms that deserve protection and the qualities of human dignity that warrant societal support. Moreover, whether acknowledged or not, rights articulate relationships among people. Every freedom of action guaranteed to an individual demands as a correlate constraints of respect by other individuals. In the context of family matters, rights-based theories need to acknowledge more fully their relational dimensions and draw on the insights of those who study care-taking.

This route – enriching rights-based theories with strong attention to relationships and their preconditions – holds more promise for family law than either contractarian or communitarian approaches. Contract-based theories promote individual freedoms but neglect social values and concerns about inequality and dignity; community-based theories articulate shared values but risk constraining individual freedoms and social pluralism and may prompt greater social conflict. While rights-based theories invigorate as social values respect for certain individual freedoms, they historically lack a rich understanding of relationships, including the preconditions, responsibilities, and consequences of human relationships. In the next section we consider whether and how a notion of relational rights, informed by theories of care-taking, might address a variety of difficult issues confronting family policy and law.

Relational Rights and Responsibilities: Elements of an Adequate Theory of Family Law

Sociological changes, rapid developments in reproductive technology, and the collapse of the common law paradigm of the family as a unitary, hierarchical, and indissoluble entity make it imperative to think anew about what social policy and law should take to be the constitutive or defining features of "family." Among the difficult policy issues that challenge current underpinnings of contemporary family law are those concerning what role genetic ties should play in establishing parental rights; the relevance or irrelevance of sexual orientation in establishing legal marriage and parental rights; the extent to which the law should allow legal family ties to be established through sale of genetic material (sperm, ova) and gestational services; the importance, if any, of racial or religious identity to decisions regarding custody, foster care, or adoption; and the relative responsibilities of government and family members to pay for childcare, respite care, and care of ill or disabled family members. The hard choices each of these issues poses for policymakers indicate the extent to which family law and family policy reflect both human social practices and institutions, and conscious political choices. These choices require argument, debate, and continual assessment and reassessment in light of experience and values.

But to say that family law is properly the product of political discussion and negotiation is not to say that it cannot be based on principle. It is, rather, to say that in a world in which social and material conditions change over time, the way in which law reflects fundamental principles will change, too.

We believe that any adequate family law must be based on principles that take account of two complex characteristics of family life and the family's relationship to the state. First, the individual must be seen simultaneously as a distinct individual and as a person fundamentally involved in relationships of dependence, care, and responsibility. For example, a woman who agrees to bear a child for someone else must be viewed both as a responsible agent and as someone who, during her pregnancy, has established some relationship to the child. A court deciding who shall have custody of the child she has borne and now wishes to keep must neither reduce the case to the enforcement of a contract nor regard the fact of childbearing alone as determining parental claims.[55] Similarly, when either same-sex or heterosexual couples who share custody of children separate or divorce, rulings determining financial support and child custody or visitation must consider the parties to such actions both as separate adults and as individuals-in-relationship. The law must allow parents to resume their independence and to remarry or form new relationships if they wish, but the law must also enforce the continuing obligations each has to their children. Those obligations are not only for financial support, but may also include requirements that one parent not take actions that would jeopardize the possibility of a continuing relationship between the other parent and the child.

Second, family law and political theory must take account of the fact that families are simultaneously private associations and entities shaped by the political order. Even confining our view to Western societies, the forms family associations take are clearly affected by law. People's views of who might be a possible marriage partner are shaped by the prohibited degrees of kinship and bans on same-sex and polygamous marriages. Laws also have affected who were regarded as parents and children; legal adoption allowed the creation of nonbiological family ties, while bastardy statutes denied any legal significance to the biological tie between offspring and parents.[56] Yet families were clearly not creatures of the state like joint-stock companies and limited partnerships. With the exception of bastardy statutes, the biological tie between an adult and his or her offspring has been taken to establish prima facie parental rights and obligations; few have proposed that children, at birth, be assigned to the best possible caretaker, rather than to their biological parents.

Moreover, peoples' lives as family members are importantly framed and influenced by practices and decisions of the larger society. Some of those practices and decisions impose burdens and allocate benefits according to generally held views about acceptable family and public behaviors; for example, nepotism laws both reflected and enforced norms against married women's working outside the home. Others reflect matters including but not limited to macroeconomic policies that set the acceptable level of unemployment, and therefore the availability of jobs; resources devoted to public transportation; and employment practices that affect equal opportunity regardless of gender, race, or other characteristics. The current practice of contract pregnancy in the United States is shaped both by cultural norms that link maternity and womanhood very closely and that regard biological ties to the children one raises as highly desirable, and by economic structures that have made paid gestational labor an attractive job relative to other available options for some women and couples.

We have argued that neither a contract-based approach nor a community-based approach takes adequate account of these tensions that are inherent in contemporary family life. While a contractarian view of marriage emphasizes the need to accommodate differences among individuals and within relationships, it does not sufficiently acknowledge the non-contractual dimension of family relationships, the social and economic contexts that influence decisions made by family members, and the weight of social and state interests affected by family-like arrangements. While community-based theories understand the importance of tradition and social context in shaping individuals and defining their relationships, they often fail sufficiently to consider individual rights and interests, the status of family as a private association, and the plurality of family-like relationships that might warrant recognition and protection. Community-based theories risk marginalizing perspectives of members of non-traditional groups that have not historically had strong political representation. A conception of relational rights and responsibilities, we believe, would not regard "rights" as belonging to individuals and arising from the imperative of self-preservation, but rather would view rights as claims grounded in and arising from human relationships of varying degrees of intimacy, what Kenneth Karst has called "intimate associations."[57]

Relational rights and responsibilities should draw attention to the claims that arise out of relationships of human interdependence. Those claims entitle people to explore a range of relationships and in so doing to draw sustenance from the larger community. A focus on relational rights and responsibilities might examine the legality of same-sex marriage by considering the place of such proposed relationships in the lives of those immediately involved and those in the surrounding community. Similarly, in thinking about cases in which a gestational mother who is party to a pregnancy contract wishes to keep the child rather than turn him or her over to the other contracting party, attention to relational rights and responsibilities requires consideration of the relationship between the gestational mother and the baby, the potential relationship between the commissioning parent(s) and the baby, and the baby's need for ongoing relationships with adults who assume full parental responsibilities. The issues for resolution thus are not simply the rights of adults who entered a contract, nor of community standards about contracts in such circumstances, but the moral and psychological dimensions of persons whose claims arise out of actual and potential relationships. In other disputes concerning child custody, a focus on relational rights and responsibilities would give great weight to preserving some continuity of relationships.

An adequate theory of family law would also have to recognize the relationship between family life and the political and economic order. Here again a vital conception of relationships and responsibilities would help. Each intimate relationship is in turn embedded in ties among members of neighbors, religious and ethnic groups, fellow citizens, all of which are deeply affected but not entirely determined by the political system and economic circumstances. Connecting these relationships to a vibrant sense of responsibility would engage wide circles of people, including even public-policy makers and voters, who would need to consider what social and economic structures are necessary to permit continuous, caring human relationships especially responsive to those most dependent on such care. As Kittay argues, "A society cannot be well-ordered, that is, it cannot be one in which all its members are sustained and included within the ideal of equality, if it fails to be a society characterized by care."[58] The polity cannot take for granted the contribution made by caregivers to maintaining the social and political order, but "must take upon itself the primary responsibility of maintaining structures that will support the principles of care."[59]

Recognizing that individuals are invariably – although to different degrees and at different times – shaped by and accountable for relationships of interdependency would invigorate private and public responses to family issues. Acknowledging the interdependence of family members and the larger polity itself is crucial, although this is simply a beginning, not an end, of the analysis. For then the society, whether through law or other means, must still address what criteria should be used to resolve disputes over what should count within the definition of "family" and what constellation of intimate relations should receive the special resources of public approval and recognition. The resolution of such issues, we argue, requires not only reasoned deliberation, but also politics and a political practice fashioned to produce maximum participation by all members of society. Exclusions and disadvantages based on gender, race, ethnicity, religion, and class historically have been reflected in public policy dealing with families. The creation of a just family policy requires reform not only of family law itself but also of the larger political and legal processes by which family law is created and applied, so that people who are presently marginalized may engage fully in the debates and decisions that frame entitlements essential to sustaining viable family lives.

A political and legal theory of family that took into account the two complex aspects of family membership, even if combined with legislative and judicial processes that worked to ensure representation of minority views and maximum participation, would not provide ready, easy, or universally acceptable answers to difficult questions such as those we raise at the beginning of this section. It would, however, provide the analytic, intellectual, and rhetorical resources for approaching such questions. It would help to ensure that the contractarian models of economic life do not take over all other areas of public life or of family relationships, and that a search for common norms would not eliminate pluralism or curtail privacy. It would also put the prerequisites of relationships of care at the center of concern, rather than treat them as incidental effects of individual choices or needs. A theory of relational rights and responsibilities would encompass not only individual freedoms but also rights to enter and sustain intimate associations consistent with public conceptions of the responsibilities those associations entail, underscoring the connection between families and the larger community. Progress in thinking about and addressing the complex issues concerning family life that have arisen from sociological changes in family structures, developments in reproductive technology, and the demise of the common law model of the patriarchal family seems most likely to develop from the conjuncture of a political and legal theory that focuses on the relationships that constitute family life and the preconditions necessary to sustain such relationships, and political practices designed to maximize inclusion, representation, and democratic participation.

Notes

1 Among those who espouse a contractual basis for thinking about family are Gary S. Becker, *A Treatise on the Family* (Cambridge: Harvard University Press, 1981); Will Kymlicka, "Rethinking the family," *Philosophy and Public Affairs*, 20, 1 (1991), pp. 77–98; Carmel Shalev, *Birth Power* (New Haven: Yale University Press, 1989); Marjorie Maguire Shultz, "Contractual ordering of marriage: A new model for state policy," *California Law Review*, 70, 2 (1982), pp. 204–334; Carol Weisbrod, "The way we live now: A discussion of contracts and domestic relations," *Utah Law Review* 1994, 2 (1994), pp. 777–815; Lenore Weitzman, "Marriage contracts," *California Law Review*, 62 (1974).

2 Among those who put forward a communitarian basis for thinking about family are Jean Bethke Elshtain, "Accepting limits," *Commonweal*, November 22, 1991; Jean Bethke Elshtain, "Feminism, family and community," in *Feminism and Community*, eds Penny Weiss and Marilyn Friedman (Philadelphia: Temple University Press, 1995); William Galston, *Liberal Purposes: Goods, Virtues, and Diversity in the Liberal State* (Cambridge: Cambridge University Press, 1991); Mary Ann Glendon, *Abortion and Divorce in Western Law* (Cambridge, MA: Harvard University Press, 1987); Milton C. Regan Jr, *Family Law and the Pursuit of Intimacy* (New York: New York University Press, 1993); Michael J. Sandel, *Liberalism and the Limits of Justice* (Cambridge: Cambridge University Press, 1982).

3 Among those who use a rights-based approach to thinking about family are Susan Moller Okin, *Justice, Gender and the Family* (New York: Basic Books, 1989); Margaret J. Radin, "Market inalienability," *Harvard Law Review*, 100, 8 (1987), pp. 1849–937; Margaret J. Radin, "What, if anything, is wrong with baby-selling?" *Pacific Law Journal* (1995), pp. 135–45; Nan Hunter, "Marriage, law, and gender: A feminist inquiry," *Law and Inequality*, 1 (1991), p. 9.

4 John Locke, *Second Treatise of Government* [1690], ed. C. B. Macpherson (Indianapolis: Hackett, 1980); John Stuart Mill, *The Subjection of Women* [1869], ed. Susan Moller Okin (Indianapolis: Hackett, 1988).

5 Carole Pateman and Teresa Brennan, "'Mere auxiliaries to the commonwealth': Women and the origins of liberalism," *Political Studies*, 27 (1979), pp. 183–200.

6 Margaret Burnham, "An impossible marriage: Slave law and family law," *Journal of Law and Inequality*, 5, 2 (1987), p. 187.

7 Michael Grossberg, *Governing the Hearth: Law and Family in Nineteenth-Century America* (Chapel Hill: University of North Carolina Press, 1985); Hendrick Hartog, "Marital exits and marital expectations in 19th century America," *Georgetown Law Journal*, 80 (1991), pp. 95–129; Martha Minow, "'Forming under everything that grows': Toward a history of family law," *Wisconsin Law Review*, 1985, 4 (1985), pp. 819–98; Carol Weisbrod, *The Boundaries of Utopia* (New York: Pantheon, 1980).

8 Minow, "'Forming under everything that grows,'" *Wisconsin Law Review*, 1985, 4 (1985), pp. 819–98.

9 Jean F. Yellin, *Women and Sisters: The Antislavery Feminists in American Culture* (New Haven: Yale University Press, 1989).

10 Michael Grossberg, *Governing the Hearth: Law and Family in Nineteenth-Century America* (Chapel Hill: University of North Carolina Press, 1985); Elaine Tyler May, *Great Expectations: Marriage and Divorce in Post-Victorian America* (Chicago: University of Chicago Press, 1980).

11 Jamil S. Zainaldin, "The emergence of a modern American family law: Child custody, adoption, and the courts, 1796–1851," *Northwestern University Law Review*, 73 (1979), pp. 1038–89.

12 Martha Albertson Fineman, *The Neutered Mother, The Sexual Family, and Other Twentieth-century Tragedies* (New York: Routledge, 1995); Kymlicka, "Rethinking the family," pp. 77–98; Carmel Shalev, *Birth Power*; Marjorie Maguire Shultz, "Contractual ordering of marriage"; Marjorie Maguire Shultz, "Reproductive technology and intention-based parenthood: An opportunity for gender neutrality," *Wisconsin Law Review* 2 (1990), pp. 297–398; Weisbrod, "The way we live now"; Weitzman, "Marriage contracts"; Lenore Weitzman, *The Marriage Contract: Spouses, Lovers, and the Law* (New York: Free Press, 1981); Lenore Weitzman, *The Divorce Revolution: Unexpected Social and Economic Consequences for Women and Children in America* (New York: Free Press, 1985).

13 Weitzman, "Marriage contracts," p. 1275 and n. 479.

14 Shultz, "Contractual ordering of marriage," p. 248.

15 Shalev, *Birth Power*; John Robertson, "Embryos, families and procreative liberty," *Southern California Law Review*, 59, 5 (1989), pp. 939–1041.

16 Lincoln Caplan, *An Open Adoption* (New York: Farrar, Strauss & Giroux, 1990); Richard Posner, *Sex and Reason* (Cambridge: Harvard University Press, 1992).

17 Shalev, *Birth Power*, p. 103.

18 John Stuart Mill, *The Subjection of Women* [1869], ed. Susan Moller Okin (Indianapolis: Hackett, 1988).

19 Carole Pateman, *The Sexual Contract* (Stanford: Stanford University Press, 1988), p. 216.

20 Young, "Pregnant embodiment: Subjectivity and alienation," in *"Throwing like a girl" and Other Essays in Feminist Philosophy and Social Theory* (Bloomington: Indiana University Press, 1990), p. 167; Adrienne Rich, *Of Woman Born: Motherhood as Experience and as Institution* (New York: Norton, Bantam, 1976), p. 47.

21 Quoted in Pateman, "The shame of the marriage contract," in *Women and Men's Wars*, ed. Judith Stiehm (New York: Pergamon Press, 1983), p. 95.

22 Pateman, "The shame of the marriage contract," p. 82.
23 Pateman, "The shame of the marriage contract," p. 95.
24 Jean Bethke Elshtain, "Accepting limits"; Jean Bethke Elshtain, "Feminism, family, and community"; William Galston, *Liberal Purposes*; Mary Ann Glendon, *Abortion and Divorce in Western Law*; Mary Ann Glendon, *Rights Talk: The Impoverishment of Politics* (Cambridge, MA: Harvard University Press, 1991); Milton C. Regan Jr, *Family Law and the Pursuit of Intimacy*; Michael J. Sandel, *Liberalism and the Limits of Justice*; Michael Walzer, *Spheres of Justice: A Defense of Pluralism and Equality* (New York: Basic Books, 1983).
25 Regan, *Family Law and the Pursuit of Intimacy*, p. 125.
26 Mary Ann Glendon, *Abortion and Divorce in Western Law*; Mary Ann Glendon, *Rights Talk: The Impoverishment of Politics*; *Michael H v. Gerald D*, opinion for the Court by Justice Antonin Scalia.
27 Philip Selznick, "Foundations of communitarian liberalism," in *The Responsive Community* 4, 4 (1994), pp. 26–8.
28 William Galston, *Liberal Purposes*; Amitai Etzioni, *The Spirit of Community: Rights, Responsibilities, and the Communitarian Agenda* (New York: Crown Publishers, 1993).
29 Galston, *Liberal Purposes*, p.14.
30 Galston, *Liberal Purposes*, p. 44 and pp. 213–27.
31 Seyla Benhabib and Drucilla Cornell, eds, "Introduction: Beyond the politics of gender," in *Feminism as Critique* (Minneapolis: University of Minnesota Press, 1987), p. 12; Virginia Held, "The non-contractual society: A feminist view," *Canadian Journal of Philosophy*, Supplementary 13 (1987), p. 113.
32 Elshtain, "Feminism, family and community," p. 268.
33 Penny Weiss, "Feminism and contractarianism: Comparing critiques of liberalism," in *Feminism and Community*, eds Penny Weiss and Marilyn Friedman (Philadelphia: Temple University Press), p. 176.
34 Marilyn Friedman, "Feminism and modern friendship: Dislocating the community," in *Friendship: A Philosophical Reader*, ed. Neera Kapur Badhwar (Ithaca: Cornell University Press, 1993), p. 285.
35 Elshtain, "Feminism, family, and community," p. 268.
36 Elshtain, "Accepting limits," p. 686.
37 Ibid.
38 Michael J. Sandel, "Moral argument and liberal toleration: Abortion and homosexuality," *California Law Review*, 77, 3 (1989), pp. 521–38.
39 Regan, *Family Law and the Pursuit of Intimacy*, p. 121.
40 Glendon, *Abortion and Divorce in Western Law*, p. 134.
41 Galston, *Liberal Purposes*, p. 287.
42 Regan, *Family Law and the Pursuit of Intimacy*, pp. 151–3.
43 Alice Hearst, "Domesticating reason: Families and good citizens," Paper presented at Law and Society Association Conference, Toronto, Ontario, June 3, 1995; Martha Minow, "We, the family: Constitutional rights and American families," in *The Constitution and American Life*, ed. David Thelen (Ithaca: Cornell University Press, 1988), pp. 222–323.

44 Elizabeth M. Schneider, "The dialectic of rights and politics: Perspectives from the women's movement," *New York University Law Review*, 61 (1986), p. 589; Elizabeth M. Schneider, "Particularity and generality: Challenges of feminist theory and practice in work on woman-abuse," *Brooklyn Law Review*, 67, 3 (1992), pp. 520–68.

45 Nan Hunter, "Marriage, law, and gender"; Sylvia Law, "Homosexuality and the social meaning of gender," *Wisconsin Law Review*, 1988 (1988), p. 187; William Eskridge, "A history of same-sex marriage," *Virginia Law Review*, 79 (1993), p. 1419.

46 Nancy Polikoff, "This child does have two mothers: Redefining parenthood to meet the needs of children in lesbian-mother and other non-traditional families," *Georgetown Law Review*, 78, 3 (1990), pp. 459–575.

47 Earl M. Maltz, "Constitutional protection for the right to marry: A dissenting view," *George Washington Law Review*, 60, 4 (1992), pp. 949–68.

48 John Robertson, "Procreative liberty and the control of contraception, pregnancy, and childbirth," *Virginia Law Review*, 69, 3 (1983), pp. 405–62; John Robertson, "Embryos, families and procreative liberty," *Southern California Law Review*, 59, 5 (1989), pp. 939–1041.

49 Margaret J. Radin, "Market inalienability"; Margaret J. Radin, "What, if anything, is wrong with baby-selling?"

50 Okin, *Justice, Gender and the Family*, pp. 89–109.

51 Okin, "Sexual orientation, gender, and families: Dichotomizing differences," *Hypatia*, 11, 1 (1996), pp. 30–48.

52 Eva F. Kittay, "Taking dependency seriously: The Family and Medical Leave Act considered in the light of the social organization of work and gender equality," *Hypatia*, 10, 1 (1995), pp. 8–30, esp. pp. 14–16.

53 Annette Baier, "Caring about caring," in *Postures of the Mind: Essays on Mind and Morals*, ed. Annette Baier (Minneapolis: University of Minnesota Press, 1985), pp. 93–104; Carol Gilligan, *In a Different Voice* (Cambridge, MA: Harvard University Press, 1982); Virginia Held, "The non-contractual society: A feminist view," *Canadian Journal of Philosophy*. Supplementary 13 (1987); Sara Ruddick, *Maternal Thinking* (Boston: Beacon Press, 1989); Joan Tronto, *Moral Boundaries: A Political Argument for an Ethic of Care* (New York: Routledge, 1993).

54 Martha Minow, *Making All the Difference: Inclusion, Exclusion, and American Law* (Ithaca: Cornell University Press, 1990); essay by Kiss in this volume.

55 Mary Lyndon Shanley, "'Surrogate mothering' and women's freedom: A critique of contracts for human reproduction," *Signs: Journal of Women in Culture and Society*, 18, 3 (1993), pp. 618–39. For further discussion of the basis for legal recognition of parental claims see Mary Lyndon Shanley, "Fathers' rights, mothers' wrongs? Reflections on unwed fathers' rights and sex equality," *Hypatia: A Feminist Journal of Philosophy*, 10, 1 (1995), pp. 74–103.

56 Grossberg, *Governing the Hearth*.

57 Kenneth L. Karst, "The freedom of intimate association," *Yale Law Journal*, 89, 4 (1980), pp. 624–92.

58 Eva F. Kittay, "Taking dependency seriously: The Family and Medical Leave Act considered in the light of the social organization of work and gender equality," p. 24.
59 Kittay, "Taking dependency seriously: Equality, social cooperation, and The Family and Medical Leave Act considered in light of the social organization of work." Paper delivered at Conference on Feminism and Social Action, University of Pittsburgh, November 1993, p. 7b.

6

Political Children: Reflections on Hannah Arendt's Distinction between Public and Private Life

Jean Bethke Elshtain

In a number of essays as well as her classic work, *The Human Condition*, Hannah Arendt eloquently worried about what she saw as the politicization of childhood. She regarded children as part of the private household, and she sought to keep the household and family life distinct from the world of political debate and action. In light of the undeniable reality of political children, past and present, I wish to revisit Arendt's argument and offer up a provisional assessment of her case (and cause) in light of the many exemplars of children cajoled, compelled, or persuaded to act politically. In doing so, I display a cluster of examples of political children of the sort Arendt would either oppose or call into question. I do not point to the nigh-universal experience encountered by those who study or observe such matters of children "liking Ike" or "loathing Nixon" because Mommy and Daddy do; rather, I have in mind children marching, chanting, courting arrest, even killing and dying under a political banner or in line with a political *imprimatur.*

Private Children:
Arendt's Case Against Political Children

The often nasty controversy surrounding Arendt's occasional piece, "Reflections on Little Rock," in which she resoundingly thumped the school desegregationists for putting children on the front line of a political battle, had its beginnings in *The Human Condition*, her 1958 book. All students of Arendt are familiar with her designation of three "fundamental human activities: labor, work, and action" as the defining features of those "basic conditions under which life on earth has been given to man."[1] Childhood enters the story with her assessment of the public and private realms, for the private sphere is the *only* space that can shelter and shield children from premature, hence devastating, entry into the public worlds, and burdens, of life. The explicit political mobilization of the young erodes natality, the birth of the new, and the possibility of a later newness that it bears. Those who indoctrinate the young politically produce controlled robots or rabid zealots, not free agents. Protection of the first natality in order to make possible the second – in the form of authentic thought and action – is a private, hidden activity: it takes place in a world not open to public scrutiny and control.

Among the many things that it is, or does, the distinction between private and public is one between the things that should be hidden and those that should be shown. Without signing on to, or challenging, Arendt's categories and conclusions in their full instantiation – that is beyond the ken of this essay – most important for my purpose is Arendt's insistence that the family, or household, is there to maintain life, to contain the initial life-world of natality, as it were. A private, hidden sphere is necessary in order that children and the labor that brings children into being and nourishes them be exempt from publicity. The private is the world made necessary, in part, by shame. Shame and its felt experience as it surrounds our body's functions, passions, and desires requires symbolic forms, veils of civility that conceal some activities and aspects of ourselves even as we boldly and routinely display and reveal other sides of ourselves when we take part in public activities in the light of day for all to see. This is not to embrace duplicity and disguise; rather, it means holding on to the concealment necessary to a rich personal life and to primary human dignity in order that one might come to know and thus work to attain that which is self-revelatory and public. For there are certain goods that can flourish only under privacy's veil, most importantly natality, love and intimacy. This, at least, is my gloss on what Arendt is up to with her insistence on keeping hidden childhood and, beyond childhood, certain adult human activities by contrast to some others.

Her insistence on a complex and many-sided public–private distinction, compounded with her lament that the category of "the social" was gobbling up much that was rightly either private or public, lies behind her much debated entries into the American fray with "Reflections on Little Rock" and the related "Crisis in Education." Although "Crisis" appeared in print first – in *Partisan Review*, Fall, 1958 – it was, in fact, a response to the criticisms of her much delayed piece, "Reflections on Little Rock," a polemic that finally saw the light of day in *Dissent*, Winter, 1959. The "Little Rock" essay had been batted around for a year before it was published. Commissioned initially by *Commentary*, whose editors were "perplexed and hostile," according to Arendt's biographer, Elisabeth

Young-Bruehl, Arendt's piece was to have been paired with a reply from Sidney Hook. After many delays, Arendt yanked the essay, in anger, deciding not to publish it. But the school desegregation crisis did not abate so Arendt accepted publication in *Dissent*.[2] She may have rued the day although, given her combativeness, she probably relished the furor, too.

Arendt's opposition to political children comes through resoundingly in "Little Rock," and is elaborated and nestled explicitly inside her *Human Condition* framework in "Crisis in Education." I begin with "Little Rock" and the hornet's nest Arendt stirred up by challenging the liberal consensus that had emerged around *Brown v. Board of Education* and the move to desegregate the schools – meaning, primarily, Southern schools. Arendt is stunned that the federal government decided to start integration in "of all places, the public schools. It certainly did not require too much imagination to see that this was to burden children, black and white, with the working out of a problem which adults for generations have confessed themselves unable to solve."[3] Arendt goes on to remind her readers of the photographs featuring a "Negro girl, accompanied by a white friend of her father, walking away from school, persecuted and followed into bodily proximity by a jeering and grimacing mob of youngsters."[4] This young girl was "asked to be a hero." The whole thing, to Arendt, smacked of a "fantastic caricature of progressive education which, by abolishing the authority of adults implicitly denies their responsibility for the world into which they have borne their children and refuses the duty of guiding them into it. Have we now come to the point where it is the children who are being asked to change or improve the world? And do we intend to have our political battles fought out in the school yards?"[5] Clearly, Arendt's concerns revolve not only around what children are being put through but about what this says concerning the adults in their immediate surround – their parents and teachers and neighbors. She hints at a mutually constitutive relationship between adult abdication of authority and premature or forced politicization of children.

Arendt moves on to a rather terse defense of social *discrimination* by contrast to political *equality*. Only in the political realm are we equals. In every other sphere we discriminate based on a variety of distinctions. In the social sphere "like attracts like." Indeed, without this sort of freedom *for* discrimination freedom *of* association could not exist. The problem, therefore, is not to abolish discrimination but to contain it to the social sphere "where it is legitimate, and prevent its trespassing on the political and the personal sphere, where it is destructive."[6] Needless to say, Arendt's sharply cast conclusions perplexed and angered her readers, many of whom disdained altogether her distinctions. Arendt took as a given the right of parents to "bring up their children as they see fit" and this is a "right of privacy, belonging to home and family." To be sure, government does have a stake in preparing children "to fulfill their future duties as citizens," but that does not extend to compelling parents and children – unwitting pawns of social engineering – to attend integrated schools against their will. This deprives "them of rights which clearly belong to them in all free societies – the private right over their children and the social right to free association." Forced integration creates terrible conflicts between home and school of the sort "children cannot be expected to handle" and "therefore [children] should not be exposed to them."[7] If parents collapse, or are stripped of their authority in relation to children, the result will be more conformism of children with their peer group, or age cohort, and a growing homogenization of society will result. Those capable of resisting will likely be few and under tremendous pressure to succumb to the wider surround.

Denounced and excoriated, Arendt was clearly somewhat perplexed at the misreading (on her view) of her essay. The horizon of Arendt's discussion was framed by her sympathy with victims of persecution and her experience of the brutal quashing of independent parental authority in totalitarian societies. She had memories of *Hitlerjugend* and the obliteration of the private sphere in the interest of an overarching (and brutal) public purpose. She had memories of the Jewish parvenu who seeks to make her way in the world of the *goyim*, going, or forced to go by others, where she is not wanted and assaulting her own dignity in the process because of the many compromises and denials she is forced to make in order to gain acceptance. These memories did not hold her in good stead as she gazed at the school desegregation aspects of America's racial battles. Arendt eventually conceded, in an exchange with Ralph Ellison, that black children were not an American version of the Jewish children of Arendt's own youth who got pushed into groups where they were unwelcome. Parvenu did not apply. Perhaps Ellison's insistence on the "Negro experience" and the Christian "ideal of sacrifice" was more apt. For Ellison, getting hurt is part of the racial situation in which Blacks find themselves.[8] Arendt conceded this but no more. She defiantly clung to the view that education should not be put at the service of ideologies for social and political change. This destroys parental and teacherly authority; it prematurely politicizes children; it threatens to erode associational diversity.

Paradoxically or, perhaps, only apparently paradoxically, the explicit political mobilization of the young eviscerates authentic politics, or the possibility of such. To preserve any possibility for profound, surprising, even revolutionary change, education must be conservative. How can this be? Arendt made the case in her essay, "Crisis in Education." Her argument, rather severely condensed, goes like this: In politics we always have to deal with those who are already educated. Education, for example, plays a tremendously important role in America as a vehicle for helping to forge commonalities from a vastly diverse society. But this is different from forcing children to expose themselves to a public existence. It is a betrayal of children thus to expose them. Examples of this betrayal abound. Europe has seen many such instances of dictatorial intervention, including "the belief that one must begin with children if one wishes to produce new conditions. ..." This latter notion "has remained principally the monopoly of revolutionary movements of tyrannical cast which, when they came to power, took the children away from their parents and simply indoctrinated them."[9] This is a horror.

Whoever wants to educate genuinely must protect children from these forms of coercion as well as that abdication of parental and teacherly authority in the benighted examples of "progressive education" Arendt so detested, schools in which children are enjoined to create their own environment for learning free from adult authority. But the whole point of education is to prepare children to enter a world that is already there, a world in and through which, for better or for worse, they must get their bearings. Children cannot, by definition, *create* an environment. The result of such attempts is the tyranny "of their own group, against which, because of its numerical superiority, they cannot rebel, with which, because they are children, they cannot reason, and out of which they cannot flee to any other world. ..."

Education must *conserve*; it must introduce children into a pre-existing world even as it shields them against the full force of publicity. To turn young people out as little platoons for this cause or that eviscerates privacy, for the light of public existence destroys those not yet able or prepared to perform in its steady glare. The newness of the child must be preserved so that it may become the platform of a second newness later. Childhood is not a political condition from which children must be (misguidedly) liberated. It is a necessary form or container for the human being in its most fragile stage, a time of concealment and preparation. We abandon and betray children if we deprive them of this protection.[10]

Arendt ties together the "loss of authority in public and political life and in the private pre-political realms of the family and the school. The more radical the distrust of authority becomes in the public sphere, the greater the probability naturally becomes that the private sphere will not remain inviolate."[11] This is the situation we – we late moderns – find ourselves in and it is quite literally world-destroying. When adults abdicate, children are cut adrift. That much of this evacuation of authority strikes "revolutionary poses" makes it more difficult to recognize the situation for what it is, hence to understand that conservatism as "conservation" is not only the "essence" of education but part of the overall task of cherishing and protecting "the child against the world."[12]

And this is done precisely *for* "the sake of what is new and revolutionary in every child." Education must "preserve this newness and introduce it as a new thing into the world. . . . We must decisively divorce the realm of education . . . most of all from the realm of public, political life." As well, there should be a line between children and adults but not a wall "separating children from the adult community as though they were not living in the same world and as though childhood were an autonomous human state, capable of living by its own laws."[13] Where this line is drawn will vary. But that it *must* be drawn is beyond question. Do we love the world enough to accept this complex and ambiguous responsibility? On this eponymous note Arendt concludes. If we are to perdure we must endure, even embrace, the need to distinguish and to define different spheres and imperatives of our complex human condition. Thus, Arendt unhesitatingly condemns politicization of childhood and education even as she embraces making children a part of the world into which they are born.

Politicizing Childhood: Past and Present

There is no end to the tales of terror. Terror against children in the name of politics; terror perpetrated by children in the name of politics. China's Maoist Cultural Revolution was the work of brutal, ardent ideologues whose childhoods had been spent waving Mao's "Little Red Book" in the air and chanting slogans in a Maoist version of the Nazi *Sprechor*. The Khmer Rouge enforcers – those on the ground who carried out the work of mass murder – were young, many of them teenagers, similarly inflamed. In today's Libya, young boys are put through rites of initiation that involve chanting and memorizing Colonel Qaddafi's "Green Book," marching and practicing military maneuvers (of sorts) that include kicking, stomping, or beating a live animal to death. Those who really want to be bloodied bite the heads off live chickens.

This is pretty far removed from, say, pledging allegiance to the flag at an assembly in a typical American school in which the kids are giggling, jostling, and smirking at the teacher or principal when he or she isn't looking. Arendt recoils at revolutionary and statist mobilization and indoctrination of youth by contrast to those practices that inculcate children into a shared *civic* culture, like the pledge of allegiance in a far less fearful and coercive situation than that in place in "revolutionary" or "totalitarian" societies. She would, however, repudiate and alert us to the dangers lurking in a good bit of the "drug war" rhetoric of recent years that encourages children to turn parents in to the state for real or imagined infractions, or the zeal of some forms of mandated "sex education" in the public schools that aims knowingly to displace familial and religious moral scruples and concerns. Arendt's own memories, as I have already indicated, were of German young people engrafted onto the Nazi state through massive mobilization efforts that had as their *explicit* aim eviscerating independent parental authority and private life.

Ten million children between the ages of 10 and 18 at the beginning of World War II belonged to the *Hitlerjugend*. A historian of this movement remarks that "Hitler was obsessed with youth as a political force in history."[14] The "youngsters" were the raw material with which he proposed to make a new world, the old being corrupt, soft, and rotten. Nazi mobilization efforts were so successful that his "uniformed army of teenagers" actually dragged "parents, teachers, and adults in general" into the Hitler cult and legend. And the *Hitlerjugend* were faithful unto death. About 5,000 children took part in the "twilight of the Gods," the last-ditch effort in Berlin. Of that 5,000 only 500 survived. Eye-witnesses describe children doing what they "believed to be their duty until they were literally ready to drop," that duty being killing and dying.[15] Historian Gerhard Rempel sees this story as one of misguided idealism and abuse of loyalty. Hitler's children, he concludes, were "exploited . . . misled . . . betrayed, deserted, and sacrificed by a party and a regime that had used them to attain power."[16] But it isn't just that, remember: it is also children intimidating, shaming, humiliating, betraying, and exposing adults – their own parents and teachers – for insufficient ideological ardor. It is this latter possibility that Arendt also aims to forestall with her strictures against political children.

Thus far the examples I have proffered seem rather clear-cut in their power to repel; hence, they too readily concede the point to Arendt. Consider, then, more complex examples of politicization of the young under the auspices of protest politics, or in the name of a particular faith or identity, rather than mobilization by, or for, revolutionary terror with or without state sponsorship. The reader should think along with me about what makes the following examples more ambiguous and difficult to sort out, whether in light of Arendt's categories or as a way of putting pressure on those categories. There are ancient stories, of course: the mass suicide of Jewish families at Masada; Christians going to martyrdom with their children; children plunging off *en masse* on pilgrimage or crusade. But I will concentrate on more recent tales of childhood activism.

Children were a central part of union activity in nineteenth-century America for families were either union or non-union. There are many vivid examples of children as victims of the wage labor system and as strikers and protestors. For example, Mother Jones, the legendary orator and all-purpose rabble-rouser, led a "Children's Crusade" of child textile workers to protest the children's working conditions and starvation wages. In July, 1903, Mother Jones marched her band (three to five hundred strong) from Philadelphia to President Theodore Roosevelt's summer home at Oyster Bay, Long Island, a 125 mile trek, to win Roosevelt's support for abolition of child labor. After the protest, she led her children to Coney Island for ice cream and mounted a bandstand to take the children's cause to beach-goers and revelers. This first "children's crusade" drew so much publicity Mother Jones decided to organize a second, also composed of striking juvenile textile workers. Tagging herself "commander-in-chief," Mother Jones spoke about her project to a reporter in this way: "The employment of children is doing more to fill prisons, insane asylums, almshouses, reformatories, slums, and gin shops than all the efforts of reformers are doing to improve society. . . . The sight of little children at work in mills when they ought to be at school or at play always rouses me. . . . I shall endeavor to arouse sleeping Christians to a sense of duty towards the poor little ones."[17]

There is an irony here we should not miss: children are politicized, drawn into protests, strikes, marches and potential danger *in order that* they may return to schools, neighborhoods and playgrounds where they belong. The fact that children have already been forced into "publicity" is made manifest in Mother Jones' strategy in a way that calls attention to this very fact and says, in effect, "Isn't this terrible? These children should be going to the beach and to school and to the playground, too. Instead, their lives are diminished and stunted. They walk around with fingers severed by dangerous machines; bodies permanently twisted by harsh labor. You think taking children on protests is shameful? No, it is shame that drives them to protest." Note that children launching their own form of union protest – with a good bit of help from the redoubtable Mother Jones – were not merely children but also workers. Perhaps this may alert us to the fact "the child" is no blank slate onto which we adults project an unblemished innocence. Perhaps the most horrific moments are those in which "the child" has been altogether supplanted or obliterated in favor of some other overarching identity.

Consider a second example, this from World War II, drawn from stories Robert Coles retells as evidence of "the inner resources of children." Throughout Nazi-occupied Europe, Coles reports, children shared in the underground and "the term 'children's front' was used by many to describe their participation." A Rotterdam newspaper from June, 1941, reports: "Children between the ages of seven and thirteen are committing offenses against the occupying forces which must be called crimes." These included booby-trapping, spying, even bombing and sniping. Coles continues of children: "They boycotted Quisling's teachers in Norway; they sang songs of protest in Danish schools; they helped derail German trains in Holland; and even murdered Gestapo agents in France."[18] The children in these stories are children *and* fighters: child-patriots prepared to sacrifice and to kill in the name of their common motherland. Coles suggests that we all "oppose mobs, and children facing them, but if children must face them, let us find out why, and what will happen to them if they don't."[19] This is an interesting move by Coles, for he intimates that *not* going public when the world is in turmoil may be much harder on children than for them to take up their share of the burden. Coles uses the story of children fighting German occupation as a way to frame his support for those children who were on the front-lines of the desegregation struggle in the American South.

Coles tells a very different story from Hannah Arendt's. In Coles' tale, the involvement of children in picketing or facing "hoses, dogs, truncheons, electric prodding poles, trials, jails, criminal records" does not "necessarily cause psychological collapse" of any sort. What Coles finds remarkable is the clear-sighted political courage of some children in some circumstances and, it must be said, the fearful and ferocious zealotry of other children in other circumstances. Perhaps what we must look at, he avers, is not the *fact* of politicization in order that we might share fully queasiness of the sort Arendt underwrites but, rather, the banner under which this "going public" takes place. In whose name? Under whose auspices? In what cause? To what ends?

Noting that children "have marched by their parents' side in racial demonstrations, both in the North and the South," Coles goes on to criticize press criticism that castigates the ostensible "cynical use" of children by adults who are more powerful, hence have no "choice" in the matter. Because the obsession with who has power is ubiquitous in contemporary political discourse, this matter bears scrutiny. Coles handles it by reminding readers of context, purpose, and the inherent ambiguity of the word "child" itself. To be a demonstrator is hard. But "responsible, nonviolent protest" is always hard and, moreover, Negro children were acting "in a region that considers them not merely children but (as Negroes) the children of children."[20] Dignity in sacrifice and danger was part and parcel of the Black struggle for self-respect, itself a necessary ingredient (not merely a "by-product") of social protest.

The most dramatic, dangerous, and ethically ambiguous example of children's desegregation protest came as part of the 1963 Birmingham Campaign launched by the Southern Christian Leadership Conference.

During the first of many youth marches, 38 elementary school children refused to disband on the orders of a police captain. The children "all said they knew what they were doing. Asked her age as she climbed into a paddy wagon, a tiny girl called out that she was six." At the end of "D-Day" 75 students "were crammed into cells built for eight." The campaign gained momentum. Soon 958 children had signed up indicating their willingness for jail and some 600 were in custody. Protest speakers extolled the courage of children. More children took to the streets and parks. Scenes of children being hit by projectiles of water from firehoses and lunged at by police dogs helped to galvanize the American conscience.

Birmingham's white leaders denounced Martin Luther King's use of children. Children, claimed the mayor, were "tools" of the movement and were being misused. The "respectable people of Birmingham," white and Black, "cannot condone . . . the use of children to these ends." Attorney General Robert Kennedy, by contrast, denounced the situation that drove children into the streets, but he added that: "School children participating in street demonstrations is a dangerous business." In the meantime, however, the fact that "a thousand Negro children had marched to jail in two days" and faced down water hoses and dogs, was hailed by King's forces. King told mothers and fathers not to worry about their children for: "They are suffering for what they believe and they are suffering to make this a better nation." Jail is a "spiritual experience" to be welcomed. Indeed, King and his cohorts plotted a strategy to put even more young people in jail.

King faced down critics by arguing that children were "going to jail for what they believed." The "children's miracle," as it got tagged in movement circles, was a tremendous success. There can be no doubt that children were knowingly placed in situations of danger and squalor. There can be no doubt that children by the hundreds, then thousands, made themselves available for this purpose.[21] It was this Arendt professed, in her exchange with Ralph Ellison, that she had not understood. How much of a dent this makes in her overall framework I will take up below but, first, consider a fracas of the present moment in the matter of political children that recalls the desegregation crisis and the political children to which it gave dramatic rebirth.

I refer to young anti-abortion protestors. I was drawn to this example in large part because of my memories of the Birmingham "children's miracle." Listening to harsh criticisms by pro-choice spokeswomen of pro-life activists for protesting with their children, hearing language similar to that proffered by pro-segregation officials in the 1960s, I grew vexed. For, by implication, the leaders of the National Organization for Women and the National Abortion Rights Action League who have pronounced on this matter, *must* retroactively condemn the strategy of the SCLC and the powerful example of Black children placing themselves in harm's way in behalf of a cause. I wonder if they are prepared to do that, to repudiate political children *tout court.* I am not thus prepared. There is, of course, far less of a moral consensus surrounding abortion than school desegregation where majority opinion rallied around the cause of integration as time went on. There is no such rallying for pro-lifers, but they, too, are routinely presented in the press as "outside agitators" and pests, labels of the sort segregationists pinned on civil rights protestors. Most interestingly, the particular stories told by child protestors are similar: a ten-year-old child is arrested, handcuffed, hauled off and booked. A press report describes "a growing number of children putting their bodies on the line in the abortion battle."[22] One of these ten-year olds, Sarah Trewhella, when queried, says: "I think I'm doing a good thing because I'm saving precious babies' lives." In the Wichita, Kansas, campaign alone (summer, 1991), 183 children under age 17 were arrested.

The response by critics? "It's a form of child abuse. It's sad to be manipulating the minds of young people. Children don't have any concept of what they're doing. Everyone who is pro-choice is disgusted [by this]," claims Susan Carone of Metropolitan Medical Services, an abortion clinic, in words that echo those of Birmingham's mayor in 1963. As well, under pressure from pro-choice forces, parents of anti-abortion children have themselves been "charged with contributing to the delinquency of a minor," if one of their children is arrested during a protest.[23] The young protestors, of course, make rejoinders to their critics – just as the young in Birmingham did or, presumably, the members of Mother Jones' "children's crusade," or underground activists in occupied Europe would have done. One 13-year-old, "who participated in her first protest when she was 7," said: "When the media is saying that our parents forced us into this, it's not true. Many of my friends got our parents into this." (Note, if you will, the reversal of the anticipated lines of influence and persuasion, something contemporary analysts who cling to rigid notions of who has power over whom can never appreciate.)

This 13-year-old girl's brother, age 9, added: "I feel if the grown-ups aren't going to do it, it's up to all the kids to do it," an uncanny echo of Arendt's plaint concerning abdication of adult responsibility. How do parents respond? The mother of these two political children says she's very concerned about the danger and it is hard for her to let her children protest in this way but "we can't stand between their hearts and their beliefs." An abortion rights activist parries: "Using children in this way is hypocritical for groups that espouse saving children," a comment that one presumes leaves the door open for pro-choice protestors to take their children on marches for they make no similar espousal, pro-choice rhetoric and justification being cast in terms of adult rights and choices.[24] The mistake pro-choice critics of pro-life child protestors make in all of this is their politically repressive embrace of the language of "child abuse" and their representation of these children as manipulated automotons with "no concept of what they're doing," charges and language of the sort used against children civic rights protestors. Let us now return to Arendt's strictures and see what we make of them in light of political children, past and present.

Political Children, Sic et Non

Many questions are on the table. How are we to evaluate political children? Do we draw the lines where we do because what is at stake is creating a *cordon sanitaire* around childhood in order that children be spared the depredations, the organized conformism and manipulation of powerful political forces, and in order that parental authority be preserved? Or, alternatively, do we evaluate the politicization of children depending upon what, or whose, politics is involved? We blanch when we see children giving a Nazi salute. We are moved when we see children singing hymns and marching off to jail in a desegregation protest. Are we bereft of ways to adjudicate these and other cases of political children? Does it come down to whether we are pro-Nazi or anti-segregation?

It must be said, first, that children are never *spared* politics. Every child must take his or her bearings in a particular time and place. Images of a homeland are nigh universal. Every culture distinguishes "us" from "them" in some manner. Robert Coles observes a "political ego" in every child, for part of a "child's awareness . . . incorporates into both the intellect and the emotions a range of nationalist values, sentiments, ideals" and uses these to "shape a life: its commitments, its purposes, its practices, and not least, its espousals."[25] A nation's or homeland's life is entangled with the personal lives of children everywhere. This I, with Coles, take as a given that can no more be wished away than the sun's rising in the East and setting in the West. It is a phenomenon that, in and of itself, neither buttresses nor undercuts Arendt's categories. She recognizes and accepts the need for a child to be inducted into his or her culture.

The problem, remember, lies elsewhere: in children facing, or being forced into, the full glare of publicity; in the abdication of adult authority; in confusing social discrimination with political inequality; in conflating violence and politics. What needs protection is the private sphere itself (hence the child) precisely in order that the child, as adult and citizen, might take his or her rightful place in the ranks of the politically equal. Political equality is the opposite of social homogenization. Premature politicization promotes, not difference, but conformity. It is the primary task of parents to induct their children into the world, not the job of the state. This guarantees that children enter the public world from many diverse sites – familial being the most diverse of all and this natal diversity, in turn, protects and nurtures that plurality essential to civic freedom.

As Margaret O'Brien Steinfels notes:

> The values embodied in any family may come from religion, race, ethnicity, class, special intellectual, artistic, or manual skills, characterological or temperamental qualities, geographic setting, and occupational preferences. The unique combination of these and other factors in a family draws on and constitutes the family's history, culture, and present social organization. A given generation may embrace those values and the rules that flow from them, adapt them to the larger social and economic conditions, or come to deplore them and rebel against them. Accepted or rejected, these values are central to the story of the family, and to the identity of its members; and they form the boundaries within which children will develop, mature, and themselves come to reshape the values and rules their parents pass on to them. Family autonomy is integral to that process.[26]

Where does this leave Arendt's analysis? First, it must be said that in misunderstanding the sacrificial dignity of the civil rights struggle, Arendt undermined her own categories perhaps more than she knew. She yearned for "the gulf that the ancients had to cross daily to transcend the narrow realm of the household," but that gulf is altogether eclipsed in modernity.[27] "Little Rock" is written with a gulf or, perhaps, a chasm, in mind. A very American devotion to a broad notion of equality together with the Christian beliefs that drove protestors, blurs distinctions between *the social* and *the political.* Too many issues blend, merge, fuse, and enmesh for things to be tidied up in the way Arendt seeks. When children *do* politics *with* their parents, or urge their parents into politics (as nearly every parent of my generation can attest in the matter of environmental concerns, it was the children that compelled recycling, energing-saving, non-smoking in many households), we are in a world that puts pressure on Arendt's categories.

But her *concerns* are nonetheless vital. In the matter of political children, I would lift up these concerns even as the burden of this essay has been to soften or to resituate Arendt's categorical distinctions between private and public, politics and everything else. Childhood does not exist, and never has existed, in a *cordon sanitaire.* There are, however, "good" and "bad" ways for children to engage politics. In politics, as in everyday life, by their fruits ye shall know them. That is why we repudiate Nazi state-dominated mobilization of the young. That and more. For it is not only the violent and repugnant ideology under which children were politicized but the fact that the method – the *necessary* method – was one of destroying any dignity and privacy, any familial authority. Children were mobilized in the name of saving a Fatherland from external and internal enemies but, in order to do so, they were first yanked out of their families, churches, and youth associations as all the autonomous arenas of social life were destroyed. The same pertains under the Maoist Cultural Revolution, the Khmer Rouge terror, or the Stalinist repression when children were enjoined to report their parents to the KGB.

By contrast, child labor protestors, desegregation children and, yes, anti-abortion children, open up a space for politics that powerful opponents would foreclose. Nazi children were instruments of a policy aimed at destroying the independence of all associations. By "doing their duty," Nazi children aided and abetted the violent anti-political impositions of the regime. This is a different phenomenon from Mother Jones' brigade, desegregation children, and anti-abortion children who fight with and for particular, plural communities of belief and memory – familial, religious, local, associational – beliefs held with their union, their church, their families. In so doing they strengthen rather than evacuate associational possibilities of a plural nature. But this is not without irony. In at least two of these cases – desegregation and pro-life – the power of the state is called upon to implement passionately held convictions that segregation and abortion are wrong, undermining the moral community.[28]

If we up the ante to anti-Nazi underground children in occupied Europe there, too, a community in the form of a homeland and its people is at stake. In two of these oppositional activities, children are responding to a military or an ethical invasion of a cherished realm and its present or future inhabitants – the country, the home – with the hope, in their eyes, of rebuilding the walls that shelter these human associations. Desegregation, more complicatedly, opposes a culturally and historically sanctioned order that itself embodies a violation of a fundamental principle of human dignity; it is, therefore, necessary to disrupt the schools and families of others temporarily in order to achieve and sustain over time a more just order of things, public and private, for all, not just for some.

There is, as well, a second irony, namely, that protests often aim at restoring or creating a zone of "protected" childhood where the primary urgency of the young would be to play, to learn, to be sustained in ways the full glare of publicity is bound to displace. The child must, for a time, be a militant labor protestor, or resistance fighter, or street marcher, or arrested placard-waver in order that childhood itself be sustained. The theme of "the child" as an innocent is most knowingly struck in pro-life protest but it echoes, it is *bound* to echo, in all stories of political children. We – we adults in late modernity – have such a stake in locating innocence somewhere, in some site or condition of being, we often assign children the task of creating or embodying such for us. It is not an easy nor an innocent burden to bear. Stories of political children draw us away from innocence into something far more complicated and morally ambiguous. Perhaps, thinking with Arendt, we can find ways to sustain childhood, not as a time of innocence, but as a time of apprenticeship that occupies a border *in-between* private and public in a sphere or zone that adults bear the heaviest responsibility for sheltering and sustaining, not to protect children *from* politics but to prepare them for politics, for all the responsibilities of adult life.

It is not only impossible to shield children entirely from political controversies that engage their parents, it may sometimes be damaging to do so. Anna Freud tells powerful tales of British children during the Blitz. Thousands of children were evacuated from London, sent to the countryside, or to Australia, or to the United States to "protect them" from the war. Shunted about in foster homes, severed from parents and siblings, many of these youngsters fell ill emotionally. Those war conditions that break up family life "deprive children of the natural background for their emotional and mental development," writes Miss Freud.[29] What Miss Freud and her co-workers at the Hampstead Nursery, where children were sustained and cared for in the most "home-like" environment possible and where parents were always welcome, found was that children who sustained severe and prolonged assault on their need for "personal attachment, for emotional stability, and for permanency of educational influence," were those who emerged from the war most traumatized, despondent, and lost.[30] But most children, in fact, reacted quite well to the war. They had a clear enemy – Hitler – and they worked his badness into their understanding of goodness. They learned to distinguish types of sounds – rockets, brands of airplanes, how far away or near were what sorts of explosions. They relished the close quarters and human warmth of bomb shelters in the tube stations. Those children who missed both the war and their families, however, incurred less danger but sustained more lasting damage. The long-range effects in depression, suicide, inability to sustain relationships and work are impressive evidence of the war's devastation to the integrity of being. Evacuated children fared *worse* overall on every scale of well-being (all other things being equal) than did children who remained at the site of danger with their families.

The film *A World Apart* (1988), set in South Africa in "June, 1963," also suggests that shielding children from their parents' political concerns and even the physical danger they risk may be futile and not without cost to the children. *A World Apart* portrays a Mother-Militant named "Diana Roth" (based on the life of Ruth First and played by Barbara Hershey), a white anti-apartheid activist whose children take second place, although what she is doing is for "their future," too. Mother, who is alternately distracted and secretive (trying to protect her children from knowing anything about her illegal activities), can't be bothered with the everyday. Her oldest child, Molly, asks questions. Mother stonewalls. Molly, in a constant state of simmering anxiety, grows more and more fraught. The film suggests that the problem isn't simply one of coveting more time with her mother in "normal" ways, but lies in the fact that Mother simply will not let her daughter in on anything of her secret, dangerous life. When she is arrested and detained, Mother is tempted with a sordid deal: "Answer our questions; make a statement and in no time you'll be back with your children." Needless to say, this is not a deal Mother will make.

At the end of her tether after release and immediate re-arrest, Mother decides to kill herself with an overdose of medication she has stockpiled. She writes a farewell note. "I haven't given in. I love you all very much." Saved at the last moment, she is sent home and recuperates slowly. Molly, relieved but angry at her Mother, invades the *sanctum sanctorum* of her Mother's study, a space forbidden her. She rummages through things and finds her Mother's suicide note inside a book. She confronts her Mother about trying to kill herself. "I told you not to go into the drawer," Mother shouts. "Stop talking about that stupid drawer. You tried to kill yourself. You tried to leave us. You should never have had us," Molly reproaches her Mother. Mother responds: "Listen, I was breaking apart. What good would I do to you in pieces?" She adds that she was so weak she might have put her "friends" in jeopardy under interrogation. Molly: "Your friends. Your work. That's all you care about." Mother: "We have to think about the country." Molly: "WHAT ABOUT ME?"

Then, and really for the first time, Mother decides to involve Molly in her militant life. The funeral of an activist killed by the police is the next day. Mother will go, defying a police ban. Molly begs to go, too. Mother agrees. The film shows the fists of both Mother and daughter raised in defiance along with those of the Black mourner-protestors at the burial site, Mother's arm encircling her daughter's thin but defiantly straight shoulders. The film ends with a freeze frame of young men throwing stones as police cars approach. Then the shocking words pop onto the screen as the film's final message: "Ruth First (Diana Roth) was assassinated August 17, 1982." There is no word on the fate of her children.

What would Hannah Arendt think of this story, of this mother, and of her decision to relent on the high-handed secretiveness and to draw her daughter – no longer a very young child but a child nonetheless – into the world of activism, danger, relentless and tireless commitment, taking her away from school, friends, the shelter of the private? Molly, of course, hasn't led much of a sheltered life prior to the moment her Mother permits her to "go public." The politics of South African apartheid permeate the four walls, we realize, in part because of Mother's politicized identity. But the film suggests that to be sheltered from and largely oblivious to the injustices of apartheid, as is Molly's best friend, is a corrupt and corrupting condition. Children, it reminds us, are never spared, not in a political world as fractured and violent as the South African reality.

Both Anna Freud's study of British children who survived the Blitz and the portrayal of South African children in *A World Apart* simultaneously confirm and put pressure upon Hannah Arendt's incisive strictures against the politicization of childhood. They confirm the vitality of the private and the need to shelter the realm of necessity. But they also challenge Arendt's insistence that "social," "political," "private," and "public" are, or must be kept, altogether distinct. *That*, I want to suggest in closing, is the way of the world – the world in which we live; that and none other. Children as workers, patriots, and protestors are powerful evidence of the ways in which these categories, and the realities towards which they gesture, bleed into one another, the most important of these being the child as apprentice citizen. Because Hannah Arendt would have us cherish and nurture this time of preparation, she might go along with the argument here presented. For it tries to be faithful to that worldliness she so cherished.

Notes

1 Hannah Arendt, *The Human Condition* (Chicago: University of Chicago Press, 1958), p. 7.
2 For the full story of the controversy see Elizabeth Young-Bruehl's biography, *Hannah Arendt. For Love of the World* (New Haven: Yale University Press, 1982), pp. 308–18.
3 Hannah Arendt, "Reflections on Little Rock," *Dissent*, 6, 1 (Winter, 1959), pp. 45–56, esp. p. 50.
4 Arendt, "Reflections on Little Rock."
5 Ibid.

6 Arendt, "Reflections on Little Rock," p. 51.

7 Arendt, "Reflections on Little Rock," p. 55.

8 Young-Bruehl, *Hannah Arendt*, p. 316.

9 Hannah Arendt, "The Crisis in Education," *Between Past and Future* (Baltimore: Penguin Books, 1968), p. 177.

10 Arendt, "The Crisis in Education," p. 181.

11 Arendt, "The Crisis in Education," p. 190.

12 Arendt, "The Crisis in Education," p. 192.

13 Arendt, "The Crisis in Education," p. 193, 195.

14 Gerhard Rempel, *Hitler's Children* (Chapel Hill, NC: University of North Carolina Press, 1989), p. 1.

15 Rempel, *Hitler's Children*, p. 241.

16 Rempel, *Hitler's Children*, p. 262.

17 Philip S. Foner, ed., *Mother Jones Speaks: Collected Writings and Speeches* (New York: Monad Press, 1983), pp. 487–8.

18 Robert Coles, *Children of Crisis*, vol. I (Boston: Little Brown, 1967), p. 325.

19 Coles, *Children of Crisis*, p. 326.

20 Coles, *Children of Crisis*, p. 319.

21 I draw here on Chapter 20 of Taylor Branch's *Parting the Waters. America in the King Years 1954–63* (New York: Simon and Schuster, 1988), pp. 756–802.

22 Arlene Becker and Mimi Hall, "It's up to all the kids to do it," *USA Today* (Tuesday, June 23, 1992), p. 3A. This widespread phenomenon has received remarkably little coverage. I mention this to apologize to the reader for my source but it is the only one I have found that cites actual figures on numbers of children arrested and imprisoned.

23 In this matter, one wishes the pro-choice forces might consider the old adage: "What goes around comes around." Why do they think building in repressive use of the police powers against political protest might not one day be turned against them or their supporters in a different climate from the one that currently prevails?

24 Becker and Hall, "It's up to all the kids to do it."

25 Robert Coles, *The Political Life of Children* (Boston: Atlantic Monthly Press, 1986), p. 65.

26 Margaret O'Brien Steinfels, "Children's Rights, Parental Rights, Family Privacy, and Family Autonomy," in *Who Speaks for the Child?* eds Willard Gaylin and Ruth Macklin (New York: Plenum Press, 1982), p. 254.

27 Arendt, *The Human Condition*, p. 33.

28 Let me add that I have no objection to children going on "pro-choice" marches with their parents and several of my friends have done precisely this with their children. Being far more ambivalent about this matter, were I still the mother of young children I would not engage with them actively in "protest politics" on either side.

29 Anna Freud and Dorothy T. Burlingham, *War and Children* (New York: Ernst Willard, 1943), p. 11.

30 There is another factor, of course, and that is the parents' — especially the mother's — steadiness. With many men off to fight the war or work in war industry, mothers tended the homefront. Those mothers who cracked under the strain imposed a double burden on their young – a broken-down mother as a presage to evacuation. The child bore the burden of the mother's breakdown as well as the trauma of separation from her.

7

The Heady Political Life of Compassion

Elizabeth V. Spelman

One important function of slave narratives and other critical depictions of North American slavery was to generate compassion in their audiences, provoke the kind of feeling that would incline readers to help relieve suffering and oppose evil. In *Incidents in the Life of a Slave Girl, Written by Herself,* the ex-slave Harriet Jacobs, writing under the pseudonym Linda Brent, expresses hope that she can "kindle a flame of compassion in your hearts for my sisters who are still in bondage, suffering as I once suffered." Having been so moved, perhaps readers will cease being silent and join others "laboring to advance the cause of humanity."

But as Harriet Jacobs herself well understood, far from tending to undermine the master/slave relation, kindliness, pity and generosity may simply reflect and reinforce it. For example, the white abolitionist Angelina Grimké exposed the political logic of certain emotions when she rightly read the "pity" and "generosity" of certain whites as indicative of their "regard[ing] the colored man as an *unfortunate inferior*, rather than as an *outraged* and *insulted equal.*" Frances Ellen Watkins Harper found it necessary to insist, in an 1891 speech to the National Council of Women of the United States, that she came "to present the negro, not as a mere dependent asking for Northern sympathy or Southern compassion, but as a member of the body politic who has a claim upon the nation for justice, simple justice."

So while Harriet Jacobs was in part hoping to arouse compassion and concern in an apathetic and neglectful white audience, she was aware, like Grimké and Harper, that appeals for compassion could be politically problematic.

There is no way to adequately understand the plea for compassion in *Incidents in the Life of a Slave Girl* without looking at Jacobs' ongoing attempts throughout the text to assert and maintain authority over the meaning of her suffering. *Incidents* is a political text not simply because it is meant to get its audience to challenge existing institutions but also because it constitutes an ex-slave's struggle against readings of her experiences of slavery that would reflect and reinforce the master/slave relationship. As Mary Helen Washington has pointed out, narratives such as Jacobs' exhibit slave women as "active agents rather than objects of pity." Jacobs wants her audience's compassion, but she wants that compassion to be well informed. She needs to have her audience understand that she and others are suffering, but she is highly attuned to the power their knowledge of her suffering can give them, and so she simultaneously instructs them about how to feel. She insists on her right to have an authoritative – though not unchallengeable – take on the meaning of her sufferings.

Jacobs is aware of the debates going on over her suffering; she knows that something is at stake in the determination of the nature of her pain, its causes, its consequences, its relative weight, its moral, religious, and social significance. And if there is such an explicit or implicit struggle, the meaning of her pain is not a given. Competing interpretations are possible, and something important hangs on which interpretation or interpretations prevail. For the meaning of someone's pain to be debatable in these ways is for it to have a place in what Hannah Arendt referred to as the "public realm," that is, for it to be a topic about which different people may well have different views and thus for it to be among the items constituting a common, public world for those different people not *despite*, but precisely *because*, their separateness is thereby revealed. Like Harriet Jacobs, though in a different context a century later, Hannah Arendt was deeply interested in the relationship between compassion and political action. But on Arendt's account the kind of debate over the meaning of suffering which I have described as a crucial context of *Incidents* should not even take place, for according to Arendt the kind of pain to which compassion is an appropriate response is not something over which different perspectives are even possible. Moreover, according to Arendt – echoing Grimké and Harper – public professions of concern about the suffering of others are by their very nature bound to degenerate into pity, which accentuates the distance and inequality between those in pain and those exhibiting feeling for them.

There is much to learn from an exploration of some of the tensions between the work of Harriet Jacobs and Hannah Arendt. While they share many worries about the political abuses to which compassion and its close emotional relatives are susceptible, they strongly differ in their treatment of pain as something about which multiple perspectives are possible, and in their willingness to regard contest over the meaning of pain as central to moral and political life.

Hannah Arendt

In *The Human Condition* Hannah Arendt describes intense physical pain as the "most private" and "least communicable" of human experiences. The degree to which something is "private" in the relevant sense, Arendt says, is the degree to which it can appear in public, the degree to which it can be seen or heard or otherwise come to the notice of and become a topic of conversation for others and oneself. Physical pain by its very nature, Arendt seems to be saying, is such that only with great difficulty can it be "transformed . . . for public appearance." Thus, however intense it may be, in an important sense it lacks reality – the kind of reality only talking about experience can provide. On the other hand, in *On Revolution* Arendt certainly doesn't doubt that we can know that others are in pain, are miserable, or in constant want, or in a state of humiliation. Indeed she reminds us that the "spectacle" of others' misery can be right before one and yet one can fail to see it or be moved by it. This appears to contradict her claims in *The Human Condition*. But there is a coherent position which emerges from a close reading of these and related texts.

First of all, in *The Human Condition* Arendt is focusing particularly on intense physical pain, and while such pain is often an ingredient of misery, want, and humiliation, these states are not identical to physical pain. Arendt doesn't say that it is impossible, but only very difficult, to communicate what she describes as the most private kind of pain. What most deeply concerns her is not an epistemological worry that we cannot know or speak about the pain and suffering of others (or of ourselves), but rather a moral and political worry about what happens to the experience of suffering and the responses to it when it becomes publicly discussed. Arendt is most emphatic about keeping private experiences private – a concern that would make no sense at all if she thought they could only remain private anyway.

Arendt, then, has no doubt that we are capable not only of being made aware of the suffering of others but of being moved by what we know or believe about their experience – and not simply because their pain has made us think about our own. But she insists that our concern for their suffering cannot become public, cannot become professed, without thereby becoming dangerously distorted. For her the prime example of such inevitable mangling of feeling is Robespierre's celebration of compassion for "*le peuple*." To really feel compassion for another, Arendt says, is to be "stricken" with the suffering of a particular person. One is so much a co-sufferer that the ordinary distance between oneself and the sufferer is abolished. And since it is precisely this distance which both allows for and requires joint talk – the joint talk which creates the common world between us – compassion is marked by a kind of mutedness. In such a state of mutedness, one has neither the inclination nor the capacity to engage in the kind of deliberation and discussion that, according to Arendt, constitutes our public and political lives together. People in the throes of compassion most likely "will shun the long drawn-out processes of persuasion and will lend their voice to suffering, which has to claim swift action and violence." Thus, according to Arendt, whatever feeling Robespierre may have had for those in the name of whose suffering he spoke and acted, it quickly degenerated into something ugly, false and dangerous when publicly professed. Robespierre's description of the object of such feeling as "*le peuple*" is very telling. It reveals that whatever he feels, it cannot be compassion, since, Arendt claims, by its nature compassion is something you feel for a particular person in the particularity of their suffering. The use of "*le peuple*" also indicates that those who are the objects of the alleged feeling have had no say in the presentation of who they are and what they are going through: the connotations of "*le peuple*" were determined "by those exposed to the spectacle of sufferings they did not share." That is, the profession of the feeling of compassion for "the people" reveals an attempt to put forth an authoritative interpretation of the experiences of those suffering, to enter into the public record not only that "*le peuple*" are suffering but what their suffering means, and to announce one's virtue by registering one's feeling about such suffering. By making public one's feeling about their suffering one offers proof of the depth of one's connection with those who are in such great pain and thus the right to speak about and for them. And since such pain is in the circumstances part and parcel of the virtue of "*le peuple*," "*les malheureux*," to present oneself as suffering with them even while not one of them becomes crucial evidence of one's possessing virtue as well.

By Arendt's lights, such profession of compassion actually amounts to pity, which involves both a looser and a tighter connection to those who are suffering than does compassion: looser, in the sense that in pity for "*le peuple*" one feels sorry for a faceless or many-faced multitude; one is not "touched in the flesh" by any particular sufferer. And insofar as pity, unlike compassion, is not a matter of co-suffering, it heightens rather than erases differences between the non-suffering and the suffering. Yet pity also has a tighter connection to sufferers than compassion: insofar as pity can so easily come to be enjoyed for its own sake, the pitier needs and seeks out others in misfortune. The suffering of others is not borne by the pitier but kept dangling at a delicious distance; hence, Arendt insists, the cruelty and inhumanity of pity.

Now we are in a position to see what I referred to earlier as Arendt's moral and political worry about the experience of suffering and the responses to it when they become public matters. She has several closely related concerns here. One is that professions of compassion all too often are barely disguised forms of pity, that what is presented as an authentic and spontaneous concern for another human being is actually a selfish and cruel wallowing in the misfortunes of others. While compassion's object is the suffering of another, pity uses the suffering of another – any old other will do – to produce or prolong a feeling in oneself.

Another reason Arendt is very doubtful about linking compassion to political action is that, as she sees it, to feel compassion is to have a stance toward someone's suffering which is completely at odds with what political life requires. A compassionate response to someone's suffering, Arendt is implying, is a response which leaves no doubt about the fact of or the meaning of that suffering. There are no doubts or uncertainties or optional responses, hence no reason to discuss, deliberate, make decisions. The reason we tend to doubt professions of care and compassion, she implies, is that the possibility of the absence of such feeling is suggested by the mere presence of public words about it. For something to be in the public eye means it is part of the world we jointly inhabit and about which we therefore can and will have different perspectives. When experiencing compassion, you don't take it to be a matter of public debate whether someone is suffering, or a matter of many possible interpretations what that suffering means. It is in this sense that for Arendt compassion is so thoroughly apolitical, indeed anti-political. She has high regard for real compassion, especially in comparison with its cruel sister, pity; but it is by definition not part of public, political life. The perception of suffering that informs it is too sure, too impervious to alteration, for it to be open to the possible change of opinion, open to the challenge to its claim to truth, which for Arendt is constitutive of public and political life. We know full well, Arendt knew full well, that there are occasions, many occasions, when we have doubts about whether someone is really in pain, or are uncertain about what their pain means; her point, I think, is simply that when one feels compassion one has no such doubts.

And this is connected to a final reason for Arendt's separation of compassion and political activity. In its definitive form, political life consists not merely of equals engaged in "discussions, deliberations, decisions," but their doing so in order to "be seen, heard, talked of, approved and respected" by people they know and regard as their worthy competitors. Arendt celebrates such desire to excel, and takes pains to distinguish it from the snuffing out of competing parties and competing views which characterizes tyranny and other invidious forms of domination. But she implicitly assumes we would share her distaste, disdain and distrust of Robespierre and anyone else who wished to excel at compassion, who extolled and claimed to exemplify compassion as a political virtue. My aim here is not to present Hannah Arendt as the final word on the proper domain of politics, the nature of compassion, the motives of Robespierre, or the political significance of the French Revolution. But she vividly alerts us to some of the dangers in professions of compassion and raises provocative questions about the place of compassion in public life.

Linda Brent

Harriet Jacobs published *Incidents in the Life of a Slave Girl, Written by Herself,* in 1861. Jacobs had by this time been living in the north almost 20 years, having escaped from North Carolina in 1842. At the suggestion of the white abolitionist Amy Post, Jacobs, using the pseudonym Linda Brent, began writing about her life in 1853. *Incidents* covers major events in Brent's life during her years as a slave in the south and a fugitive in the north, including her attempts to rebuff and put an end to the incessant sexual advances of her *de facto* owner, Dr Flint, as well as to avoid the emotional and physical cruelty of Dr Flint's jealous wife; and her struggles to free her two children. The text ends at what Brent considers the self-contradictory moment at which her freedom is purchased by the northern white woman by whom she was employed.

Incidents is explicitly addressed to northern whites, particularly northern white Christian women. Well aware that most northerners were ignorant, misinformed, or simply complacent about the meaning of slavery for slaves themselves, Brent wanted to provide the kind of information that would generate the sort of feeling likely to lead to abolitionist action on behalf of slaves.

Linda Brent's anxiety about the extent of her audience's knowledge of events in her life, and the accuracy of their interpretation of her experience, is expressed throughout the text. For example, sometimes she worries that they can't possibly know what slavery is like (p. 55; and see pp. 141, 173). At other times she insists that surely the mothers in particular in her audience can know what it is like to have your children torn from you (for example, pp. 16, 23). *Incidents* is a sustained attempt to give shape to and control the meaning of the compassion of its white audience. Brent tries to shape her audience's knowledge of and responses to the suffering of slaves through (a) tacitly alerting her audience to the kinds of misunderstandings to which they are likely to be subject; (b) trying to establish herself as a moral agent and political commentator and not simply a victim; and (c) encouraging her audience to think of not only compassion but outrage as appropriate responses to slavery. She wishes to contribute to determinations of what the actual harms of slavery are and what, in considerable detail, ought to be the response to such harms. In this way she is subverting the logic of the "helper/helped" about which Grimké, Harper, Arendt and others rightly were so concerned, whereby feeling for the others in their suffering can simply be a way of asserting authority over them, to the extent that such feeling leaves no room for them to have a view about what their suffering means or what the most appropriate response to it is.

Brent, then, was keenly aware of the risks she was taking in pleading for compassion. Her recognition of these risks, and the lengths she went to counteract them, tell us a lot about the moral and political dangers of becoming the object of compassion. In many ways *Incidents* is a lesson in how to assert your status as moral agent, and maintain authorship of your experiences, even as you urge your audience to focus on the devastating suffering to which you have been subjected against your will. Brent is well aware that in the process of getting her audience to feel for her and other slaves as crushed victims of an evil institution supported by cruel people, she may simply provoke hostile disapproval of her actions and character, or an anemic kindliness, mistakenly understood by those who feel it to be proof of their Christian virtue. So she takes great care *instructing* her audience about what they are to feel.

(a) First of all, Brent distinguishes the response she is looking for from other responses with which it has been or could easily be confused, especially in the social and political climate of the United States in mid-nineteenth century. She makes it clear that she does not wish to be understood to be asking for the kinds of feelings in whites which are simply weapons demonstrating their cruel power. She provides instructive examples of the kind of feeling she *does* value.

Having decided to put herself and other slave women forward as very much in need of the compassion of white northerners, Linda Brent faced what we might call the dilemma of compassion: she could keep to a minimum the information necessary to invoke compassion, relying on stock images of trembling fugitives and kindly rescuers, and hence risk playing into the very master–slave relationship she deplored; or, she could reveal much more, in hopes of presenting herself as something more than a mere victim, but at the risk of incurring hard questions about her behavior. That is, on the one hand she could try to invoke the aid of others without providing much contextual information. But this risks inviting people to think of you only in terms of how you have suffered or been victimized; it risks forfeiting the possibility of establishing other facts about yourself which you don't want your audience to lose sight of, such as the ways in which you are a moral agent. It also risks giving up your chance to question and critically appraise your would-be helper as a moral equal. The extent to which one imploring the help of another dare not simultaneously criticize the helper is a measure of the extent to which the sufferer is at the mercy of the savior.

In order to avoid the narrow roles of sufferer/savior, you can leap to the other horn of the dilemma and provide the kind of information about your state which will not only make your helper adequately informed about important details but also will preclude the helper's seeing you simply as someone to whom horrible things have happened. By presenting yourself as not only in need of great help, but simultaneously as someone who makes decisions and judgments, you open up the possibility to your helper that despite your being in great need you are still capable of and insist on the right to make judgments about him or her even as he or she helps you. However, this course has serious risks, too: you cannot take on the benefits of being considered such an agent without also being subject to its burdens. The more you reveal about yourself and the more you establish yourself as something other than a victim, the more likely you are to be the object of others' critical judgments. Linda Brent, then, instructs her audience about what they are to feel by distinguishing the responses she hopes for from others which she distrusts, by talking about exemplary responses, and by indicating her recognition of the risks she takes in providing the kind of information she does.

(b) While Linda Brent despairs at the morally precarious situations slavery put her in, she also is unhappy about some of her own reactions to being in such situations. She carves out a moral position somewhere between excusing herself, on the one hand, and presenting herself as unqualifiedly deserving of blame, on the other. She suggests to her audience that there are indeed standards by which she ought to be judged, but perhaps they are *not* those by which free people, free women, are to be judged (p. 56). She takes pains to make clear that she has standards by which she appraises her own actions, even those toward whites: she takes pride in never "wronging" or ever wishing to wrong her cruel mistress Mrs Flint (p. 32); she worries about the harm that may come to those helping her escape, and insists that being caught would be better than "causing an innocent person to suffer for kindness to me" (p. 98).

We may be inclined to regard some of this as evidence of her heightened awareness of the need to convince her audience of her moral stature. But that is the point: she doesn't want her plea for help to erase her status as someone who has had to make some painful decisions for which she bears some responsibility. For example, she takes responsibility for having made the extremely difficult decision to separate herself from her children in order to try to save them (pp. 85, 91, 141). She puts herself forward as someone who has moral standards, who wishes to live under conditions in which she can be "a useful woman and a good mother" (p. 133). She is ready to rebuke herself for selfishness (p. 135). If she doesn't want her call for help to erase or exclude her status as someone who has moral standards to live up to, neither does she want it to render her ineligible as a moral critic of whites, southern or northern. For example, she does not hesitate to make cutting and sarcastic remarks about her mistress Mrs Flint, who prides herself on her Christian charity but enjoys inflicting mental and physical pain on Linda and other slaves even while pretending to be moved by their sorrows. While she wonders aloud about the extent to which slavery forces slaves into morally compromising dilemmas, she also has an eye for the moral damage slavery does to whites, who pay more attention to "blighted cotton crops" than to the "blight on their children's souls" (p. 52).

Brent thus establishes herself in the moral community in a variety of ways. She expresses worry about the immoral acts slavery pushed slaves to commit. She presents herself as subject to moral standards. But she also exercises the right to contribute to examination of what those standards ought to be, not only by introducing the possibility that people living under slavery ought not to be held to *all* the same standards as free people, but also by frequently offering biting critiques of the character and actions of southern and northern whites.

(c) While there is no doubt that Linda Brent values and hopes to succeed in prompting compassion from her audience, she also frequently suggests, directly or indirectly, that outrage would be an appropriate response to the conditions under which slaves (and fugitives) live. Often her inventory of slavery's wrongs seems intended not so much to promote compassion for slaves as to evoke outrage at slaveowners and the northerners who are duped by them – particularly when she describes the unspeakable horrors of slavery in such a way that readers' attention is directed not so much to those who had to endure them as to the people and the institutions that are responsible for them.

In taking on the task of providing information about slavery to her audience that will evoke outrage and sustained indignation about such things taking place in their country, Brent is further instructing her audience about how they ought to feel. Here she seems to be resisting (self-consciously or not) two fairly strong forces. (1) While appealing to the compassion of white northern women played to a virtue which, according to a powerful stereotype for women of their class and race and religion, they were supposed to have and cultivate, appealing to their sense of outrage did not. (2) Slave narratives and other abolitionist literature had a very wide readership. But at least some of those readers seemed to find pleasure in the kinds of depictions of cruelty and pain we've just seen examples of above. For such readers some of the narratives were what Robin Winks has referred to as "pious pornography." Lydia Maria Child, who edited *Incidents*, perhaps was referring to such tastes in this comment about some of her rearranging of Jacobs' manuscript: "I put the savage cruelties into one chapter . . . in order that those who shrink from 'supping upon horrors' might omit them, without interrupting the thread of the story."

Describing slave experience in such a way as to provoke outrage thus could expand some readers' emotional responses even as it checked those of others. Those comfortable in their role as agents of care and compassion might think about whether reluctance to become angry or indignant was keeping them from some kinds of political action. Those finding delight in the revelation of cruelty might find obstacles to their pleasure in hearing moral outrage, not simple pleas for mercy, in the voices of those on whom the cruelty is inflicted.

Linda Brent was highly attuned to the political logic of the variety of emotions her account of slavery was likely to stir up. Knowing the risks she was taking, she at every turn did what she could to minimize the dangers, instructing her readers about the differences among "kindly" responses and about the special moral burdens slavery placed on both slave and slaveowner. Instead of allowing her plea for compassion to become an invitation to her audience to take pride in their good feelings, or to demean her as a helpless victim, she uses it as an occasion to exhibit the significance of the slave as moral agent and social critic. And yet she never for a moment suggests that she and other slaves do not need (though they should not "make capital out of") the good feelings of the very audience receiving lessons from her about what those feelings ought to be.

Compassion and Politics

Let us recall briefly Hannah Arendt's worries about attempts to mix compassion and politics. Compassion, she insists, is by its very nature non- or anti-political: when one is stricken by the suffering of another, there is not the plurality of subjects, the plurality of perspectives, or the need for speech definitive of political life. Since there is no reason for speech, presenting oneself as compassionate is highly suspect, especially if one attempts to excel or shine at such feeling. When pity parades as compassion and is touted as proof of one's political virtue, the actual needs of particular suffering people are lost in scandalous posturing.

Linda Brent would agree with Arendt's warning about the high stakes involved when some people try to capitalize on other people's suffering. That seems to be why at the very moment of pleading for compassion for herself and other slaves, she offers a disquisition about the difference between real compassion and its insidious imitators. She is responding to the fact of there being any number of possible and actual perspectives on the meaning of the suffering of slaves, including the view that Black slaves are not capable of feeling the kind of pain to which whites are subject. She is announcing her entry into the explicit and implicit battles over what her suffering and the suffering of other slaves means – to them, to whites, to the country, to God.

Brent thus sees suffering as much more deeply political, in Arendtian terms, than Arendt herself does. After all, for Arendt what enables something to become part of the public realm is not whether it can be seen or touched, but whether it can be talked about from a variety of perspectives. To be sure, Arendt doesn't exactly deny that different perspectives about someone's pain or suffering are possible. After all, on her own reckoning not all reactions to pain are what Arendt describes as compassionate; but can these other reactions involve the taking up of a perspective in the sense crucial for political life as she understands it? As she describes it, pity is not so much another perspective on pain as it is a glomming onto it, an unquenchable thirst for the suffering of others, too passionate a pleasure to brook the challenge of any other perspective. While Arendt applauds solidarity as a way that non-sufferers "establish deliberately and, as it were, dispassionately a community of interest with the oppressed and exploited," such solidarity "may be aroused by suffering [but] is not guided by it." Solidarity focuses on what non-sufferers and sufferers have in common – for example, their shared humanity or dignity – not on the conditions of want, deprivation, misery, or humiliation which distinguish them. Nor is suffering the focus of the robust discussions of political life, the deliberations for which a plurality of perspectives are crucial. Arendt strongly implies that there is no need to deliberate over the existence or significance of suffering; if people are hungry you feed them, if they are without shelter you house them. The only question is whether the technological means are there to do it.

In short, Arendt doesn't treat pain and suffering as matters on which there will be a variety of perspectives, topics for the "discussions, deliberations, [and] decisions" of those engaged in "public business." In trying to lead her audience to understand what the right feelings are about the suffering entailed by slavery, Brent seems to be deeply engaged in just the kind of persuasive speech characteristic of Arendt's political domain. For Brent, her freedom, the freedom of other slaves, and the moral health of the nation hinges on her audience getting the right perspective on slaves' experience of suffering; hence while she is asking for compassion she simultaneously provides a treatise on its meaning. In asking for the compassion of her audience, Brent seems not at all to want a perspectiveless co-feeling – perspectiveless in part because there is only one subject, in a "dumb" state – but informed passion from someone who is without doubt another subject, occupying quite a different position. Brent agrees with Arendt that the gap between non-sufferer and sufferer is not to be bridged by pity; but she doesn't believe or hope that there will be a collapse of the difference between them. While Arendt sees compassion as being stricken with another's pain, Brent insists that it has to do with understanding it properly. Her plea for compassion in the context of accompanying instruction suggests that she regards compassion as involving cognition but nevertheless having a kind of cognitive slack or cognitive recklessness. Unlike Arendt, she seems to believe that feeling responses to others' pain can stand in need of and thus must be formatted for fine tuning. Unlike Arendt, whose strict distinction of passion from reason seems to entail that compassion as a passion is incapable of adjustment, Brent treats compassion as capable of being informed by knowledge and hence capable of change, of enlightenment.

Indeed, as Ronald Hepburn has argued, it is precisely this feature of our emotions (or at least some of them) that makes us responsive to and educated by good literature. The more carefully a situation is delineated, the more particularized the emotional response it brings forth; and the more thoughtfully an emotional response is rendered, the more closely depicted the situation to which it is a response.

Brent is not unwilling to employ stock images of anguished mothers and trembling fugitives, but *Incidents* as a whole provides a context in which the audience can correct and expand the naive, stereotyped emotional response such imagery calls forth. *Incidents* pleads for the audience's compassion, but describes in considerable detail the persons for whom such compassion is to be felt. We are to understand that such persons themselves have complicated reactions to the suffering they have had to undergo; they are not necessarily so brutalized by the conditions under which they live that they have ceased to regard themselves as moral agents who bear the burdens and enjoy the rights pertaining thereto (for example, being subject to moral standards themselves; evaluating the behavior of both slave owners and slaves as they see fit).

Arendt, we recall, insisted that compassion is a response to a particular person in a particular situation. Brent would seem to agree. But she would also seem to believe that compassion becomes particularized – beyond simply being directed toward one person – in the process of an exchange between the non-sufferer and the sufferer in which the non-sufferer's passion is honed by growing awareness of the details of the sufferer's being and situation.

So for Brent, compassion, far from being a perspectiveless co-feeling with sufferers, is a matter of getting the right perspective. Her work strongly suggests that struggles over what that perspective ought to be – and more generally, over whose pain counts, what such pain means, and who gets to provide answers to these questions – is at the heart of political life.

Compassion and Politics: Current Controversies

Hannah Arendt's and Linda Brent's worries about the political dangers involved in offering and in being the object of compassion provide instructive background for some of the important struggles among feminists and others at the end of the twentieth century: debates over welfare, "victim" status, and the place of care and compassion in political life. Let us look briefly at them, since the filaments of compassion that readily lend themselves to becoming politically hotwired are unmistakably present in all of them.

The political valence of compassion is perhaps easiest to see in some of the ongoing debates about welfare. As Nancy Fraser and Linda Gordon have demonstrated in the case of the meaning of "dependency," semantic disputes often are politically driven and their resolution can be of considerable political consequence: who counts as a dependent, and whether dependency is or is not seen as a moral failure, has everything to do with battles over how to allocate the political, economic and emotional resources of a community. Similar disputes over the meaning of "compassion" have been part of the same debate. So for example in *The Tragedy of American Compassion*, Marvin Olasky insists that the very definition of "compassion" tells us that our current welfare policies are terribly misguided. According to Olasky, only when we understand the crucial distinction between "real compassion" and misguided sentimentality will we know who deserves our compassion and who the appropriate agents of compassion ought to be. As he sees it, the moral high ground in the political debate over welfare belongs to those who properly understand the meaning of compassion. It is not always virtuous to offer compassion, not always safe to receive it. We must distinguish between the worthy and unworthy poor; those who receive compassion should also be prepared to receive admonishment; and it is wrong, indeed it is tragic, to allow the compassionate care voluntarily offered by individuals to come to be regarded as something the government should supply as a matter of right.

Since compassion by its very nature involves focus on suffering, it also has been implicated in recent allegations about widespread abuse of "victim" status. More and more individuals and groups, so the complaint goes, are trying to persuade us that they are victims and thus deserving of our compassionate concern and accompanying legal or economic relief. In "Surviving Victim Talk," Martha Minow neatly captures some of the current struggles to claim the title to victim – for example, is it the person who was the object of the crime, or the deprived criminal? the target of hate speech, or the speaker threatened with the denial of free expression? the abused child, or the unfairly suspected adult? Minow does not want to be included among those who attack "victim rhetoric" out of a lack of concern about oppression (p. 1413) or out of a desire simply to "blame the victim" (p. 1417). But she is worried about how tricky it is to claim victim status: on the one hand, you run the risk of portraying yourself as lacking agency; but on the other, if you allow for or insist on your own capacity for agency, you may invite others to "minimize real facts of victimization" (p. 1427). Indeed, as we have seen, this is one of the dilemmas faced by the ex-slave Harriet A. Jacobs when she appealed to her white northern Christian audience to have compassion for her and other slaves.

Some critics of "victimolatry" worry that our critical capacities are being subverted by the cry for compassion for victims: if people really are victims, isn't criticism of them out of the question? And when so many make claim to being victims, and as such entitled to our attention, how are legal remedies and economic resources to be parcelled out in any thoughtful way? Compassion appears to be both that which ought to direct the distribution of such goods and that which makes unevenness of such distribution monstrous when all the competing parties are victims.

This raises more generally the question of what role, if any, compassion ought to play in the distribution of valued social goods. Joan Tronto's recent work provides an illuminating sample from a variety of recent feminist answers to that question. In *Moral Boundaries: A Political Argument for an Ethic of Care*, Tronto is concerned to unsettle both definitions of compassion that sequester it from political life, and definitions of the political that disguise the place compassion has in the allocation of public resources.

On the one hand she criticizes those who "dismiss from the outset ways in which care [including compassion] can function socially and politically in a culture" (p. 103). Tronto is highly attuned to the legion of ways in which a relationship of care and compassion can exacerbate, rather than ameliorate, inequalities of condition – when, for example, the care recipient has no say in the determination of her needs (pp. 139–40). But the solution to this, she urges, is not to insulate compassion from social and political contexts in which care can be corrupted (p. 167), but rather to make sure that our understanding of care and compassion are inseparable from a theory of justice (p. 171).

At the same time, Tronto is worried about notions of 'the political' that fail to recognize how existing institutions allocate social and political resources in response to perceived needs: someone must be setting priorities as to who gets what care and in what order (p. 110). Surely we ought to be thinking about whether the "distribution of caring tasks and benefits" is just (p. 169). And, since it turns out that among the decisions citizens have to make is how best to distribute care and compassion, the more thoughtful people are as carers the more thoughtful they will be as citizens (pp. 167ff.).

Even this very brief review of some of the terms of current debates over welfare, "victim" status, and the place of care in political life tell us what Linda Brent and Hannah Arendt knew so well: the political stakes in the definition, evaluation, location and distribution of compassion are very high. Compassion, like so many of our other complex emotions, has a heady political life.

References

Arendt, Hannah, *The Human Condition* (Garden City: Doubleday Anchor, 1959).

Arendt, Hannah, *On Revolution* (New York: Penguin, 1977).

Brent, Linda (pseudonym of Harriet A. Jacobs), *Incidents in the Life of a Slave Girl, Written by Herself,* Edited by Lydia Maria Child; edited and with an introduction by Jean Fagan Yellin (Cambridge: Harvard University Press, 1987).

Fraser, Nancy, and Linda Gordon, "A Genealogy of *Dependency*: Tracing a Keyword of the U.S. Welfare System," *Signs: Journal of Women in Culture and Society*, 19, 2 (1994), pp. 309–36. See also their essay in this volume.

Grimké, Angelina, Letter VII to Catharine Beecher. In *The Public Years of Sarah and Angelina Grimké. Selected Writings 1835–1839*, edited and annotated by Larry Ceplain (New York: Columbia University Press, 1989).

Harper, Frances Ellen Watkins. "Duty to Dependent Races." National Council of Women of the United States, *Transactions* (Philadelphia, 1891). Quoted in Loewenberg, Bert James, and Ruth Bogin, *Black Women in Nineteenth-Century American Life* (University Park: The Pennsylvania State University Press, 1976).

Hepburn, R. W., "The arts and the education of feeling and emotion," *Education and Reason*, ed. R. F. Dearden, P. H. Hirst, and R. S. Peters (London: Routledge & Kegan Paul, 1972).

Minow, Martha, "Surviving Victim Talk," *UCLA Law Review* 40, 1411–59 (1993).

Olasky, Marvin, *The Tragedy of American Compassion* (Washington, DC: Regnery Publishing Inc., 1992).

Tronto, Joan C., *Moral Boundaries: A Political Argument for an Ethic of Care* (New York: Routledge, 1994).

Washington, Mary Helen, "Introduction: Meditations on History: The Slave Woman's Voice," *Invented Lives: Narratives of Black Women 1860–1960* (Garden City: Doubleday Anchor, 1987).

Winks, Robin, *Four Fugitive Slave Narratives* (Reading, MA: Addison-Wesley, 1969). Quoted in Foster, Frances Smith, *Witnessing Slavery: The Development of the Ante-Bellum Slave Narratives* (Westport, CT: Greenwood Press, 1979).

8

Feminism and Power

Anna Yeatman

Introduction

As an emancipatory movement which seeks to end a particular kind of power relationship, feminism is deeply concerned with issues of how power should be conceived and understood. A great deal depends on how an emancipatory movement engages with different conceptions of power. Historically, feminism has been a central politico-ethical force for the development of more democratic social relationships in both public and private domains. By democratic, I mean self-regulated or self-governed relationships. At the same time, feminism has relied on a state-centric "power over" to bring about a greater degree of democratization of public and private relationships between men and women. It is the state's power of legitimate domination which has created an equal civil standing within marriage for men and women, and which has required such things as equal opportunity and anti-discrimination in the workplace.

However, feminism confronts a difficulty in this use of state-centric domination to "democratize" social relations. When the state works in different ways to constitute the personhood of women, is it "protecting" or "respecting" the personhood of women? Or perhaps both? Protection is a state-centric form of "power over" which reconstitutes the standing of those who are to be protected as subjects in need of protection, and as subjects who are likely to be victimized without this protection. When women are included within the category of such subjects, this particular type of "feminization" of women functions to inscribe them discursively as subjects who depend on the protective power of the state.

Respect, on the other hand, is a state-centric form of "power over" which constitutes the capacities of women as self-determining and self-regulating beings. To date, feminism is ambiguous in its requirement of state "power over" to improve the status of women: it has wanted both protection from patriarchal practices, *and* respect for women. This ambiguity, I argue here, is a significantly unresolved aspect of feminism's relationship to how power is conceived. To the extent that feminism requires the state to protect women from men it generates a paternalistic-patriarchal rather than a democratic state. To the extent that feminism requires the state to respect the personhood of women, it can become a force for developing self-regulated social relationships. Out of this rich, complex and ambiguous relationship to concepts of power, we can distill three strands within feminism's relationship to power: (1) power as coercion; (2) power as protection; (3) power as capacity.

Feminism and Power as Coercion

Feminism, like all other emancipatory social movements, tends to collapse power into domination, and then to collapse domination into undemocratic force. Before we proceed it is important to make the distinction between democratic and undemocratic uses of "power over." Domination can be used to control others in order to serve the interests of the powerful, or, domination can work democratically to extend or even constitute the powers of its subjects. Paul Patton elaborates upon this distinction.

> One frequent purpose served by states of domination is to enable some to extract a benefit from others . . . However, while extractive power may always presuppose some system of domination, states of domination may occur in situations where the flow of capacities or benefits is non-extractive . . . In Hobbes's account, the relationship of domination which obtains between State and citizens is a condition of maintaining the rule of law . . . The purpose of this system of domination is not further extraction but the enhancement of the powers of its subjects.[1]

Historically, emancipatory social movements have not made this distinction between democratic and undemocratic types of domination. Rather, power is identified with all the coercive and non-benign senses of "power over." On this approach to power, the emancipatory movement sees itself as representing those who are dominated and exploited by some kind of ruling class: the bourgeoisie, the colonialists, men, etc. The focus for change thereby becomes this movement's efforts to throw off this relationship of domination and exploitation by a mix of various means: ideological contestation of this relationship, mobilization of mass resistance, revolutionary struggle. Since power is equated with force, counter-power has to be a counter-force. This being the case, the emancipatory movements including feminism tend to pursue an undemocratic and often non-political practice of counter-force.

This is a politics which cannot discern *within* modern statist systems of domination the difference between the democratic and undemocratic features of such systems. When the dominant exploiter class's power is equated with the various forms of force (economic, physical, moral, ideological), it follows that established democratic procedure and process cannot be accorded face value. Instead the achievements of modern democracy are construed as the false appearance of a systemically coercive set of relations which is the "base" or truth of this society. Even if an emancipatory movement declares its interest in promoting a more democratic society, this interest is rendered null and void by its inability to accord reality to such democratic achievements as have been made, for example, the rule of law, freedoms of speech and assembly, and representative government. Moreover, since the oppressor class is homogenized as a class committed to the domination of others, "at bottom," its members are accorded only an interested and instrumental relationship to their professions of modern democratic values. It is assumed that the powerful have no interest in democratic process, but manipulate a pseudo-democratic process to serve their own ends of domination. This means that the emancipatory movement needs to make no effort to work with the powerful in the development of democratic values. It makes very little sense to work to develop a politics with those whom one assumes are oriented fundamentally to power as undemocratic domination.[2]

Historically, emancipatory movements have contributed enormously to the terms of critique of relationships of domination, for they show how different groups are constituted as marginal by being wronged by the established modes of governance. These constructions of wrong establish directions for particular projects of democratization. Without a positive relationship to a democratic politics, however, emancipatory movements have failed to contribute to the development of modern democratic institutions and values. This has been a major historical weakness. For example, feminist consciousness-raising is not intrinsically democratic. Even though it is structured by a democratic form of turn-taking in discussion, it functions in terms of face-to-face relations oriented by the desire to find what it is the members of the group have by way of experience and feelings in common. This is a totalizing politics which can easily be made over to particular kinds of moral blackmail and personal tyranny.[3]

There is no doubt that the powerful – those we may term the aristocracies of history – combine both power as capacity and undemocratic domination in their relationship to power. That is, they combine their own distinctive historical project of self-government with their undemocratic domination of others. These, however, are separable aspects of their relationship to power. To separate them means that we can come to appreciate the historical achievements in regard to self-government that different of these aristocracies have made. We can ask what their constructions of freedom of action may offer to us now. We can recognize as Nietzsche called it their "triumphant self-affirmation," namely their capacities to *act* as distinct from being trapped in various forms of reaction.[4] These include the capacities for violence, joy, sensual abandon, and disciplined physical or mental virtuosity.

The historical weakness of emancipatory movements in regard to positive conceptions of power, including those which are associated with democratic procedures and politics, is indicated in their worldlessness, and their tendency to practice a politics of *ressentiment*.[5] I borrow the term worldlessness from Hannah Arendt.[6] When a movement understands itself as representing those who are powerless, the victims of the powerful, it neither permits itself responsibility for, nor engagement in the affairs of the world. It maintains an innocence of worldly affairs, and in particular an innocence in regard to power. It does not confront the truths that power inheres in all relationships, that any interpretation of reality is itself a manifestation of power, and that those who are relatively powerless still participate in power.

Worldlessness preempts enquiry into how these subject positions of victimizer and victim are constituted through historically specific practices. Sharon Marcus argues this point powerfully in relation to established feminist approaches to rape:

> To take male violence or female vulnerability as the first and last instances in any explanation of rape is to make the identities of rapist and raped preexist the rape itself. If we eschew this view and consider rape as a scripted maneuver in which one person auditions for the role of rapist and strives to manoever another person into the role of victim, we can see rape as a *process* of sexist gendering which we can attempt to disrupt.[7]

In a politics of *ressentiment,* the dynamic energies of action are given over to the difficult and demanding work of reaction. As Nietzsche says of this subject, "all its action is reaction."[8] Such reaction means that these subjects interpret their powerlessness as moral virtue, and in casting their oppressors as evil, seek in some way to be rescued from this evil by someone more powerful than they. It is this paradox – that the powerful rescue the victims – which underwrites the vicious circle in which this kind of powerlessness and its politics are caught.

We must use this term complicity carefully. A politics of *ressentiment* is a politics which makes sense to a subject who is systematically brutalized and exploited by more powerful forces, and who proceeds to translate a reactive project of survival into the more generalized moral–political passion and world-view of *ressentiment.* This is especially the case in situations where democratic institutions are lacking and, accordingly, such victims can have no recourse to institutional support for their rights.

Worldlessness shields those who construct themselves as passive and innocent victims of world history from any responsibility for their fate. It also permits them to locate their resistance to their relatively powerless status in a hatred of those to whom they attribute all power, and, it follows, all evil. The politics of *ressentiment* is a negative politics. All that is identified with the world of the powerful is rejected as participating in the oppressor's evil. Thus, feminism tends to identify all that is worldly with the evil of patriarchy, and thereby to reject all values – including reason, an individualized striving for excellence, heroism, dispassionate judgment, ambition – that are associated with the "triumphant self-affirmation" of the powerful class, men.[9]

This is a politics of rancor, and a feminism oriented by rancor and *ressentiment* casts women as good, men as evil. Such a feminism is committed to discovering what is good in women's distinctive ways of relating and doing things. It extends critical insight into the mix of power and undemocratic domination that characterizes men's distinctive ways of relating and doing things. But it is not transformative. All that is permitted a feminism oriented by rancor is a separatist retreat from the world, understood in Arendtian terms as the shared terms of our coexistence in relation to differently positioned subjects. The world understood in this way demands of us a political agency oriented to working out how the terms of this coexistence can be justly worked out.

A feminism of rancor accords value to the oppressed subject because it views the subject as beyond domination. As we have seen, the confusion of power with domination means that the emancipatory movement ends up celebrating as virtues all those aspects of the identity of the oppressed which are associated with strategic self-preservation in a condition of weakness: acuity of perception of the other's feelings; the masking of assertive and direct modes of leadership in those of indirect suggestion and persuasion; the assertion of power through goodness where this works to occlude the subject's interest in power and makes it appear that all they are doing is operating on behalf of the needs of others.

This is a politics of reaction oriented more to the preservation of the identity of the oppressed subject than it is to a project of social transformation that encourages all individuals and groups to assume a positive relationship to power. Encouraging such a positive relationship to power would challenge the attribution of identity to individuals and the correlative requirement that their identity is the expression of their condition as a member of a group.[10] Instead individuals would be encouraged to explore their capacities, to discover the contingencies and multiplicity of identity, and to celebrate those moments of transformative practice when their sense of self completely changes. These are moments, indeed, when individual selfhood may or may not be oriented in terms of shared identities and affiliations.

Feminism and Power as Protection

Women's liberation from patriarchal despotic authority in individual households has come at the hands of the modern, democratic state. The rights of women – for example, the rights of married women to own property, to sue and be sued, to have custody of their children, etc. – were all conferred by the state, and were rhetorically understood to be rights which empowered women against the despotic excesses of their husbands. In general, women's accession to the rights of the modern individual is understood to have followed from the state's conferral of these rights. This is in direct contrast to the origins myth of men's rights as modern individuals. In the case of men, the state is held not to confer rights but to recognize rights already held, "natural" rights.

This prominence of the state in the construction of women as right-bearing subjects bears scrutiny. Liberalism interprets state intervention on behalf of women's rights as the legitimate extension of state protection to a vulnerable group. This being the case, women's right-bearing status may be a qualified one, namely one that exists only to the extent that it is reconcilable with the idea of state-sponsored patriarchal protection of women. While the patriarchal paternalism of the modern state is deployed to enhance the rights of women against abusive men, this paternalism is qualified by being harnessed to a democratic principle of governance, one that enhances rather than diminishes individual rights. Where non-democratic paternalism works on behalf of maintaining the communal household economy of the patriarchal lord or master, democratic paternalism is justified by reference to the individualized needs and rights of those who are perceived as needing protection from abusive patriarchal power.

Democratic paternalism, thus, is paradoxical and ambiguous. To illustrate this, let us take the example of successful feminist argument for state intervention against domestic violence. In Australia in the 1970s the feminist movement successfully argued that the federal government should fund emergency accommodation for women who were seeking to leave men who abused either them and/or their children. This program was complemented by the introduction of the Sole Supporting Parents Benefit. Together both programs were significant in extending the capacity of individual women to resist domestic violence. For the first time, many women had a real alternative to their dependency on an abusive partner.

At the same time, argument for such use of state funds and intervention was couched in terms of women's vulnerability to domestic violence. Feminist advocates of state support for victims of domestic violence had to refuse any legitimacy to patriarchalist ideas of rape and violence as normal aspects of relationships between men and women. In particular, they could not countenance patriarchalist extension of the liberal doctrine of consent to domestic rape and violence. Feminists, indeed, had to contend with a difficult fact, namely the seeming passivity and inability of many battered and abused women to leave their situation. This was not a case of "consent," feminists came to argue, but a complex psycho-dynamic process whereby battered women did not possess any sense of efficacious independent agency in the face of the continuing presence of their abusive male partner.

The feminist argument, then, was that the liberal notion of consent did not apply to the case of the battered woman. There is now a repertoire of sophisticated argumentation which indicates that use of physical force by a dominant subject in conditions of an unequal power relationship is antipathetic to the sense of efficacy as an agent of the weaker subject. Thus, not only do women need to be supported in sufficient economic independence to permit them genuine choice as to where and with whom they live, but both abused women and abusive men need support to learn to practice their personal relationships in non-violent ways. Effective choice and consent, in short, need a range of different kinds of state-sponsored support.

Growing insight into the conditions for the constitution and enhancement of individual agency allows another perspective on male abusers, one that shows how their own capacities for choice and consent have been deformed by a culture of patriarchal violence in which their psycho-dynamic development has occurred.[11] It is as arguable that the male abuser/batterer is not choosing/consenting to abuse his female partner, as it is that she is not choosing/consenting to this abuse. While he is morally responsible for socially unacceptable and illegal acts of violence, it seems unreasonable, for complex psycho-dynamic reasons, to exempt her from complicity in this situation and not extend to him a parallel effort to explain his self- and other-destructive behaviors.

Most feminist thinking proceeds on the assumption that men always already have the power to rape and to batter women. As Sharon Marcus puts it, this assumption concedes to men this "primary power" over women, "implying that at best men can secondarily be dissuaded from using this power by means of threatened punishment from a masculinized state or legal system."[12] On this thinking, good men are those who restrain themselves from acting on their potential to exercise such primary power over women. Bad men are those who do not exercise such restraint. The former are to protect women as potential victims from the latter, where this protection is exercised by means of a paternalistic state and legal system.

Feminist thinking has tended to equate women's victim status with goodness, and men's aggressor status with badness. On this approach, democratic state intervention into domestic violence is designed both to rescue and protect women from violent men, *and* to constitute the rights of women not to be battered or raped. Whether these rights can have any effectiveness under conditions where it is assumed that men already have such a primary power to abuse women is a moot point.

When protectionist conceptions of power are operating, women are reconstituted as no longer agents, who in some complex way are involved in their oppression, but as simply "innocent victims." Here victim status requires the suppression rather than the constitution of the capacities for agency of the subjects concerned. In this way, protectionist feminism is undemocratic.

Several assumptions appear to operate in the protectionist approach to power. On the first, women are assumed both to lie outside power and to be powerless. Therefore, they need the powerful to protect them against those who threaten them. This is a non-political relationship to power. Women do not have to take responsibility for themselves as both implicated in patriarchal domination and as subjects whose capacity for positive, self-governing action can be developed.

On the second assumption, power is assumed to be benign, and in this sense not power at all, if it is directed by enlightened, benevolent, protective motives. Goodness is attested to by the effort made to control evil. Such effort is all. Good people thereby do not have to be responsible for the consequences of their actions, and thus do not have to be politically accountable for them. Nor do they have to become aware of their own tendencies to exploit, abuse and oppress others. This is a recipe for allowing the ends to justify the means.

On the third assumption, those who are weak become powerful only as they are "empowered" by the strong arm of the patriarchal state. On the natural law approach to rights, men do not need to be empowered by the state. They represent a masculinist and democratic version of an old idea: aristocrats by nature.

Empowerment is an idea we may have good reason to wish to retain. However, we need to ask what meanings this term acquires given that it tends to be used of those who are positioned as powerless, who are to be "empowered" by or through the benign, paternalistic agency of the state. We may wonder whether this term reproduces the relationship of tutelage between powerful protector and those who, being powerless, are seen to need help. Against this, it may be argued that "empowering" – like "enabling" and "capacitating" – is a term which suggests that a "power over" is required to constitute an individualized capacity for self-regulating social relationships. This power over does not have to assume the form of paternalistic protection of those who are cast as vulnerable in relation to those who are cast as strong. Instead, it can be expressed as the inclusive requirement that *all* individualized agency requires to be socially constituted and supported. In particular, this includes the social resourcing and support of alternative discourses to the one which naturalizes men's primary power to rape and batter women. These would be discourses where men do not always already have this primary power, and where women as active, powerful subjects are like men in their capacity to resist any other person's attempt to exercise undemocratic domination, physical or otherwise, over them.

Feminism and Power as Capacity

Protectionist and negative conceptions of power have not been the only ways of conceiving power within feminism. As we have seen they make good sense in reflecting the conditions of strategic survival for women as a relatively powerless group. As an emancipatory movement, feminism has also developed a long and sophisticated politics of advocacy for the inclusion of women within modern democratic freedoms.

This is a reactive politics to the extent that inclusion is sought within the established conception of democratic freedoms. For as feminists have come to recognize, these established freedoms reflect the ways in which the powerful and dominant class has conceived freedom. Thus, we discover a thoroughgoing conflation of the very idea of self-governance with private propertied status as master of a household and of all who live within the household. As a consequence, when feminists work for the right of women to be included within the established model of self-governance ("freedom"), they are effectively also working for women to become like men in this sense of patriarchal private propertied householder status. As we know, precisely because of the terms of the gender division of labor entailed in patriarchal households, the vast majority of women are positioned in ways which mean they cannot become like men in this sense.[13]

One response to the discovery of the patriarchally inflected models of self-governance is, as we have seen, to reject them altogether in favor of an equally reactive but separatist orientation to the virtue of women. Another response is evident in an emerging feminist response which permits itself an active and experimental relationship to established and not-yet-established models of self-governance.

This response is evident in the poststructuralist feminist literature which disrupts the binaries of power/powerlessness, masculinity/femininity, good/evil, and so on. Judith Butler's work for example brings out the performative aspects of who we are as sexed and gendered beings: gender is not something we are but something we *do*.[14] When we "do" rather than express gender, our action contributes to a politics of contested gender relations.

Sharon Marcus exemplifies such a politics of power as capacity in her argument that a feminist anti-rape politics should not adopt the reactive position of persuading men not to use their power to rape, but instead should work to prevent rape. This depends on contesting the established discourse of rape which scripts men as always already possessing this power, women as always already potentially violable, and, thus, as subjects of fear. Marcus argues that we need to stop assuming these discursive subject positions, and instead to pay attention to how it is that an intention to rape occurs, and how it is able to become the act of rape. If we ask how different kinds of rape occur and under what conditions, we can develop strategies for women to sabotage effectively the power this script has given men to rape women.

Marcus emphasizes the importance of a feminist counter-discourse or script which enables women to see, and thus externalize, how the dominant discourse/script casts them as always already "subjects of fear," and, in this way, as objects of men's violence. The critical capacity which Marcus emphasizes women must develop if they are to change the script which positions them as subjects of fear is the "will, agency, and capacity for violence."[15] Men respect other masculine subjects as others who will resist their violence with violence of their own. Women, Marcus argues, need to make men see them in the same way.

The transgressive force of this suggestion is obvious, its symptom being a knee jerk response of rejection by those of us who have been positioned as subjects of fear, objects of violence. Ours has been the reactive morality of those who eschewed violence in favor of the weapons of the weak: for example, empathy with or efforts to stay within the limits set by the violent subject.[16] We mistake our historical incapacity for violence as virtue.

If feminists are to develop a conception of power as capacity, we need to accept the whole repertoire of action, including as this does the capacity for violence. Acceptance of this kind will lead us to be suspicious of a politics which would do away with violence. There are many ways of practicing violence, and some of them inevitably inflect our passionate attachments, however peaceable these seem to be. This is not to say that we should become indiscriminate in our attitude to violence. Indeed it is to argue that, historically, women at least have been positioned as subjects who were unable to discriminate between different kinds of violence. Specifically, they have not been able to accept and even celebrate their own capacities for violence, strategic cunning and all kinds of wickedness, those which are playful and satirical as well as those which are harmful to others.

Without such celebration, power as capacity is not to be had. Of course, this is to surrender the virtues of reaction in order to assume the moral complexities of agency or capacity. In these, the agent is an individualized agent whose own needs are thoroughly imbricated in all their socially oriented actions. This is not to reduce agency to a utilitarian calculus of ego-centric action, but to insist on the inseparability of self- and other-regarding components of individualized agency.

A feminist counter-discourse of women as subjects of power, capable of exercising the full range of agentic capacities, including that of violence, can come into being only in the context of the development of a demo-cratic state which *respects*, not simply protects, the rights of women. Such a state constitutes women as agents in their own right who are entitled to the status of a rights-bearing person.

There is a whole panoply of recent legislation in contemporary demo-cratic state-societies which cannot be understood in terms of either the liberal discourse of extension of private propertied personhood to women, or the paternalistic discourse of state protection of the rights of women as potential objects of men's violence and exploitation. I am referring to anti-discrimination, affirmative action and equal employment types of legisla-tion. The significance of this legislation is the statutory constitution of women as right-bearing subjects, where these rights are attached neither to property nor to protection but to personhood. Legislation of this kind creates the space for a discourse of what it means to be constituted as a person, how this constitution works, in what ways and in what contexts.[17] Instead of it being assumed that there are always already natural persons – the discourse of "natural rights" – the implication of this type of legislation is that persons have to be positively constituted through the agency of the state in ways that are not prejudicial to some for reasons of their sex, or any other assumed aspect of identity.

Power as capacity, then, depends on the democratic deployment of legitimate state domination. Without feminism's demands for women to be included within the status of personhood, the legislation of the kinds referred to above would not have come into being. At the same time, it is unreasonable to ask feminism to give up its conceptions of power as force and power as protection – conceptions which are driven by women's historical positioning as relatively powerless subjects – *without* the power of the democratic state to constitute and underwrite women's agency or capacities as persons in their own right.

Conclusion

In identifying these three distinct strands within feminist conceptions of power, my intention is not to suggest that it could be otherwise. The historical inevitability of each of these strands is clear. Their coexistence is uneasy and contradictory. Different feminisms effect this coexistence in different ways, but it would be impossible to find a feminism that did not evince all three strands to more or less extent.

Feminist conceptions of power as protection and power as coercion are made increasingly problematic within a political environment shaped by contemporary values of self-regulation. For example, the contemporary state has adopted an equal opportunity approach to income support in so far as it now requires women on welfare to participate in labor market programs regardless of whether they are mothers of small children or not.[18] This is a market-oriented version of self-regulation which withdraws paternalistic protection from women, and thereby challenges the patriarchal division between a master and his dependents. Feminism, of course, legitimized this extension of the tyranny of market freedom to women workers even though the employment contract is still governed by the employer's prerogative. This being the case, feminism cannot argue for a reinstatement of women as economic dependents of either individual patriarchs or of the state as a corporate patriarch. In order to intervene to show that this kind of equal opportunity approach to welfare disadvantages women on welfare, feminism will have to work with rather than against the self-regulatory features of this situation. Among other things, this requires feminism to argue that the employment contract become more adequately contractual, namely no longer subject to the undemocratic and patrimonial component of employer prerogative.

This is not an easy challenge for feminism given its complex and contradictory relationship to power. However, it is arguable that feminism has developed a reflexive relationship to its own history and contradictions, and that this means that it has already moved beyond a naive and reactive relationship to power. It has become too conscious of its own complex and contradictory historical agency to engage in a politics driven by *ressentiment*, and by a desire for protection from what are taken to be benign, all-powerful forces beyond itself. At the least, this reflexive relationship permits a more thoroughgoing and useful conception of the different meanings and uses of power.

Notes

This paper is a substantially revised version of "Women and Power," *Women's Studies Journal* (New Zealand), 10, 1 (1994), pp. 79–101. In its earliest version, it was a paper titled "Women, Communication and Power," presented to Women in Leadership National Conference, Edith Cowan University, Perth, November 1992, and published in the Conference Proceedings, *Women, Communication and Power,* Edith Cowan University 1993. This version is indebted to Barbara Sullivan for some excellent substantive editing advice.

1 From Paul Pattons' "Foucault's Subject of Power," *Political Theory Newsletter,* 6, 1 (1994), pp. 64–5. See also his "Politics and the Concept of Power in Hobbes and Nietzsche," in *Nietzsche, Feminism and Political Theory,* eds Paul Patton (New York and London: Routledge, 1993), pp. 144–62.

2 For more elaboration of this argument, see my "Voice and Representation in the Politics of Difference," in *Feminism and the Politics of Difference,* eds Sneja Gunew and Anna Yeatman (St. Leonards: Allen & Unwin, 1993), pp. 228–46.

3 For further critical discussion of the ideal of face-to-face community, see Iris Marion Young, "The Ideal of Community and the Politics of Difference," in *Feminism/Postmodernism,* ed. L. Nicholson (New York and London: Routledge, 1990), pp. 300–24. See also Ch. 8 "City Life and Difference," in Iris Marion Young, *Justice and the Politics of Difference* (Princeton: Princeton University Press, 1990).

4 Friedrich Nietzsche, "The Genealogy of Morals," in *The Birth of Tragedy and the Genealogy of Morals* (New York: Doubleday Anchor, 1956), p. 170.

5 See also Marion Tapper, "Ressentiment and Power: Some Reflections on Feminist Practices," in Paul Patton, *Nietzsche, Feminism and Political Theory,* pp. 130–44.

6 See Ron Feldman, ed., *Hannah Arendt: the Jew as Pariah* (New York: Grove Press, 1978), pp. 24–5.

7 Sharon Marcus, "Fighting Bodies, Fighting Words: A Theory and Politics of Rape Prevention," in *Feminists Theorize the Political,* eds Judith Butler and Joan Scott (New York and London: Routledge, 1992), p. 391.

8 Nietzsche, "The Genealogy of Morals," p. 171.

9 Nietzsche, "The Genealogy of Morals," p. 170.

10 On this point see Bonnie Honig, "Towards an Agonistic Feminism: Hannah Arendt and the Politics of Identity," in *Feminists Theorize the Political,* eds Judith Butler and Joan Scott (New York and London: Routledge, 1992), pp. 215–39.

11 The important New Zealand film *Once Were Warriors* shows this clearly for its Maori male protagonist. See also the book, Alan Duff, *Once Were Warriors* (Auckland: Tandem Press, 1990).

12 Sharon Marcus, "Fighting Bodies, Fighting Words," p. 388.
13 For the working of what Carole Pateman calls "the sexual contract" in organizations see Cynthia Cockburn, *In the Way of Women: Men's Resistance to Sex Equality in Organizations* (London: Macmillan, 1991).
14 See Judith Butler, *Gender Trouble: Feminism and the Subversion of Identity* (New York and London: Routledge, 1990).
15 Marcus, "Fighting Bodies, Fighting Words," p. 395.
16 See Marcus "Fighting Bodies, Fighting Words," p. 393.
17 For development of this idea see Anna Yeatman, "Interpreting the New Contractualism," in Jonathon Boston, ed., *The State Under Contract* (Wellington: Bridget Williams Books, 1995).
18 See Nancy Fraser and Linda Gordon, "Decoding 'Dependency': Inscriptions of Power in a Keyword of the US Welfare State," in this volume, for a genealogy of the processes by which legitimate dependency has been withdrawn from all groups with the exception of children.

9

Rethinking Anarchism/Rethinking Power: A Contemporary Feminist Perspective

Martha Ackelsberg

The collapse of socialism in the Soviet Union and Eastern Europe, combined with the growing popularity of postmodernist criticism in the academy, has left both activists and theorists largely bereft of models for social and political transformation. The old formulas no longer compel. Neither class, nor race, nor gender seems, on its own, sufficient to offer a foolproof basis for transforming pervasive relationships of oppression and inequality. At the same time, however, the postmodernist suspicion of "totalizing" discourses has not provided an alternative way of thinking about the categories of political struggle that enables us to deal simultaneously with the complexities of identity while developing a strategy for action.[1]

A focus on eradicating domination links many formulations of feminism with anarchist perspectives. Classic communalist anarchism (in the collectivist tradition of Proudhon, Bakunin, Kropotkin, Malatesta, Goldman and, more recently, Murray Bookchin) offered a critique of contemporary society that focused on relations of domination and subordination, a vision of an ideal (egalitarian, non-hierarchical) society, and a strategy for achieving it, based on direct action and what Colin Ward has termed "spontaneous organization".[2]

To an extent, one could argue that anarchism participated in the same Enlightenment-inspired search for "primary causes" and "universalizing theories" that characterized the socialism, radical feminism, and other theories so profoundly criticized by postmodernist theorists: communalist anarchists have tended to focus on hierarchy, as such, as *the* manifestation of oppression, and to direct their strategic attention to the state. Yet, at the same time, anarchist theories and practices challenge the claim that there exists one "primal cause" or most basic form of domination and subordination. A focus on hierarchy can lead to exploration of the *multiplicity* of relations of domination and subordination, and of the connections among them.

Still, to the extent that much anarchist theorizing envisioned a mutualist society *without* relations of power and domination, its discourse grates against contemporary sensibilities.[3] In an intellectual and political climate in which we are constantly made aware of the pervasiveness of power and of domination, it may be difficult to take seriously those who call for an end to all such relationships. This chapter offers a brief overview of communalist anarchism, and then explores its analyses of power and domination, and of strategies for change, through the lens of feminist criticism and activism. Finally, it turns to what an anarchism revised in the light of these critiques might have to offer to contemporary political analysis and political strategy.

Communalist Anarchism: A Brief Overview

The main tenets of the communalist anarchist tradition can be summarized fairly simply. First, communalist anarchists are committed to freedom and community: they insist that freedom is a social product, and that people become free to develop themselves fully only when they are members of an appropriately organized, supportive, community. Personal freedom and social life are not mutually antagonistic, but interdependent and mutually supportive.

Second, an anarchist society would be one without hierarchical relationships, and without institutionalized patterns of authority. Anarchists claim that people can organize and associate themselves on the basis of need, that individuals or small groups can take the necessary initiative, and that centralized *political* coordination is both harmful and unnecessary. Anarchists criticize both the so-called neutrality of the state, and the actual practice of politics: neither is free of relations of domination. That is not to say that there never can or will be leaders, or those who take initiative. It is to say, however, that the right or authority to direct or command a situation should not inhere in roles or offices to which some people have privileged access, or from which others are systematically excluded.[4]

Third, the anarchist vision is of a society characterized by diversity: one that not only tolerates, but positively supports, differences among groups of people, and also among people within such groups. It is a society in which, as Colin Ward has described it, harmony is achieved through complexity.[5] And, along with a commitment to non-dominating relationships among people, anarchism has a commitment to non-dominating relationships with the environment.[6]

In addition, the anarchist vision is of an egalitarian society. Not only should there be no one who (by virtue of sex, race, class, etc.) has the authority to order others around, but neither social nor economic inequality is necessary to sustain social organization. In place of economic inequality, anarchists propose mutualism and reciprocity. People can organize themselves on the basis of mutual interdependence, and need neither centralized work authority nor inegalitarian work incentives and salaries to keep social and economic life on an even keel.

Finally, anarchism implies a theory of social change, a revolutionary strategy, which can best be termed the theory and practice of direct action. That strategy means, first, that the process that creates the new society must be consistent with the aims and relationships in the society which is the goal. Thus, there can be no leadership or hierarchy in the process of social change. And, second, the way to create a new society is to *create* a new reality. The new society is to be built up from and, in fact, the revolutionary process *consists* of, social organizations which change existing reality (specifically relations of domination and subordination). It is only *by* participating in communal, mutualist, institutions that people learn *how* to participate in them, that is, how to live in a communalist, anarchist society. And it is only by acting in ways consistent with mutualism and reciprocity that those institutions and practices can be created.[7]

Power and Domination

Classical anarchist theorists argued that the exercise of power (particularly the unrestrained power that accompanies holding specific positions in political, economic, religious, or social life) brutalizes both the wielder of power and the one over whom it is exercised. With respect to the first, anyone who holds power tends only to develop an ever-increasing desire to maintain it. The powerful come, ultimately, either to think of themselves as indispensable or to act as if they did. Bakunin argued, for example, that "nothing is as dangerous for personal morality as the habit of commanding . . . Two feelings inherent in the exercise of power never fail to produce . . . demoralization: contempt for the masses, and, for the one in power, an exaggerated sense of his own worth."[8] Kropotkin made the point equally strongly: "any group of people entrusted with deciding a certain set of activities . . . of an organizational quality always strives to broaden the range of these activities and its own power in these activities."[9] Formal hierarchical authority structures may well create the conditions they are supposedly designed to combat: rather than preventing disorder, anarchists have argued, governments are among its primary causes. Hierarchies make some people dependent on others, blame the dependent for their dependency, and then use that dependency as a justification for the further exercise of authority.[10]

Conversely, to be always in a position of being acted upon, and never to be allowed to act, is to be doomed to a state of dependence and resignation. Those who are constantly ordered about and not allowed to think for themselves, the anarchists insisted, soon come to doubt their own ability to think or act for themselves. Bakunin argued that political authority debases the individual by not allowing one to make one's own free choices (thus negating freedom). And Kropotkin faulted political authority for preventing that spontaneous cooperation among people which he saw as the foundation of moral action.[11] Thus, government becomes its own justification: the more we are governed, the less we feel we can do without it. Mutual aid is replaced by a one-way dependence on external authority.

Many anarchist theorists and activists have devoted attention to the way participation in relationships of domination and subordination undermines the sense of self, of self-confidence, and of possibility, on the part of those in subordinate positions. In 1903, for example, the Spanish anarchist, José Prat argued that "Women's 'backwardness' is a consequence of the way she has been, and still is, treated. 'Nature' has nothing to do with this . . . If woman is backward, it is because in all times man has kept her inferior. . . ."[12] While the subordination of women has social roots, it also has psychological effects. Emma Goldman went so far as to argue that "true emancipation [for women] begins neither at the polls nor in courts. It begins in woman's soul. . . ."[13] In short, relationships of domination and subordination have complex and multiform consequences for those who participate in them.

Classical anarchists recognized that there are different kinds of power and that it is important to distinguish the sort of *institutionalized* power I have been discussing from other sorts of authority. Even these anarchists, who rejected the argument that formal authority is necessary for social order,[14] acknowledged that, in many situations, someone will know more than others about a particular task and how to do it, so others will defer to him or her on that basis. Or, as Bakunin and Kropotkin argued, some may have greater knowledge or understanding of natural or scientific laws, and be able to exercise what they term "natural authority" on the basis of such knowledge. Or, some people may have overwhelming personalities that seem to "compel" obedience. But anarchists distinguish sharply between these sorts of authority – which people may decide *freely* to follow or not – and formal, institutionalized authority, which there are sanctions for disobeying.[15]

Classical anarchist theory, then, seems to imply a discernible distinction between *formally* recognized power or authority, on the one hand, and a kind of "free followership," based on acknowledgment of superior knowledge or understanding, on the other. The former is considered incompatible with freedom (or the vision of an ideal anarchist society); the latter is not only not incompatible, but possibly even necessary for its smooth functioning.

A number of contemporary anarcha-feminists have argued that one of the most significant (for feminists) aspects of anarchism is precisely its critique of power relationships. Thus, in the words of Carol Ehrlich, "Social anarchists and radical feminists share the belief that power relationships (that is relationships in which one has the ability to compel another's obedience or control another's actions) are inherently coercive, competitive, and inegalitarian, and that institutionalized forms of inequality are rooted in power relationships. . . . Anarchist feminism works to end all forms of inequality, beginning (but not ending) with patriarchy."[16]

It is *power* that is "key to class and sex inequality alike, and to all the other forms of inequality as well. . . ."[17] The goal for (anarchist) feminists is the elimination of those organizational forms that institutionalize unequal access to resources; that is, that support and manifest relationships of power and domination.

Marsha Hewitt argues, similarly, that "the core of both anarchist and feminist theory is an ongoing preoccupation with power . . . feminism and anarchism complement each other because they are both concerned with, and struggle against, domination in its every form," and attend to the impact of power on both the political and the personal/internal levels.[18] Most dramatically, perhaps, L. Susan Brown argues that "anarchism goes beyond feminism in its ceaseless attempts to annihilate power itself."[19]

But what does this mean? In the context of many contemporary feminist efforts to "empower" women (or to define feminism as the empowerment of women), or to reconceive power as capacity, is it appropriate even to *aim* at "annihilating" power?[20] And in an era defined significantly by the legacy of Michel Foucault, and by the feminist insistence that "the personal is political" (and, therefore, is not free from relationships of power), can we even imagine that it would be possible to end all relationships of domination and subordination?

It is precisely the effort to make a sharp distinction between "formal" and "informal" power which is difficult for many contemporary feminists (postmodernist and otherwise) to accept. As Marx, Foucault and many others have made clear, power is much more complex than such a formulation would imply. "Informal power," for example, is almost invariably concentrated in the hands of individuals who are otherwise socially privileged. Further, there is virtually no arena of our lives free from the exercise of power of some sort; and, at the same time, virtually no context in which there is not also resistance. What, then, does it mean to advocate the "annihilation" of power, or to suppose that such a goal is even desirable? Is it possible to imagine new understandings of power (such as power as capacity, or "empowerment") that would not be imbued with relations of domination?

Kathleen Jones has suggested that one key to the problem is the definition of power as *sovereignty* that demands, or depends upon, an enforced unity.[21] Jones argues that it was the construction of sovereignty (by Hobbes) as the overcoming of difference that has been fundamental to "establishing authority as a 'command–obedience relationship.'"[22] In its place, she draws on Hannah Arendt to call for an understanding of authority as an "augmentation of our common life": "contrary to the restricted understanding of authority as contingent on conflicting individual and, primarily, male wills, authority is here seen as the construction of a meaningful world . . . the vitalizing of community itself." Authority, then, becomes a way of describing shared meanings, "cohering and sustaining connectedness."[23]

The attempt to think about power *other* than as a mechanism for enforcing unity is one component of a more complex understanding of power. But contemporary debates have also highlighted other necessary dimensions of such a reconceptualization – specifically, the multiple faces of power and resistance. Here, feminist questions focus on how to analyze relationships of domination (and resistance) so as to recognize the multiple domains and dimensions of power while not succumbing to analytical incoherence and/or political resignation.

Perhaps the most serious (and strategically compelling) charges levelled against the various interpretations of "feminism" that have been developed over the past two decades is that each focuses on one particular relationship of domination and subordination as critical, effectively ignoring or marginalizing the others. Increasing numbers of feminist activists and theorists, however, have found these approaches inadequate. Either they could not account for differences of class or race or sexual orientation among women, or they treated one or another of these characteristics as "secondary." But women who exist in a world characterized by multiple "fault-lines," who find themselves members (or non-members!) of a variety of collectivities, with multiple loyalties, have found such approaches overly simplified and oblivious to the complexity with which they live.[24]

The problem is clear. In the words of Ernesto Laclau and Chantal Mouffe, the problem facing contemporary radical activists is the loss of "privileged points of rupture": contemporary US and Western European societies are characterized by a "diffusion of social conflictuality to more and more numerous relations."[25] Neither Marxism's claim to explain all relations of domination and subordination on the basis of class, nor radical feminism's claim to explain it all on the basis of sex, is adequate: on the one hand, there are too many other lines of cleavage which seem to generate challenges to existing structures of power and, on the other, there are too many ways in which the supposed grounds of resistance are undermined and constrained. "There is no *unique* privileged position from which a uniform continuity of effects will follow. . . . There is therefore no subject . . . which is absolutely radical and irrecuperable by the dominant order, and which constitutes an absolutely guaranteed point of departure for a total transformation."[26]

If there is no one privileged "point of rupture," no necessary assumption of homogeneity of experience or consciousness, no particular form of domination and subjection that can or will guarantee the final degree of resistance, whence comes the will or force to change, to overcome the relations of domination and subordination that limit us?

Like a number of contemporary activist/theorists, Laclau and Mouffe insist that the recognition that there is no "fundamental contradiction" signals not an end to politics, but its beginning. If any and all perspectives are necessarily partial, then effective political action requires what they term "articulation" – the successful linking of one's struggles with those of others – in short, "coalition-building."[27] We can see this perspective foreshadowed in the communalist anarchist insistence that the focus of analysis (and of resistance) need not be on any *single* relationship of domination and subordination (that is, one based on class, on race, on gender, on age, or on religious affiliation, for example), but rather on *relations of domination and subordination as such*[28] – a perspective about power that fits well with contemporary understandings of its multiple faces and dimensions. And we see it named, again, in Gail Stenstad's call for what she terms "atheoretical," "anarchic thinking" that is characterized by "openness to ambiguity and multiple interpretations, attentiveness to the strange-within-the-familiar . . ." and that "empowers a multiplicity of voices and of possibilities for thought and action."[29]

Another context in which feminist explorations of the ambiguities of power have been developed quite extensively in recent years is in theories of the state. Anarchists, of course, are best known for their anti-state perspective, the insistence that there can be *no* legitimate political authority, and that the so-called neutrality of the state is always a mask for relations of domination and subordination.[30] Contemporary feminists have been quite divided about the role of the state and its particular implications for women; and many of these critical writings can be helpful in exploring anarchist approaches.

For example, it is now a commonplace that the welfare state has ambiguous consequences for its clients. On the one hand, beginning with Piven and Cloward's *Regulating the Poor*, some critics have viewed welfare programs as mechanisms for the exercise of state control. They, and other more recent critics, have focused specifically on the impacts of state policies generally, and of state-sponsored welfare programs in particular, on family and sexual lives. Some emphasize the ways contemporary welfare state policies organize family life and sexuality, in Balbus' view, transforming "citizens of a limited state" into "clients of an unlimited state."[31] Others have explored the ways legal structures legitimize certain definitions of "family" and acceptable sexuality, and marginalize others.[32] And still others have focused more specifically on the ways state welfare programs have created and/or reinforced hierarchical relationships of gender and race, specifically through the creation of a two-channel welfare system.[33]

On the other hand, state programs can also provide sources of empowerment.[34] Many such programs have been of tremendous value to women – whether by providing employment within the welfare-state bureaucracy, or by providing needed, albeit often inadequate, benefits to those who are clients. Further, women and poor people have been able to use programs and institutions created by the welfare state precisely to organize *against* the state, demanding better services and benefits. In the process, "clients" can come to experience, for themselves, precisely the stronger self-image and the collective sense of empowerment which many anarchists have taken as a goal. Thus, these critics argue, state programs could serve as the contexts for major organizing against the state, not only on behalf of greater welfare benefits, but also for more equality. The welfare state comes to be seen not just as a mechanism of control over the poor, but as a product of the demands made, and resistance offered, by poor and working-class people to changes in the class relations of advanced capitalism.[35]

In short, the state is a much more complex set of institutions and practices than early anarchist theory acknowledged. While contemporary feminists are hardly agreed about what to make of this complexity, or how best to relate to "the state," most seem convinced that issues of power must be addressed in all their complexity. The state can neither be ignored, nor simply opposed in the sense that anarchism (at least as traditionally understood) would have advocated. In that respect, contemporary feminist perspectives pose important challenges to those anarchist views. Unlike traditional anarchists who wanted to eliminate the state, many feminists advocate a state that is accountable to its citizens, and genuinely responsive to, and representative of the interests of, *all* its citizens.

Strategies for Change

The key question for all theories of domination and resistance (of which socialism is one, feminism another, and anarchism yet another) is to develop an analysis not only of the workings of domination, but of the possibilities of resistance and transformation. For both socialism and feminism, that process has generally been referred to as the problem of "consciousness-change." How do people come to recognize (collective) grievances and their capacity to take action to overcome them? How can such consciousness and action be coordinated and sustained into a more broadly based movement? It has become clear that a simple "oppression/resistance" or "oppression/consciousness" model is inadequate. While, on the one hand, as theorists as different as Michel Foucault and Piven and Cloward have noted, power is never exercised without there being resistance to it, it is also the case that resistance is never automatic, and a consciousness of grievances does not necessarily follow from even the most horrific abuses of power.[36]

Anarchist analyses of resistance and the strategic prescriptions deriving from it center on direct action and the consistency of means and ends. Recognizing the existence of conflicting realities in the world is central to the anarchist strategy for social change. Just as there is no power without resistance, there is no hierarchy without a variety of understandings of those relationships.[37] For anarchists, the perspectives of those subject to domination and oppression provide the bases for social change. To overcome domination is, in fact, to create a new reality, and to do so by asserting, and acting upon, a different conception of what constitutes knowledge, one's own nature, and the relationships in which one finds oneself. In addition, through such action, people effectively *change themselves*. By acting differently, they convince both themselves and others that they are not "naturally subordinate," that the dependency or submissiveness that has characterized them, for example, is not definitive of their being.[38]

This relationship between "personal" change and "political" change helps to explain why anarchists argue so strongly for the consistency of means and ends. One cannot establish an egalitarian society through hierarchical organizations which re-create in different form long-standing patterns of subordination. To live as members of an egalitarian, communalist society, people must resocialize themselves as new persons. They must come to see themselves, and to act, on the basis of a new (alternate) reality. And this they can do only by acting – with others, and on a non-dominating basis.

For anarchists, previously dependent people come to recognize their grievances and their capacity to take action to combat them, by a combination of education (including "propaganda by the deed," exemplary action that recruits adherents by the power of the positive example it sets) and engaging in action, both of which reflect new understandings and manifestations of "power," and which become self-sustaining activities.

But how can these actions and consciousness be sustained and coordinated into a broad movement? The anarchists' answer to this question differs significantly from that of Marxists – and fits well with much feminist practice. For anarchists argue that change cannot be achieved through centralized organizations that manifest the traditional, hierarchical understanding of power, but must develop out of the widest possible sort of participation. This must be so because particular action or organization is necessarily *partial*, even as it is also potentially a building-block of a new society. People must act "locally," that is, where they feel called to act; and no centralized organization can direct that.

This is what both anarchists and many feminists have meant by strategies of "empowerment," what Spanish anarchist women termed *capacitación*.[39] When people join together to exert control over their workplace, their community, the conditions of their day-to-day lives, they experience the changes they make as their own. Instead of reinforcing the sense of powerlessness that often accompanies modest improvements granted from the top of an hierarchical structure, a strategy of direct action enables people to *create their own power*. This is not power in the sense of domination; but power/authority in Kathleen Jones' sense of "augmentation" or connection, power that both enables and constitutes the work of what Laclau and Mouffe refer to as "articulating" differences. Acting in this way increases people's self-confidence, and fortifies them to continue to act.[40] It is not surprising, in this context, that so many women felt *strengthened* by the consciousness-raising sessions that were characteristic of early stages of the "second wave" of the women's movement – sessions that enabled people to share a different reality, and then to act upon it. That acting together strengthened women further, and gave them the power to continue to act, even against obstacles. The women of Mujeres Libres (a Spanish anarchist women's organization, active in Spain during the time of the Spanish Civil War, and committed to "emancipating women from their triple enslavement to capital, to illiteracy, and as women") reported similar experiences of overcoming their own embarrassment and timidity about speaking in public, for example. Those who act together with others in non-traditional ways are often perceived as threatening (and ridiculed or dismissed as "hysterical" or "disorderly") precisely because they are challenging some long- and dearly-held beliefs about how the world does and should operate.[41]

Laclau and Mouffe challenge us to redefine understandings of domination and subordination in more complex ways. In their view, the problem of "consciousness" must be renamed: "Our central problem is to identify the discursive conditions for the emergence of a collective action, directed towards struggling against inequalities and challenging relations of subordination . . . our task is to identify the conditions in which a relation of subordination becomes a relation of oppression. . . ."[42]

They take "relation of subordination" to mean "that in which an agent is subjected to the decisions of another" – the relationship of employee to employer, for example, or of women to men in "certain forms of family organization." By "relations of oppression," they refer to "those relations of subordination which have transformed themselves into sites of antagonism." The problem then becomes to explain that process of transformation.[43]

For both Laclau and Mouffe and for Piven and Cloward – although in different ways – that process is fundamentally *political*. If there is nothing automatic about resistance – and, in particular, about resistance expressed in collective forms – then it must be created or constructed. But what are the conditions for doing so? Both sets of authors look to the larger context in which the relationships are located. Laclau and Mouffe, and Anna Yeatman, focus on "discursive conditions," in particular, the "profound subversive power of democratic discourse" that enables those experiencing relationships of subordination to understand them *as subordinating*, and therefore unjust according to commonly accepted democratic principles, and then to resist.[44] For Piven and Cloward, as well, the larger political context matters, but these authors tend to focus on the state of relationships/consensus/alignments among those who are *exercising* power, rather than on the discursive context, noting that the possibilities for successful resistance and realignment of power relationships is greatest when disruptive protest can splinter existing alignments and allegiances.[45] While anarchist writers have tended to focus on the ways action, in itself, can help to develop alternative perspectives, contemporary writer/activists such as Piven and Cloward, Boyte and Evans, and others have argued that openings for successful resistance are often quite fleeting: it is only in the (often temporary) interstices of power that alternative views and practices can really begin to develop and flourish.[46]

Here is where feminist *practice* has much to offer to anarchist theory. Consciousness-raising groups brought together women who – consistent with the dominant cultural consensus – had perceived dissatisfaction with their lives as their "personal problems," and enabled them to recognize both the "commonness" of those issues and their socially constructed aspects. The recognition that "the personal is political" became the watchword of the women's movement, and allowed people to develop and then to share changing perceptions of self and world. But consciousness-raising, and the making of connections between "personal problems" and social/political practices, was not limited to the privacy of living rooms. To give just two examples: self-help health clinics enabled people to recognize that they *could* understand at least some of what is going on inside their bodies, and that they could *participate* in making decisions about how to care for themselves. Food co-ops arose from a growing recognition of the ways food production and distribution were designed to further the interests of distributors, rather than of either producers or consumers; and, at the same time, they effectively empowered the women (and others) who created and participated in them by enabling them to work with others and to take greater responsibility for the context of their daily lives. Here we can see important connections with much contemporary feminist postmodernist theorizing about "local" actions, the importance of what Laclau and Mouffe term "articulation," and what others discuss as the work of "politics" in a context of partial and unstable identities.[47]

Barbara Epstein's recent study of the non-violent, direct action movement makes a number of similar claims. She emphasizes the importance to movement activists of *personal* transformation as well as the achievement of more broadly "political" goals. On her view, "in late twentieth-century United States, protest politics must be utopian, in the sense that it must hold out a vision of a nonviolent and egalitarian society, and that it must build the new society within the shell of the old by creating a space within which these values can be realized as far as possible."[48] She sees most contemporary movement groups as anarchist in inspiration and practice. Yet she argues that it is another side of that anarchist legacy which poses the greatest problem for the movement: "there is an assumption running through the direct action movement that constructing an egalitarian, nonviolent society requires abolishing power relations and doing away with conflict. . . . [But the] movement's suspicion of power and conflict makes it difficult to make strategy and to build the kinds of organizations that can weather changes in issues or tactics."[49] While she favors eliminating centralized state power, she thinks it fanciful "to believe that power itself should be or can be abolished."

My own sense is that the wariness of "power" expressed in Epstein's analysis, and manifest both in the movements she studied and in so much of feminist and anarchist theorizing, reflects the complexities of power explored earlier. On this point, Jones' call for us to rethink power/authority in more "woman-friendly" ways that do not assume that unity must be enforced through the repression of differences becomes particularly relevant. Critics of both anarchism and feminism, for example, have warned of the dangers of their communalist/collectivist side. All too often, these critics argue, the consensus-oriented decision-making strategies associated with both movements have either faltered because of differences, or else reinforced the power of the majority in the name of the collective. Of course, these problems are not limited to consensus-based organizations: they are surely manifest, as well, in liberal democratic systems such as that of the United States.

Much of the discussion of the coercive nature of "community" has focused, in recent years, on these more "collectivist approaches."[50] Nira Yuval-Davis and Floya Anthias, Iris Young, Audre Lorde, Patricia Hill Collins, Elizabeth Spelman, Gloria Anzaldúa, and a host of contemporary feminists have all pointed to the dangers of basing feminist utopian visions on some unitary/homogeneous notion of "community" which is almost necessarily exclusive of differences among women.[51] The question then becomes, how to develop a conception of community/politics that is multivocal, and based on diversity, rather than on univocal concepts of power that are rooted in enforcing homogeneity or conformity.

Conclusion

And so we return, in the end, to the questions of difference, conflict and strategy we raised earlier. How can we realize the goal of collective action that unites people across differences, but does so without creating new, centralized, hierarchical structures, and without either denying the differences or reifying them into permanent identities?

Contemporary feminist perspectives offer crucial rethinkings of locally based, direct action strategies. For, it is *through politics* – that is to say, efforts to coordinate perspectives and activities with others – that we come to develop our own identities (however temporary and unstable) and capacities, and to learn about others'. Laclau and Mouffe are correct in saying that "articulation" is all. While we may not be able to eliminate power, we can move toward challenging the dominating, hierarchical, structures of power in and through which we interact. Much progressive protest politics, in fact, consists of actions that express such challenges. Further, people do (and seemingly will) question and resist those forms of dominating power by which they are oppressed and to which they have access, once the possibility of such resistance becomes a reality (a process that happens through what has been described as changing discourse – for example, the spread of democratic ideas; as "propaganda by the deed"; or as finding the "cracks" in existing patterns or institutions of control).[52]

Those who resist dominating power (and, in the process, create a different kind of power) — whether in their daily lives, or in more formal protest organizations – do not necessarily have fully developed long-term strategies formulated in their minds. While the absence of such strategizing has often tended to make us doubt the legitimacy or effectiveness of the resistance, feminist/anarchist perspectives challenge us to recognize that such skepticism is unwarranted. In fact, I would argue, "local action" – action taken not on the basis of some universalized narrative about "revolution," but on the basis of challenging (a) particular oppressive relationship(s) – partial and limited though it might seem, is the only politics consistent with a commitment *not* to deny the differences among us.[53] Such a politics – for example, of women's health collectives, food co-ops, of bus boycotts, lunch-counter protests, ACT-UP demonstrations – recognizes the *particular* circumstances in which people live their lives, and in which they experience relations of domination, at the same time that it provides a context to challenge those relationships and to participate with others in creating a "new self."

There is yet another side to this "local" politics. In a recent paper on "Coyote Politics," Shane Phelan has described both lesbians and feminists as "shape-shifters," who not only *do* shift perspectives, behaviors, attitudes, etc., in response to changing circumstances, but ought to celebrate and take pride in that multiplicity, as it is the only way to deal with a world of great complexity.[54] Similarly, María Lugones has used the language of "mestizaje," and metaphors of "curdling," to address the complexities of identity and resistance, specifically the "impure resistance to interlocked, intermeshed oppressions." She urges us to think in terms of "multiplicity" (which communicates a sense of the "messiness" of identity), rather than of "fragmentation," which, in the guise of attending to differences, implies the possibility of a "clean separation" between parts of a self, a separation that can be accomplished – if at all – only through domination.[55] And Gloria Anzaldúa writes of the spiritual, sexual, and psychological borderlands where cultures, classes, and races touch, "where the space between two individuals shrinks with intimacy," and calls upon her readers to live with the contradictions, *in* those borderlands, to live "without borders" to "be a crossroads."[56] It is not coincidental that such calls for action that is open to difference, and for a politics that does not freeze people into particular identities, come from those who have been "marginalized," or "particularized" by the traditional universalizing discourses. Yet it is from these margins that we find arising both theory and practice/resistance.

For too long – blinded by efforts to understand this resistance in terms of conventional theories of protest and organization – feminists and progressives have denied the significance of seemingly disparate and fragmented activities. If a rethinking of anarchist perspectives does nothing more, it should at least make us aware of the importance of such forms of resistance, and offer a framework within which to understand it. Partial, fragmented, identities may not seem to offer as sound and solid a basis for organizing and resistance as did traditional claims to class, race, or sex-based unities. But they *do* form the basis of actual resistance struggles. The task now is to explore the ways those struggles challenge domination while attempting to create new, more mutualist, expressions of power.

Notes

1 This formulation of the issues owes much to conversations and writing with Irene Diamond.
2 Colin Ward, *Anarchy in Action* (London: Freedom Press, 1988).
3 See, for example, John P. Clark, "What Is Anarchism," in *Anarchism*, Nomos XIX, ed. J. Roland Pennock and John W. Chapman (New York: New York University Press, 1978), especially p. 17; Peggy Kornegger, "Anarchism – The Feminist Connection," *The Second Wave*, 4, 1 (Spring 1975), pp. 26–37; Carol Ehrlich, "Socialism, Anarchism, and Feminism," *The Second Wave*, 5, 1 (Spring/Summer 1977), pp. 29–35, and "The Unhappy Marriage of Marxism and Feminism: Can It Be Saved?" in *Women and Revolution*, ed. Lydia Sargent (Boston: South End Press, 1981), especially pp. 114, 116, 131; Marsha Hewitt, "Emma Goldman: The Case for Anarcho-Feminism," *Our Generation*, 17, 1 (Fall/Winter 1985–6), pp. 167–75, and "Is Sexism Genetic?" *Our Generation*, 16, 2 (Spring 1984), pp. 13–14; and L. Susan Brown, "Anarchism, Existentialism, Feminism, and Ambiguity," *Our Generation*, 19, 2 (Spring/Summer 1988), pp. 1–18.
4 I have developed these arguments more fully in *The Posssibility of Anarchism: The Theory and Practice of Non-Authoritarian Organization*, PhD dissertation, Department of Politics, Princeton University, 1976; in *Free Women of Spain: Anarchism and the Struggle for the Emancipation of Women* (Bloomington: Indiana University Press, 1991), especially Ch. 1; (with Kathryn Pyne Addelson) in "Anarchist Alternatives to Competition," in *Competition: A Feminist Taboo?*, eds Valerie Miner and Helen E. Longino (New York: The Feminist Press, 1987), pp. 221–33; and (with Kathryn Pyne Addelson and Shawn Pyne), "Anarchism and Feminism," in Kathryn Pyne Addelson, *Impure Thoughts: Essays on Philosophy, Feminism, and Ethics* (Philadelphia: Temple University Press, 1991).
5 Ward, *Anarchy in Action*, Ch. 4.
6 See, for example, Peter Kropotkin's attempt to develop an alternative to social-Darwinist understandings of evolutionary theory that emphasized co-operation rather than competition in *Mutual Aid* (London: William Heinemann, 1902) and *Fields, Factories and Workshops Tomorrow*, introduced and edited by Colin Ward (New York: Harper and Row, 1974); also Myrna Breitbart, "Peter Kropotkin: Anarchist Geographer," in *Geography, Ideology and Social Concern*, ed. David Stoddart (New York: Oxford University Press, 1982), pp. 134–53; David Miller, "The Neglected (II) Kropotkin," *Govern-*

ment and Opposition, 18 (Summer 1983), pp. 119–38; and William M. Dugger, "Veblen and Kropotkin on Human Evolution," *Journal of Economic Issues*, XVIII, 4 (December 1984), pp. 971–85.

7 On this point, see Ackelsberg and Addelson, "Anarchist Alternatives"; also Kropotkin, "Expropriation" (pp. 160–209) and "Must We Occupy Ourselves with an Examination of the Ideal of a Future System?" (pp. 46–117), both in *Peter Kropotkin: Selected Writings on Anarchism and Revolution*, ed. Martin A. Miller (Cambridge: MIT Press, 1970).

8 "Federalism, Socialism, and Anti-Theologism," p. 145; see also "Representative Government and Universal Suffrage," p. 221; and "The Program of the Alliance," pp. 245–6, all in *Bakunin on Anarchism*, ed. Sam Dolgoff (Montreal: Black Rose Books, 1980).

9 "Must We Occupy Ourselves?", p. 62. See also Pierre-Joseph Proudhon, *Du principe fédératif et de la nécessité de reconstituer le Parti de la Révolution* (Paris: E. Dentu, Libraire-Editeur, 1863), p. 42.

10 See my *Free Women of Spain*, pp. 18–20.

11 M. Bakunin, *God and the State*, With a New Introduction and Index of Persons by Paul Avrich (New York: Dover, 1970), pp. 31–2; and "Letters on Patriotism," in *Oeuvres* (Paris: Stock, 1895), vol. I, pp. 222–4; and Kropotkin, "The State: Its Historic Role," in *Selected Writings*, p. 252.

12 José Prat, *A las mujeres*, Conferencia leída en el "Centro Obrero" de Sabadell y en el "Centro Fraternal de Cultura" de Barcelona, October 18 and 24, 1903 (Barcelona: Biblioteca Editorial Salud, 1923), pp. 14–15. See also Mariano Gallardo, "Tendencias del instinto sexual humano," *Estudios*, 136 (December 1934), and "Influencia de las instituciones sociales sobre el carácter humano," *Estudios*, 137 (January 1935), p. 63.

13 "The Tragedy of Woman's Emancipation," in Emma Goldman, *Anarchism and Other Essays* (New York: Dover, 1969), p. 224.

14 I discuss these arguments at some length in *The Possibility of Anarchism*, Ch. 1.

15 I discuss the concept of "natural authority" in *The Possibility of Anarchism*, pp. 42–54. For Bakunin's views see *God and the State*, pp. 28–35; "Federalism, Socialism, and Anti-Theologism," p. 129, and "The Paris Commune and the Idea of the State," pp. 261–2, both in *Bakunin on Anarchism*. For Kropotkin, "Law and Authority," especially pp. 202–3; "Modern Science and Anarchism," especially pp. 146, 149, 152, 179; and "Anarchism: Its Philosophy and Ideal," especially pp. 120–1, 141, all in *Kropotkin's Revolutionary Pamphlets*, ed. Roger Baldwin (New York: Dover, 1969). For more contemporary anarchist perspectives, see Richard T. De George, "Anarchism and Authority," in *Anarchism*, Nomos XIX, eds J. Roland Pennock and John Chapman (New York: New York University Press, 1978), especially, pp. 98–100; Alan Ritter, "The Anarchist Justification of Authority," in Pennock and Chapman, eds, *Anarchism*, pp. 130–40; and Clark, "What Is Anarchism?" especially pp. 8ff.

16 "The Unhappy Marriage," pp. 114, 116.

17 Ibid., p. 131. See also "An Anarcha-Feminist Looks at Power Relationships," *Quest* 5, 4 (1982), pp. 76–83.

18 Hewitt, "Is Sexism Genetic?" pp. 13–14, and "Emma Goldman," p. 169.

19 Brown, "Anarchism, Existentialism, Feminism and Ambiguity," p. 18.

20 See, for example, Ann Bookman and Sandra Morgen, eds, *Women and the Politics of Empowerment* (Philadelphia: Temple University Press, 1988). My own work on the Spanish anarchist organization, Mujeres Libres, focuses on their goal of *capacitación,* which I translated "empowerment." Barbara Cruikshank criticizes the concept (and the strategy) of empowerment in "The Will to Empower: Technologies of Citizenship and the War on Poverty," paper presented at the 1994 Annual Meeting of the Western Political Science Association, Albuquerque, New Mexico, March 10–12, 1994.

21 See Kathleen Jones, *Compassionate Authority: Democracy and the Representation of Women* (New York: Routledge, 1993), pp. 46, 69, 157.

22 Ibid., p. 70.

23 Ibid., pp. 157, 159, 160; see also pp. 230–1 and 245 and Jones, "Citizenship in a Woman-Friendly Polity," *Signs: Journal of Women in Culture and Society,* 15 (1990), pp. 781–812.

24 I have discussed these questions in "Identity Politics, Political Identities: Reclaiming Politics," *Frontiers: A Journal of Women's Studies* 16, 1 (1996); see also María C. Lugones and Elizabeth V. Spelman, "Have We Got a Theory for You!" *Women's Studies International Forum* 6, 6 (1983), pp. 573–81; and Gloria Anzaldúa, *Borderlands/La Frontera: The New Mestiza* (San Francisco: Spinsters/Aunt Lute, 1987).

25 Ernesto Laclau and Chantal Mouffe, *Hegemony and Socialist Strategy: Towards a Radical Democratic Politics* (London: Verso, 1985), p. 159; see also Mouffe, "The Sex/Gender System and the Discursive Construction of Women's Subordination," in *Rethinking Ideology: A Marxist Debate,* International Socialism – Discussion 3, ed. Sakari Hänninen and Laena Paldán (Berlin: Argument-Verlag, 1983), p. 142.

26 Laclau and Mouffe, *Hegemony and Socialist Strategy,* p. 169.

27 See Bernice Johnson Reagon, "Coalition Politics: Turning the Century," in Barbara Smith, ed. *Home Girls: A Black Feminist Anthology* (New York: Kitchen Table Press, 1983) pp. 356–68; also Judith Butler, *Gender Trouble: Feminism and the Subversion of Identity* (New York: Routledge, 1990), p. 148; Lee Quinby, "Ecofeminism and the Politics of Resistance," in *Reweaving the World: The Emergence of Ecofeminism,* eds I. Diamond and G. Orenstein (San Francisco: Sierra Club Books, 1990), p. 123; and Jana Sawicki, "Identity Politics and Sexual Freedom," ibid., pp. 185–7. I have explored these issues in some detail in "Identity Politics, Political Identities."

28 See Ackelsberg, *Free Women of Spain,* especially pp. 18–33; and Clark, "What Is Anarchism?"

29 Gail Stenstad, "Anarchic Thinking," *Hypatia,* 3, 2 (Summer 1988), pp. 96, 99.

30 Carole Pateman has offered a powerful contemporary articulation of this position in *The Problem of Political Obligation: A Critique of Liberal Theory* (Berkeley: University of California Press, 1985) (originally published by John Wiley, 1979), especially Ch. 7. See also Robert Paul Wolff, *In Defense of Anarchism* (New York: Harper and Row, 1970).

31 See, for example, Isaac Balbus, *Marxism and Domination* (Princeton: Princeton University Press, 1982), p. 333. See also Jean B. Elshtain, "Feminism, Family, and Community," *Dissent* (Fall 1982), pp. 442–9, and "Reclaiming the Socialist-Feminist Citizen," *Socialist Review,* 74 (1984),

pp. 1–27; Kathy E. Ferguson, *The Feminist Case Against Bureaucracy* (Philadelphia: Temple University Press, 1984); Irene Diamond, "American Feminism and the Language of Control," in *Feminism and Foucault: Reflections on Resistance,* eds Irene Diamond and Lee Quinby (Boston: Northeastern University Press, 1988), pp. 193–206, and *Fertile Ground* (Boston: Beacon Press, 1994).

32 See Susan Moller Okin, *Justice, Gender, and the Family* (New York: Basic Books, 1989); Frances Olsen, "The Myth of State Intervention in the Family," *University of Michigan Journal of Law Reform,* 835 (1985); Margaret Burnham, "An Impossible Marriage: Slave Law and Family Law," *Law and Inequality,* 5 (1987), pp. 187–225; Maxine Baca Zinn, "Family, Race, and Poverty in the Eighties," *Signs: Journal of Women in Culture and Society,* 14, 4 (Summer 1989), pp. 856–74; and Butler, *Gender Trouble.*

33 See, especially, Barbara Nelson, "The Origins of the Two-Channel Welfare State: Workman's Compensation and Mothers' Aid," in *Women, the State and Welfare,* ed. Linda Gordon (Madison: University of Wisconsin Press, 1990); Gwendolyn Mink, "The Lady and the Tramp: Gender, Race, and the Origins of the American Welfare State," in Gordon, ed., *Women, the State, and Welfare,* and "Welfare Reform in Historical Perspective," in *Social Justice* (forthcoming), and *The Wages of Motherhood: Inequality in the Welfare State, 1917–1942* (Ithaca, NY: Cornell University Press, 1995) and Linda Gordon, *Pitied But Not Entitled* (New York: Basic Books, 1994).

34 See, for example, Frances Fox Piven and Richard A. Cloward, *The New Class War* (New York: Pantheon, 1982); Zillah Eisenstein, "The Patriarchal Relations of the Reagan State," *Signs: Journal of Women in Culture and Society,* 10, 2 (Winter 1984), pp. 329–37, and "The Sexual Politics of the New Right," *Signs: Journal of Women in Culture and Society,* 7, 3 (Spring 1982), pp. 567–88; Ida Susser, "Working Class Women, Social Protest, and Changing Ideologies" and Sandra Morgen, " 'It's the Whole Power of the City Against Us,' " both in *Women and the Politics of Empowerment,* eds Bookman and Morgen; Linda Gordon, "Family Violence, Feminism, and Social Control," *Feminist Studies,* 12, 3 (Fall 1986), pp. 453–78; and Kathryn Kish Sklar, "The Historical Foundations of Women's Power in the Creation of the American Welfare State, 1830–1930," in *Mothers of a New World,* eds Seth Koven and Sonya Michel (New York: Routledge, 1993), pp. 43–93.

35 I have explored these and related issues in some detail in "Review Article: Feminist Analyses of Public Policy," *Comparative Politics* (July 1992), pp. 477–93.

36 Again, the literature here is almost too vast to cite. Piven and Cloward have written of these issues most directly in *Poor People's Movements: How They Succeed, Why They Fail* (New York: Pantheon, 1977), in *The Politics of Turmoil* (New York: Pantheon, 1972), especially Part Two, and in "Normalizing Collective Protest," in *Frontiers in Social Movement Theory,* ed. Aldon D. Morris and Carol McClurg Mueller (New Haven: Yale University Press, 1992), pp. 311–12. See also Laclau and Mouffe, *Hegemony,* pp. 152–3, 169. On class consciousness see E.P. Thompson, *The Making of the English Working Class* (New York: Vintage, 1966), and Aldon Morris' discussion of it in "Political Consciousness and Collective Action," in Morris and Mueller, eds, *Frontiers in Social Movement Theory,* pp. 352–3. There has also been

extensive discussion among feminist historians about what constitutes "resistance" by women. See, for example, "Politics and Culture in Women's History: A Symposium," *Feminist Studies*, 6 (1980), pp. 26–64.

37 Kathryn Addelson, Shawn Pyne, and I developed this argument more fully in "Anarchism and Feminism." We drew there, also, on W.E.B. DuBois' analysis of the "doubled" nature of Black consciousness under racism in *The Souls of Black Folk* (Chicago: A.C. McClurg, 1953). Such doubled consciousness is also the focus of some of Simone de Beauvoir's discussion in *The Second Sex*, translated and edited by H.M. Parshley (New York: Bantam Books, 1961).

38 See, for example, Emma Goldman, "Woman Suffrage," in *Anarchism*, p. 211.

39 See Ackelsberg, *Free Women of Spain*, especially Ch. V.

40 Many examples of this sort of empowerment are to be found in Bookman and Morgen, eds, *Women and the Politics of Empowerment*. See also Sara Evans and Harry Boyte, *Free Spaces* (New York: Harper and Row, 1986) and Bettina Aptheker, *Tapestries of Life: Women's Work, Women's Consciousness, and the Meaning of Daily Experience* (Amherst: University of Massachusetts Press, 1990), especially Ch. V. Of the classical anarchist theorists, Kropotkin is, perhaps, the most eloquent on this point. See, especially, "The Spirit of Revolt" and "The Commune of Paris," both in *Selected Writings*.

41 On this point see, especially, Jacquelyn Dowd Hall, "Disorderly Women: Gender and Labor Militancy in the Appalachian South," *Journal of American History* (September 1986), pp. 354–62; Jacquelyn Dowd Hall, Nancy Hewitt, Ardis Cameron, and Martha Ackelsberg, "Disorderly Women: Gender, Politics and Theory," roundtable presentation, Berkshire Conference of Women Historians, Wellesley College, June 1987; Amrita Basu, *Two Faces of Protest: Contrasting Modes of Women's Activism in India* (Berkeley: University of California, 1992); and Ackelsberg, *Free Women of Spain*, especially pp. 171–2. For a view reflecting the position that such behavior is, simply, "disorderly," see Edward C. Banfield, "Rioting Mainly for Fun and Profit," in *The Unheavenly City Revisited* (Boston: Little Brown, 1974).

42 Laclau and Mouffe, *Hegemony*, p. 153. See also Anna Yeatman's discussion of new social movements as engaging in symbolic challenges, opening up "public spaces of openly-contested representations." *Postmodern Revisionings of the Political* (New York: Routledge, 1994), pp. 114–15.

43 Laclau and Mouffe, *Hegemony*, pp. 153–4.

44 Laclau and Mouffe, *Hegemony*, pp. 155, 159–60.

45 See, especially, *The Politics of Turmoil* and "Normalizing Collective Protest," pp. 319–22.

46 On this point, see also Martha A. Ackelsberg and Myrna Margulies Breitbart, "Terrains of Protest: Striking City Women," *Our Generation*, 19, 1 (Fall/ Winter 1977–8), pp. 151–75; also Yeatman, *Postmodern Revisionings*.

47 See, for example, Donna Haraway, "A Manifesto for Cyborgs," in Linda Nicholson, ed. *Feminism/Postmodernism* (New York: Routledge, 1990), p. 199; Butler, *Gender Trouble*, p. 148; Biddy Martin and Chandra Talpade Mohanty, "Feminist Politics: What's Home Got to Do With It?" in Teresa de Laurentis, ed., *Feminist Studies, Critical Studies* (Bloomington: Indiana University Press, 1986), p. 210; Shane Phelan, "(Be)Coming Out: Lesbian Identity and Politics," *Signs: Journal of Women in Culture and Society*, 18, 4 (Summer 1993), pp. 778, 783–4; Arlene Stein, "Making It Perfectly Queer,"

Socialist Review, 22, 1 (January–March 1992), p. 26; Barbara Epstein, *Political Protest and Cultural Revolution: Nonviolent Direct Action in the 1970s and 1980s* (Berkeley and Los Angeles: University of California Press, 1991), pp. 260–1; Anna Yeatman, *Postmodern Revisionings of the Political,* and my "Identity Politics, Political Identities."

48 Epstein, *Political Protest,* p. 269; see also pp. 109, 116, 123, 159.

49 Epstein, *Political Protest,* p. 269.

50 See, especially, Amy Gutman, "Communitarian Critics of Liberalism," *Philosophy and Public Affairs,* 14, 3 (Summer 1985). See also Jane Mansbridge, *Beyond Adversary Democracy* (New York: Basic Books, 1980), pp. x, 10; Kathleen P. Iannello, *Decisions Without Hierarchy: Feminist Interventions in Organization Theory and Practice* (New York: Routledge, 1992), pp. 28–9. For a related study, see Helen Brown, *Women Organising* (London and New York: Routledge, 1992).

51 See, among others, Floya Anthias and Nira Yuval-Davis, "Contextualizing Feminism – Gender, Ethnic and Class Divisions," in Yuval-Davis and Anthias, eds, *Woman-Nation-State* (New York: St. Martin's, 1989); Iris Young, "The Ideal of Community and the Politics of Difference," *Social Theory and Practice,* 12, 1 (Spring 1986), pp. 1–26, and *Justice and the Politics of Difference* (Princeton: Princeton University Press, 1990); Audre Lorde, *Sister Outsider* (Trumansburg: The Crossing Press, 1983); Patricia Hill Collins, *Black Feminist Thought* (Boston: Unwin Hyman, 1990); Gloria Anzaldúa, ed., *Haciendo Caras: Making Face, Making Soul* (San Francisco: Aunt Lute, 1990); Cherríe Moraga and Gloria Anzaldúa, eds, *This Bridge Called My Back: Writings by Radical Women of Color* (Watertown, MA: Persephone Press, 1981); and Elizabeth V. Spelman, *Inessential Woman: Problems of Exclusion in Feminist Thought* (Boston: Beacon Press, 1990).

52 On this point, see also Yeatman, *Postmodern Revisioning,* especially 114–22.

53 Shane Phelan makes a similar argument about "local politics" in *Getting Specific: Postmodern Lesbian Politics* (Minneapolis: University of Minnesota Press, 1994), especially pp. 145–7.

54 Shane Phelan, "Coyote Politics," paper prepared for delivery at the 1994 Annual Meeting of the Western Political Science Association, Albuquerque, NM, March 1994.

55 María Lugones, "Purity, Impurity, and Separation," *Signs: Journal of Women in Culture and Society,* 19, 2 (Winter 1994), pp. 458–79, especially pp. 459–69.

56 Anzaldúa, *Borderlands/La Frontera,* preface, and p. 195.

10

Intersectionality and Identity Politics: Learning from Violence Against Women of Color

Kimberlé Crenshaw

Introduction

Over the past two decades, recognizing that the political demands of many speak more powerfully than the pleas of a few isolated voices, women have organized against the almost routine violence that shapes their lives. This politicization in turn has transformed the way we understand violence against women. For example, battering and rape, once seen as private (family matters) and aberrational (errant sexual aggression), are now largely recognized as part of a broad-scale system of domination that affects women as a class.[1] This process of recognizing as social and systemic what was formerly perceived as isolated and individual has also characterized the development of what has been called the "identity politics" of African Americans, other people of color, and gays and lesbians, among others. For those who engage in or advocate identity-based politics, membership in a group – defined by race, sex, class, sexual orientation or other characteristics – both helps to explain the nature of the oppression experienced by members of that group and serves as a source of strength, community, and intellectual development.

The problem with identity politics is that it frequently conflates or ignores intragroup differences. In the context of violence against women, this elision of difference is problematic because the violence that many women experience is often shaped by other dimensions of their identities, such as race, class, and sexual orientation. Moreover, ignoring difference *within* groups contributes to tension *among* groups, another problem of identity politics that bears on efforts to politicize violence against women. Feminist efforts to politicize experiences of women and anti-racist efforts to politicize experiences of people of color have frequently proceeded as though the issues and experiences they each detail occur on mutually exclusive terrains. Although racism and sexism readily intersect in the lives of real people, they seldom do in feminist and anti-racist theories and practices. And so, when those theories and practices expound identity as "woman" or "person of color" as an either/or proposition, they relegate the identity of women of color to a location that resists telling.

My objective in this article is to advance the telling of that location by exploring the race and gender dimensions of violence against women of color.[2] I consider how the experiences of women of color are frequently the product of intersecting patterns of racism and sexism, and how these experiences tend not to be represented within the discourses of either feminism or anti-racism, discourses that are shaped to respond to one *or* the other, leaving women of color marginalized within both. I do not mean to imply that the disempowerment of women of color is singularly or even primarily caused by feminist and anti-racist theorists or activists. Rather, I hope to capture, at least in part, how prevailing structures of domination shape various discourses of resistance. Although there are significant political and conceptual obstacles to moving against structures of domination with an intersectional sensibility, I argue that the effort to do so should be a central theoretical and political objective of both anti-racism and feminism.

Although this article deals with violent assault perpetrated by men against women, women are also subject to violent assault by women. Violence among lesbians is a hidden but significant problem.[3] Lesbian violence is often shrouded in secrecy for similar reasons that have suppressed exposure of heterosexual violence in communities of color – fear of embarrassing other members of the community, which is already stereotyped as deviant, and fear of being ostracized from the community. There are nonetheless distinctions between heterosexual violence against women and lesbian violence that warrant more analysis than is possible in this essay. I will therefore focus on the intersectionality of race and gender in the context of heterosexual violence.

In an earlier article, I used the concept of intersectionality to denote the various ways in which race and gender interact to shape the multiple dimensions of Black women's employment experiences.[4] My objective there was to illustrate that many of the experiences Black women face are not subsumed within the traditional boundaries of race or gender discrimination as these boundaries are currently understood, and that the intersection of racism and sexism factors into Black women's lives in ways that cannot be captured wholly by looking at the race or gender dimensions of those experiences separately. I build on those observations here by exploring the various ways in which race and gender intersect in shaping structural, political, and representational aspects of violence against women of color.

I end by addressing the implications of the intersectional approach within the broader scope of contemporary identity politics, and argue that we must recognize that the organized identity groups in which we and others find ourselves are in fact not monolithic but made up of members with different and perhaps competing identities as well. Rather than viewing this as a threat to group solidarity, we should view it as an opportunity for bridge building and coalition politics.

Intersectionality is not being offered here as some new, totalizing theory of identity. I consider intersectionality a provisional concept linking contemporary politics with postmodern theory. In mapping the intersections of race and gender, the concept does engage dominant assumptions that race and gender are essentially separate categories. By tracing the categories to their intersections, I hope to suggest a methodology that will ultimately disrupt the tendencies to see race and gender as exclusive or separable.[5] While the primary intersections that I explore here are between race and gender, the concept can and should be expanded by factoring in issues such as class, sexual orientation, age, and color. Indeed, factors I address only in part or not at all, such as class or sexual orientation, are often as critical in shaping the experiences of women of color. My focus on the intersections of race and gender only highlights the need to account for multiple grounds of identity when considering how the social world is constructed.

Structural and Political Intersectionality and Battering

I observed the dynamics of structural intersectionality during a brief field study of battered women's shelters located in minority communities in Los Angeles.[6] In most cases, the physical assault that leads women to these shelters is merely the most immediate manifestation of the subordination they experience. Many women who seek protection are unemployed or underemployed, and a good number of them are poor. Shelters serving these women cannot afford to address only the violence inflicted by the batterer; they must also confront the other multilayered and routinized forms of domination that often converge in these women's lives, hindering their ability to create alternatives to the abusive relationships that brought them to shelters in the first place. Many women of color, for example, are burdened by poverty, childcare responsibilities, and the lack of job skills. These burdens, largely the consequence of gender and class oppression, are then compounded by the racially discriminatory employment and housing practices women of color often face, as well as by the disproportionately high unemployment among people of color that makes battered women of color less able to depend on the support of friends and relatives for temporary shelter.

Where systems of race, gender, and class domination converge, as they do in the experiences of battered women of color, intervention strategies based solely on the experiences of women who do not share the same class or race backgrounds will be of limited help to women who face different obstacles. Such was the case in 1990 when Congress amended the marriage fraud provisions of the Immigration and Nationality Act to protect immigrant women who were battered or exposed to extreme cruelty by their spouses who were United States citizens or permanent residents. Under the marriage fraud provisions of the Act, a person who immigrated to the United States to marry a United States citizen or permanent resident had to remain "properly" married for two years before even applying for permanent resident status, at which time applications for the immigrant's permanent status were required of both spouses. Predictably, under these circumstances, many immigrant women were reluctant to leave even the most abusive of partners for fear of being deported. Reports of the tragic consequences of this double subordination put pressure on Congress to include in the Immigration Act of 1990 a provision amending the marriage fraud rules to allow for an explicit waiver for hardship caused by domestic violence.[7]

Yet many immigrant women, particularly immigrant women of color, have remained vulnerable to battering because they are unable to meet the conditions established for a waiver. The evidence required to support a waiver "can include, but is not limited to, reports and affidavits from police, medical personnel, psychologists, school officials, and social service agencies."[8] For many immigrant women, limited access to these resources can make it difficult for them to obtain the evidence needed for a waiver. And cultural barriers often further discourage immigrant women from reporting or escaping battering situations. Tina Shum, a family counselor at a social service agency, points out that "[t]his law sounds so easy to apply, but there are cultural complications in the Asian community that make even these requirements difficult. . . . Just to find the opportunity and courage to call us is an accomplishment for many." The typical immigrant spouse, she suggests, may live "[i]n an extended family where several generations live together, there may be no privacy on the telephone, no opportunity to leave the house and no understanding of public phones."[9] As a consequence, many immigrant women are wholly dependent on their husbands as their link to the world outside their homes.

Language barriers present another structural problem that often limits opportunities of non-English-speaking women to take advantage of existing support services. Such barriers not only limit access to information about shelters, but also limit access to the security shelters provide. Some shelters turn non-English-speaking women away for lack of bilingual personnel and resources. These examples illustrate how patterns of subordination intersect in women's experience of domestic violence. Intersectional subordination need not be intentionally produced; in fact, it is frequently the consequence of the imposition of one burden that interacts with preexisting vulnerabilities to create yet another dimension of disempowerment. In the case of the marriage fraud provisions of the Immigration and Nationality Act, the imposition of a policy specifically designed to burden one class – immigrant spouses seeking permanent resident status – exacerbated the disempowerment of those already subordinated by other structures of domination. By failing to take into account the vulnerability of immigrant wives to their husbands' control, Congress positioned these women to absorb the simultaneous impact of its anti-immigration policy and their spouses' abuse.

The enactment of the domestic violence waiver of the marriage fraud provisions similarly illustrates how modest attempts to respond to certain problems can be ineffective when the intersectional location of women of color is not considered in fashioning the remedy. Cultural identity and class affect the likelihood that a battered spouse could take advantage of the waiver. Although the waiver is formally available to all women, the terms of the waiver make it inaccessible to some. Those immigrant women least able to take advantage of the waiver – women who are socially or economically the most marginal – are the ones most likely to be women of color.

The concept of political intersectionality highlights the fact that women of color are situated within at least two subordinated groups that frequently pursue conflicting political agendas. The need to split one's political energies between two sometimes opposing groups is a dimension of intersectional disempowerment that men of color and white women seldom confront. Indeed, their specific raced *and* gendered experiences, although intersectional, often define as well as confine the interests of the entire group. For example, racism as experienced by people of color who are of a particular gender – male – tends to determine the parameters of anti-racist strategies, just as sexism as experienced by women who are of a particular race – white – tends to ground the women's movement. The problem is not simply that both discourses fail women of color by not acknowledging the "additional" issue of race or of patriarchy but that the discourses are often inadequate even to the discrete tasks of articulating the full dimensions of racism and sexism. Because women of color experience racism in ways not always the same as those experienced by men of color and sexism in ways not always parallel to experiences of white women, anti-racism and feminism are limited, even on their own terms.

That the political interests of women of color are obscured and jeopardized by political strategies that ignore or suppress intersectional issues is illustrated by my experiences in gathering information for this essay. I attempted to review Los Angeles Police Department statistics reflecting the rate of domestic violence interventions by precinct because such statistics can provide a rough picture of arrests by racial group, given the degree of racial segregation in Los Angeles.[10] LAPD, however, would not release the statistics. A representative explained that one reason the statistics were not released was that domestic violence activists both within and outside the Department feared that statistics reflecting the extent of domestic violence in minority communities might be selectively interpreted and publicized so as to undermine long-term efforts to force the Department to address domestic violence as a serious problem. I was told that activists were worried that the statistics might permit opponents to dismiss domestic violence as a minority problem and, therefore, not deserving of aggressive action.

The informant also claimed that representatives from various minority communities opposed the release of these statistics. They were apparently concerned that the data would unfairly represent Black and Brown communities as unusually violent, potentially reinforcing stereotypes that might be used in attempts to justify oppressive police tactics and other discriminatory practices. These misgivings are based on the familiar and not unfounded premise that certain minority groups – especially Black men – have already been stereotyped as uncontrollably violent. Some worry that attempts to make domestic violence an object of political action may only serve to confirm such stereotypes and undermine efforts to combat negative beliefs about the Black community.

This account sharply illustrates how women of color can be erased by the strategic silences of anti-racism and feminism. The political priorities of both were defined in ways that suppressed information that could have facilitated attempts to confront the problem of domestic violence in communities of color.

Domestic Violence and Anti-racist and Feminist Discourses and Politics

Within communities of color, efforts to stem the politicization of domestic violence are often grounded in attempts to maintain the integrity of the community. Yet the violence that accompanies these attempts at unity is devastating, not only for the Black women who are victimized, but also for the entire Black community. The recourse to violence to resolve conflicts establishes a dangerous pattern for children raised in such environments. It has been estimated that nearly 40 percent of all homeless women and children have fled violence in the home, and an estimated 63 percent of young men between the ages of 11 and 20 who are imprisoned for homicide have killed their mothers' batterers. And yet, while gang violence, homicide, and other forms of Black-on-Black crime have increasingly been discussed within African-American politics, patriarchal ideas about gender and power preclude the recognition of domestic violence as yet another compelling incidence of Black-on-Black crime.

A common problem is that the political or cultural interests of the community are interpreted in a way that precludes full public recognition of the problem of domestic violence. While it would be misleading to suggest that white Americans have come to terms with the degree of violence in their own homes, race adds yet another dimension to why the problem of domestic violence is suppressed within non-white communities. People of color often must weigh their interests in avoiding issues that might reinforce distorted public perceptions against the need to acknowledge and address intracommunity problems. Yet the cost of suppression is seldom recognized in part because the failure to discuss the issue shapes perceptions of how serious the problem is in the first place. Suppression of some of these issues in the name of anti-racism imposes real costs. Where information about violence in minority communities is not available, domestic violence is unlikely to be addressed as a serious issue.

The political imperatives of a narrowly focused anti-racist strategy support other practices that isolate women of color. For example, activists who have attempted to provide support services to Asian- and African-American women report intense resistance from those communities. At other times, cultural and social factors contribute to suppression. Nilda Rimonte, director of Everywoman's Shelter in Los Angeles, points out that in the Asian community, saving the honor of the family from shame is a priority.[11] Unfortunately, this priority tends to be interpreted as obliging women not to scream rather than obliging men not to hit.

Race and culture contribute to the suppression of domestic violence in other ways as well. Women of color are often reluctant to call the police, a hesitancy likely due to a general unwillingness among people of color to subject their private lives to the scrutiny and control of a police force that is frequently hostile. There is also a more generalized community ethic against public intervention, the product of a desire to create a private world free from the diverse assaults on the public lives of racially subordinated people. The home is not simply a man's castle in the patriarchal sense, but may also function as a safe haven from the indignities of life in a racist society. However, but for this "safe haven" in many cases, women of color victimized by violence might otherwise seek help.

There is also a general tendency within anti-racist discourse to regard the problem of violence against women of color as just another manifestation of racism. Gender domination within the community is reconfigured as a consequence of discrimination against men. Of course, it is probably true that racism contributes to the cycle of violence, given the stress that men of color experience in dominant society. It is therefore more than reasonable to explore the links between racism and domestic violence. But the chain of violence is more complex and extends beyond this single link. Racism is linked to patriarchy to the extent that racism denies men of color the power and privilege that dominant men enjoy. When violence is understood as an acting-out of being denied male power in other spheres, it seems counterproductive to embrace constructs that implicitly link the solution to domestic violence to the acquisition of greater male power. The more promising political imperative is to challenge the legitimacy of such power expectations by exposing their dysfunctional and debilitating effect on families and communities of color. Moreover, while understanding links between racism and domestic violence is an important component of any effective intervention strategy, it is also clear that women of color need not await the ultimate triumph over racism before they can expect to live violence-free lives.

Not only do race-based priorities function to obscure the problem of violence suffered by women of color; feminist concerns often suppress minority experiences as well. Strategies for increasing awareness of domestic violence within the white community tend to begin by citing the commonly shared assumption that battering is a minority problem. The strategy then focuses on demolishing this strawman, stressing that spousal abuse also occurs in the white community. That battering occurs in families of all races and all classes seems to be an ever-present theme of anti-abuse campaigns.[12] Such disclaimers seem relevant only in the presence of an initial, widely held belief that domestic violence occurs primarily in minority or poor families. A few commentators have even transformed the message that battering is not *exclusively* a problem of the poor or minority communities into a claim that it *equally* affects all races and classes. I would suggest that assertions that the problem is the same across race and class are driven less by actual knowledge about the prevalence of domestic violence in different communities than by advocates' recognition that the image of domestic violence as an issue involving primarily the poor and minorities complicates efforts to mobilize against it. These comments seem less concerned with exploring domestic abuse within "stereotyped" communities than with removing the stereotype as an obstacle to exposing battering within white middle- and upper-class communities.

Women working in the field of domestic violence have sometimes reproduced the subordination and marginalization of women of color not only by speaking in universal terms about "batterers" and "victims" but also by adopting policies, priorities, or strategies of empowerment that either elide or wholly disregard the particular intersectional needs of women of color. While gender, race, and class intersect to create the particular context in which women of color experience violence, certain choices made by "allies" can reproduce intersectional subordination within the very resistance strategies designed to respond to the problem.

This problem is starkly illustrated by the inaccessibility of domestic violence support services to many non-English-speaking women. Diana Campos, Director of Human Services for Programas de Ocupaciones y Desarrollo Económico Real, Inc. (PODER), detailed the case of a Latina in crisis who was repeatedly denied accommodation at a shelter because she could not prove that she was English-proficient. The woman had fled her home with her teenage son, believing her husband's threats to kill them both. She called the domestic violence hotline administered by PODER seeking shelter for herself and her son. Because most shelters would not accommodate the woman with her son, they were forced to live on the streets for two days. The hotline counselor was finally able to find an agency that would take both the mother and the son, but when the counselor told the intake coordinator at the shelter that the woman spoke limited English, the coordinator told her that they could not take anyone who was not English-proficient. All of the women at the shelter are required to attend a support group and they would not be able to have her in the group if she could not communicate. The intake coordinator restated the shelter's policy of taking only English-speaking women, and stated further that the woman would have to call the shelter herself for screening.[13]

Despite this woman's desperate need, she was unable to receive the protection afforded English-speaking women, due to the shelter's rigid commitment to exclusionary policies. Perhaps even more troubling than the shelter's lack of bilingual resources was its refusal to allow a friend or relative to translate for the woman. This story illustrates the absurdity of a feminist approach that would make the ability to attend a support group without a translator a more significant consideration in the distribution of resources than the risk of physical harm on the street. The point is not that the shelter's image of empowerment is empty, but rather that it was imposed without regard to the disempowering consequences for women who didn't match the kind of client the shelter's administrators imagined. And thus they failed to accomplish the basic priority of the shelter movement – to get the woman out of danger.

Here the woman in crisis was made to bear the burden of the shelter's refusal to anticipate and provide for the needs of non-English-speaking women. Said Campos, "It is unfair to impose more stress on victims by placing them in the position of having to demonstrate their proficiency in English in order to receive services that are readily available to other battered women."[14] The problem is not easily dismissed as one of well-intentioned ignorance. The specific issue of monolingualism and the monistic view of women's experience that set the stage for this tragedy were not new issues in New York. Indeed, several women of color reported that they had repeatedly struggled with the New York State Coalition Against Domestic Violence over language exclusion and other practices that marginalized the interests of women of color.[15] Yet despite repeated lobbying, the Coalition did not act to incorporate the specific needs of non-English-speaking women, many of whom are women of color, into their central organizing vision.

The struggle over which differences matter and which do not is neither an abstract nor an insignificant debate among women. Indeed, these conflicts are about more than difference as such; they raise critical issues of power. The problem is not simply that women who dominate the anti-violence movement are different from women of color but that they frequently have power to determine, either through material or rhetorical resources, whether the intersectional differences of women of color will be incorporated at all into the basic formulation of policy. Efforts to politicize the issue of violence against women challenge beliefs that violence occurs only in homes of "others." While it is unlikely that advocates and others intend to exclude or ignore the needs of poor and colored women, the underlying premise of this seemingly universalistic appeal is to keep the sensibilities of dominant social groups focused on the experiences of those groups. This strategy permits white women victims to come into focus, but does little to disrupt the patterns of neglect that permitted the problem to continue as long as it was imagined to be a minority problem. The experience of violence by minority women is ignored, except to the extent it gains white support for domestic violence programs in the white community. Unless policymakers ask why violence remained insignificant as long as it was understood as a minority problem, it is unlikely that women of color will share equally in the distribution of resources and concern. The struggle over incorporating these differences is not a petty or superficial conflict about who gets to sit at the head of the table. In the context of violence, it is sometimes a deadly serious matter of who will survive and who will not.

Conclusion

This essay has presented intersectionality as a way of framing the various interactions of race and gender in the context of violence against women of color. Yet intersectionality might be more broadly useful as a way of mediating the tension between assertions of multiple identity and the ongoing necessity of group politics. It is helpful in this regard to distinguish intersectionality from the closely related perspective of anti-essentialism, from which women of color have critically engaged white feminism for the absence of women of color on the one hand, and for speaking for women of color on the other.

One rendition of this anti-essentialist critique – that feminism essentializes the category woman – owes a great deal to the postmodernist idea that categories we consider natural or merely representational are actually socially constructed in a linguistic economy of difference.[16] While the descriptive project of postmodernism of questioning the ways in which meaning is socially constructed is generally sound, this critique sometimes misreads the meaning of social construction and distorts its political relevance.

One version of anti-essentialism, embodying what might be called the vulgarized social construction thesis, is that since all categories are socially constructed, there is no such thing as, say, Blacks or women, and thus it makes no sense to continue reproducing those categories by organizing around them. But to say that a category such as race or gender is socially constructed is not to say that the category has no significance in our world. On the contrary, a large and continuing project for subordinated people – and indeed, one of the projects for which postmodern theories have been very helpful – is thinking about the way power has clustered around certain categories and is exercised against others. This project attempts to unveil the processes of subordination and the various ways those processes are experienced by people who are subordinated and people who are privileged by them. It is, then, a project that presumes that categories have meaning and consequences. And this project's most pressing problem, in many if not most cases, is not the existence of the categories, but rather the particular values attached to them and the way those values foster and create social hierarchies.

This is not to deny that the process of categorization is itself an exercise of power, but the story is much more complicated and nuanced than that.

First, the process of categorizing – or, in identity terms, naming – is not unilateral. Subordinated people can and do participate, sometimes even subverting the naming process in empowering ways. One need only think about the historical subversion of the category "Black" or the current transformation of "queer" to understand that categorization is not a one-way street. Clearly, there is unequal power, but there is nonetheless some degree of agency that people can and do exert in the politics of naming. And it is important to note that identity continues to be a site of resistance for members of different subordinated groups. At this point in history, a strong case can be made that the most critical resistance strategy for disempowered groups is to occupy and defend a politics of social location rather than to vacate and destroy it.

Vulgar constructionism thus distorts the possibilities for meaningful identity politics by conflating at least two separate but closely linked manifestations of power. One is the power exercised simply through the process of categorization; the other, the power to cause that categorization to have social and material consequences. While the former power facilitates the latter, the political implications of challenging one over the other matter greatly. We can look at debates over racial subordination throughout history and see that in each instance, there was a possibility of challenging either the construction of identity or the system of subordination based on that identity.

Consider, for example, the segregation system in *Plessy v. Ferguson.*[17] At issue were multiple dimensions of domination, including categorization, the sign of race, and the subordination of those so labeled. There were at least two targets for Plessy to challenge: the construction of identity ("What is a Black?"), and the system of subordination based on that identity ("Can Blacks and whites sit together on a train?"). Plessy actually made both arguments, one against the coherence of race as a category, the other against the subordination of those deemed to be Black. In his attack on the former, Plessy argued that the segregation statute's application to him, given his mixed race status, was inappropriate. The Court refused to see this as an attack on the coherence of the race system and instead responded in a way that simply reproduced the Black/white dichotomy that Plessy was challenging. As we know, Plessy's challenge to the segregation system was not successful either. In evaluating various resistance strategies today, it is useful to ask which of Plessy's challenges would have been best for him to have won – the challenge against the coherence of the racial categorization system or the challenge to the practice of segregation?

The same question can be posed for *Brown v. Board of Education.*[18] Which of two possible arguments was politically more empowering – that segregation was unconstitutional because the racial categorization system on which it was based was incoherent, or that segregation was unconstitutional because it was injurious to Black children and oppressive to their communities? While it might strike some as a difficult question, for the most part, the dimension of racial domination that has been most vexing to African Americans has not been the social categorization as such, but the myriad ways in which those of us so defined have been systematically subordinated. With particular regard to problems confronting women of color, when identity politics fail us, as it frequently does, it is not primarily because that politics takes as natural certain categories that are socially constructed but rather because the descriptive content of those categories and the narratives on which they are based have privileged some experiences and excluded others.

Consider the Clarence Thomas/Anita Hill confrontation during the Senate hearings for the confirmation of Clarence Thomas to the Supreme Court. Anita Hill, in bringing allegations of sexual harassment against Thomas, was rhetorically disempowered in part because she fell between the dominant interpretations of feminism and anti-racism. Caught between the competing narrative tropes of rape (advanced by feminists) on the one hand and lynching (advanced by Thomas and his anti-racist supporters) on the other, the raced and gendered dimensions of her position could not be told. This dilemma could be described as the consequence of anti-racism's essentializing Blackness and feminism's essentializing womanhood. But recognizing as much does not take us far enough, for the problem is not simply linguistic or philosophical in nature. It is specifically political: the narratives of gender are based on the experience of white, middle-class women, and the narratives of race are based on the experience of Black men. The solution does not merely entail arguing for the multiplicity of identities or challenging essentialism generally. Instead, in Hill's case, for example, it would have been necessary to assert those crucial aspects of her location that were erased, even by many of her advocates – that is, to state what difference her difference made.

If, as this analysis asserts, history and context determine the utility of identity politics, how then do we understand identity politics today, especially in light of our recognition of multiple dimensions of identity? More specifically, what does it mean to argue that gendered identities have been obscured in anti-racist discourses, just as race identities have been obscured in feminist discourses? Does that mean we cannot talk about identity? Or instead, that any discourse about identity has to acknowledge how our identities are constructed through the intersection of multiple dimensions? A beginning response to these questions requires that we first recognize that the organized identity groups in which we find ourselves in are in fact coalitions, or at least potential coalitions waiting to be formed.

In the context of anti-racism, recognizing the ways in which the intersectional experiences of women of color are marginalized in prevailing conceptions of identity politics does not require that we give up attempts to organize as communities of color. Rather, intersectionality provides a basis for reconceptualizing race as a coalition between men and women of color. For example, in the area of rape, intersectionality provides a way of explaining why women of color have to abandon the general argument that the interests of the community require the suppression of any confrontation around intraracial rape. Intersectionality may provide the means for dealing with other marginalizations as well. For example, race can also be a means to create a coalition of straight and gay people of color, and thus serve as a basis for critique of cultural institutions, including churches, that reproduce heterosexism.

With identity thus reconceptualized, it may be easier to understand the need for and to summon the courage to challenge groups that are after all, in one sense, "home" to us, in the name of the parts of us that are not made at home. This takes a great deal of energy and arouses intense anxiety. The most one could expect is that we will dare to speak against internal exclusions and marginalizations, that we might call attention to how the identity of "the group" has been centered on the intersectional identities of a few. Recognizing that identity politics takes place at the site where categories intersect thus seems more fruitful than challenging the possibility of talking about categories at all. Through an awareness of intersectionality, we can better acknowledge and ground the differences among us and negotiate the means by which these differences will find expression in constructing group politics.

Notes

For their kind assistance in facilitating my field research for this article, I wish to thank Maria Blanco, Margaret Cambrick, Joan Creer, Estelle Cheung, Nilda Rimonte and Fred Smith. I benefitted from the comments of Taunya Banks, Mark Barenberg, Darcy Calkins, Adrienne Davis, Gina Dent, Brent Edwards, Paul Gewirtz, Lani Guinier, Neil Gotanda, Joel Handler, Duncan Kennedy, Elizabeth Schneider, and Kendall Thomas. A very special thanks goes to Gary Peller and Richard Yarborough. Jayne Lee, Paula Puryear, Yancy Garrido, Eugenia Gifford, and Leti Volpp provided valuable research assistance. I gratefully acknowledge the support of the Academic Senate of UCLA, Center for Afro-American Studies at UCLA, the Reed Foundation and Columbia Law School. Earlier versions of this article were presented to the Critical Race Theory Workshop and the Yale Legal Theory Workshop. This article is dedicated to the memory of Denise Carty-Bennia and Mary Joe Frug.

1 See Susan Schechter, *Women and Male Violence: The Visions and Struggles of the Battered Women's Movement* (Boston: South End Press, 1982); R. Emerson Dobash and Russell Dobash, *Violence Against Wives: A Case Against the Patriarchy* (New York: Free Press, 1979); Lenore E. Walker, *Terrifying Love: Why Battered Women Kill and How Society Responds* (New York: Harper & Row, 1989).

2 For a body of legal scholarship that investigates the connections between race and gender, see, e.g., Regina Austin, "Sapphire Bound!", *Wisconsin Law Review* (1989), p. 539; Angela P. Harris, "Race and Essentialism in Feminist Legal Theory," *Stanford Law Review*, 42 (1990), p. 581; Marlee Kline, "Race, Racism and Feminist Legal Theory," *Harvard Women's Law Journal*, 12 (1989), p. 115.

3 See Jane Garcia, "The Cost of Escaping Domestic Violence: Fear of Treatment in a Largely Homophobic Society May Keep Lesbian Abuse Victims from Calling for Help," *Los Angeles Times*, May 6, 1991, at 2; see also Kerry Lobel, ed., *Naming the Violence: Speaking Out About Lesbian Battering* (Seattle: Seal Press, 1986); Ruthann Robson, "Lavender Bruises: Intralesbian Violence, Law and Lesbian Legal Theory," *Golden Gate University Law Review*, 20 (1990), p. 567.

4 Kimberlé Crenshaw, "Demarginalizing the Intersection of Race and Sex," *University of Chicago Legal Forum* (1989), p. 139.

5 Professor Mari Matsuda calls this inquiry "asking the other question." For example, we should look at an issue or condition traditionally regarded as a gender issue and ask, "Where's the racism in this?" Mari J. Matsuda, "Beside My Sister, Facing the Enemy: Legal Theory Out of Coalition," *Stanford Law Review*, 43 (1991).

6 During my research in Los Angeles, California, I visited Jenessee Battered Women's Shelter, the only shelter in the Western states primarily serving Black women, and Everywoman's Shelter, which primarily serves Asian women. I also visited Estelle Chueng at the Asian Pacific Law Foundation and I spoke with a representative of La Casa, a shelter in the predominantly Latino community of East Los Angeles.

7 Immigration Act of 1990, Pub. L. No. 101–649, 104 Stat. 4978. The Act, introduced by Representative Louise Slaughter (D-N.Y.), provides that a battered spouse who has conditional permanent resident status can be granted a waiver for failure to meet the requirements if she can show that "the marriage was entered into in good faith and that after the marriage the alien spouse was battered by or was subjected to extreme mental cruelty by the U.S. citizen or permanent resident spouse." H.R. Rep. No. 723(I), 101st Cong., 2d Sess. 78 (1990), reprinted in 1990 U.S.C.C.A.N. 6710, 6758.

8 H.R. Rep. No. 723(I) at 79, reprinted in 1990 U.S.C.C.A.N. 6710, 6759.

9 Ibid.

10 Most crime statistics are classified by sex or race but none are classified by sex *and* race. Because we know that most rape victims are women, the racial breakdown reveals, at best, rape rates for Black women. Yet, even given this head start, rates for other non-white women are difficult to collect. While there are some statistics for Latinas, statistics for Asian and Native American women are virtually non-existent. G. Chezia Carraway, "Violence Against Women of Color," *Stanford Law Review*, 43 (1991).

11 Interview with Nilda Rimonte, Director of the Everywoman Shelter, in Los Angeles, California (April 19, 1991). Also see Nilda Rimonte, "Cultural Sanction of Violence Against Women in the Pacific-Asian Community," *Stanford Law Review*, 43 (1991).

12 Natalie Loder Clark, "Crime Begins At Home: Let's Stop Punishing Victims and Perpetuating Violence," *William and Mary Law Review*, 28 (1987), pp. 263, 282 n. 74 ("The problem of domestic violence cuts across all social lines and affects 'families regardless of their economic class, race, national origin, or educational background.'")

13 Letter of Diana M. Campos, Director of Human Services, PODER, to Joseph Semidei, Deputy Commissioner, New York State Department of Social Services (Mar. 26, 1992).

14 Ibid.

15 Roundtable Discussion on Racism and the Domestic Violence Movement (April 2, 1992) (transcript on file with the *Stanford Law Review*). The participants in the discussion – Diana Campos, Director, Bilingual Outreach Project of the New York State Coalition Against Domestic Violence; Elsa A. Rios, Project Director, Victim Intervention Project (a community-based project in East Harlem, New York, serving battered women); and Haydee Rosario, a social worker with the East Harlem Council for Human Services and a Victim Intervention Project volunteer – recounted conflicts relating to race and culture during their association with the New York State Coalition Against Domestic Violence, a state oversight group that distributed resources to battered women's shelters throughout the state and generally set policy priorities for the shelters that were part of the Coalition.

16 I follow the practice of others in linking anti-essentialism to postmodernism. See generally Linda Nicholson, *Feminism/Postmodernism* (New York: Routledge, 1990).

17 *Plessy v. Ferguson*, 163 U.S. 537 (1896).

18 *Brown v. Board of Education*, 347 U.S. (1954).

The Theory and Practice of Freedom:
The Case of Battered Women

Nancy J. Hirschmann

Of all the concepts that feminists are analyzing in this volume and elsewhere,[1] freedom would seem to be the least contestable. After all, freedom from patriarchal restrictions to choose lies at the heart of contemporary feminist struggles, such as that over abortion. Yet I believe that freedom is conceptually gender biased, and that examining the concept in the context of women's concrete experiences reveals it to be problematic.

The problem of domestic violence particularly illustrates the uncomfortable fit between women's experiences and liberty discourse. Domestic violence presents a fundamental challenge to existing liberty discourse because it raises questions about the construction of choice: not only what a woman's choices are – how those choices are actually, materially constructed – but also how the *concept* of "choice" itself is constructed, what the conceptual parameters are to different definitions of choice, how certain actions are or are not considered "genuine" choice. A feminist perspective is necessary to understand the relationship of women's experience not only to existing notions of liberty, but also to a new notion of liberty that can accommodate such experiences. The example of a battered woman who remains with her abuser strikingly reveals the inadequacy of existing freedom theory from a feminist perspective.

The Discourse of Male Liberty

There are, broadly speaking, two theoretical orientations in the conceptualization of choice and the agents that make them, articulated by Isaiah Berlin in his famous essay, "Two Concepts of Liberty." According to Berlin, the first of these, "negative liberty," consists in an absence of external constraints. The individual is free to the extent that he or she is not restrained by external forces, primarily viewed as law, physical force and other overt coercion. "By being free in this sense I mean not being interfered with by others," Berlin says. "The wider the area of non-interference, the wider my freedom." Berlin's general notion that restraints come from outside the self, that they are "other," is an important tenet of negative liberty; other people's direct (or, in some cases, indirect) participation "in frustrating my wishes" is the relevant criterion in determining restraint.[2] For this reason, negative liberty is sometimes called an "opportunity concept": the significant factor in determining whether I am free is that no other person or thing is actually preventing me from taking advantage of opportunities that I would otherwise pursue but for this restraint.[3]

Furthermore, these desires which I must be able to pursue unimpeded if I am to be free, are seen as coming from me and from me alone. Desires may be reactions to external stimuli, of course – for instance, I may not desire chocolate until I smell the brownies you have taken from the oven – but the important fact is that I can identify a desire as *mine*, regardless of *why* I have it. Negative liberty draws clear-cut lines between inner and outer, self and other, subject and object: desires come from within, restraints from without, desires are formed by subjects, by selves, they are thwarted by objects, by others.

In contrast, "positive liberty," according to Berlin, attends to what might be called "internal barriers": fears, addictions, compulsions which are at odds with my "true" self can all inhibit my freedom. This notion involves qualitative evaluation about our desires: we can have desires that are higher or lower, good or bad, significant or trivial, genuine or false. Because of this, it is not enough to experience an absence of external restraints, because the immediate desires I have may frustrate my true will. For instance, if I am combatting bulimia, and an argument with a colleague sends me on a binge, we could argue that the immediate, short-term desire to eat violates my long-term desire to stop such behavior, which I honestly feel is more important. So being able to binge uninhibited does not mean I am free. Indeed, engaging in such acts means I am *unfree* (and not just weak willed) because I am violating my "real" will. Positive liberty is thus sometimes called an "exercise concept"; we have to exercise our full capacities if we are to be free.[4]

Logically, then, positive liberty also requires that this evaluation can be performed by others who know my true will as well as I; indeed, sometimes better than I, particularly when I am in the grip of these self-destructive, short-term desires. This leads to the conclusion that these others can interfere with (or "guide") my actions in order to help me realize my true will and hence to realize my freedom. So as you snatch the brownie from my lips, positive liberty says that you enhance my liberty.

While both conceptions inform popular understandings of liberty – most of us can understand how the cheating smoker is *both* free and unfree – it is also obvious that negative liberty is more common in our everyday understanding of liberty, as it is in political theory.[5] As a central element of the ideology of individualism and rights that emerged from the Enlightenment, negative liberty plays a prominent part in the ideological and political landscape of Western democracies.[6] Positive liberty has developed as more of a leftist (though sometimes rightist) reaction to liberalism's individualistic tendencies. As such it might seem, as Diana Coole suggests, that it has more to offer feminism.[7] But I also agree with Coole that both models are gender biased. Furthermore, the dualistic typology itself is theoretically inadequate to deal with many questions raised by women's historical and material experience.

Indeed, while these two orientations toward liberty are generally seen by political theory as opposed, even mutually exclusive, from a feminist perspective they can be seen to embody similar approaches and assumptions, and demonstrate similar problems. Historically, theorists of both persuasions generally denied women both the "opportunities" and the "exercise" of freedom. Negative liberty theorists such as Hobbes and Locke barred women from public life because they were less able than men to form and act on rational choice.[8] Women's diminished humanity disqualified them from taking advantage of the "opportunities" of liberal society, and required that they be ruled by men. Indeed, women's restraint in the private sphere was one of the things that made negative liberty in the public sphere possible for men. That is, freedom could be defined as abstract choice for men only because women were bound to the aspects of life that are not necessarily chosen.

Positive libertarians such as Rousseau, Kant, and Hegel also denied women's rationality, requiring them to adopt very particularized and structured roles within the family as a means of guaranteeing the stability of the state. All people could be free only by following their true will; but women were too emotional to know what their will was. Furthermore, their irrationality confused men, and impeded *their* ability to know their true will. So women could "exercise" their greatest freedom only by being restrained in the private realm, and allowing men to act for them in the public realm.

Of course, women are not the only ones excluded from these theories; but to define the world in terms of a concept that is denied to a majority of the population (namely women, people of color, and the poor), and that takes white, economically privileged men as the standard for "humanity," suggests fundamental difficulties in terms of representation and applicability. Domestic violence highlights this inadequacy in a particularly clear fashion. It suggests that one cannot simply apply existing liberty theories to excluded groups. Rather, it suggests the need to rethink what we mean by freedom.

Liberty Theory and Domestic Violence

How can this model illuminate the problem of battered women's freedom? There are several restraints faced by victims of domestic violence which most of us would call external. Certainly, violence or physical abuse itself is an external restraint, even on the narrowest Hobbesian reading of negative liberty; but as Hobbes might argue, the violence in a battering relationship is (usually) not constant, so unless a man has physically enslaved, bound, or trapped a woman, she is free to leave. On a less strict reading, however, many negative libertarians could agree that *fear* of a repeat of violence, a major reason why women stay with abusive mates, also presents an external barrier.[9] Economic dependence is a second factor cited by most researchers; women often do not work and lack employment skills, often because the batterer prevented the woman from working during their relationship. Finding a job that pays enough to support herself and her children may be very difficult given sexual discrimination in employment opportunities and pay scales. Alternatively, women who already have good-paying jobs may have to quit if they leave their partners, who will otherwise harass them at their place of employment.[10] Or, they may be fired because of work disruption or adverse publicity.[11] Finally, a woman may have nowhere to go: relatives may be unable or afraid to take her in, battered women's shelters are too few and inadequately funded, and affordable housing that is also safe is often extremely difficult to locate.[12] Force, fear, economic dependence and lack of resources can all present effective external obstacles to a woman's leaving.

But there are other reasons which most of us would consider internal, or "intrapsychic," that explain why women stay with abusive mates.[13] For instance, women who as girls observed their mothers being beaten by their fathers, or who were themselves abused as children, may internalize a belief that violence is a "normal" expression of love, as contradictory as that belief may seem.[14] Love may persuade women to believe an abuser's promises of reform and his displays of remorse and affection. Depression, feelings of low self-worth and guilt, all stemming from her beliefs that she deserved or even provoked the violence, are all too common, and may keep a woman from leaving her abuser.[15] These feelings often coincide with a woman's traditional values about women's and men's roles and about the stigma of divorce.[16] Indeed, women who feel guilt or shame may be reluctant to come forward at all, or even to admit to themselves that they *are* battered women.[17] Ofei-Aboagye's work on domestic violence in Ghana suggests that battering is barely even identifiable *as* a social phenomenon in cultures where it is considered a normal part of marriage.[18]

Do these experiences of battering lend themselves to a conventional understanding of women's freedom? Citing the internal barriers, positive liberty would hold that the battered woman who returns to or remains with her abuser is unfree on several levels. It would point to notions of diminished agency; the woman appears not to understand her motivations, which psychiatrists, psychologists, or social workers may. By staying in a relationship with patterns of violence that are not likely to change, the woman not only acts unfreely, but abdicates future liberty of action; by subjecting herself to physical force and violence, she severely limits her choices and options. The decision to return is thus an act of "false consciousness," the positive libertarian might argue; it violates her true will and perverts her ability for self-development and self-realization.

Given this unfreedom, positive liberty would justify preventing a battered woman from going back to her partner. It would not only make prosecution mandatory, as is the case now in Connecticut and Minnesota,[19] it would further *require* her to go to a shelter; undergo job training, counseling, therapy; and develop her sense of self-worth, her skills, her economic and psychic independence. By preventing her from acting out her *apparent* preference, we would help her realize her *true* preference, that is (at the minimum), not to be battered; and we would, to borrow from Rousseau, only be forcing her to be free.

It is precisely such ideas that are displayed by the "therapeutic" approach to domestic violence in Britain and the United States. "Family violence" therapists, though differing in the specific causes to which they attribute violence, all consistently describe it as a pathology of diseased individuals, women as well as men. Pizzey and Shapiro suggest that women are "addicted to violence," that they "obtain sexual excitement from being abused."[20] Others such as Shainess subscribe to "masochist" theories of domestic violence; Norwood hypothesizes that women "choose dangerous men and dangerous situations" in order to achieve adrenaline highs.[21] Even the British Women's National Commission declared that "battered wives . . . tend to be passive, dependent, inhibited and acquiescent in their behavior . . . [and] prefer men who are older or superior to them in various ways."[22] And in 1986 the American Psychiatric Association tried to classify battered women as "masochistic personalities."[23] Perhaps more benignly, many feminists writing on domestic violence agree with Mildred Pagelow that victims "are lacking in ego-strength or have low self-esteem."[24]

Such theories, of course, claim to promote the interests of women, and many of them claim to be feminist; indeed, the first battered women's shelter in England, Chiswick Women's Aid, founded by Erin Pizzey, overtly adopted such an approach. Pizzey says battered women come to *need* "chaotic behavior interspersed with hazardous adventures" and suggests that "the crisis refuge must act as a deescalating [*sic*] station and hold these families sometimes for as long as two to four years before they can be safely reintegrated into the community."[25] What Dobash and Dobash call "philanthropic" shelters – which they distinguish from "activist" shelters – similarly focus on "restructuring the individual" rather than social and legal institutions and practices.[26]

Central elements of positive liberty are obvious in these accounts, and feminists advocate them with some consistency. After all, unless one actually does subscribe to "masochist" theories, it is difficult to believe that any human being actually chooses to be beaten. Even if we say that the majority of battered women return to or stay with their abusers because of external barriers, how does one explain the fact that some battered women defend or excuse their abusers as well, unless it is by emotional or psychological imprisonment?[27] It is often difficult for those who are not battered, even feminist women who work in shelters, to believe that battered women are exercising full agency when they act in such ways.

Yet the feminist distaste for such a response should be obvious. Such approaches locate the problem of violence exclusively in individual pathologies and locate the solution in therapies directed at changing individual personalities. Indeed, in true positive liberty fashion, such approaches deny that a battered woman can even know what she wants – and hence make choices – because of these pathologies. But in forcing such women to be free, the therapeutic response does exactly what patriarchy has *always* done to women, namely tell them what it is they "really" want. It denies the agency of the woman and fails to respect her capacity to make choices and act on them.

Negative liberty, in contrast, places such respect at its core. While it might require that currently rare resources such as shelters be made more available, in their absence a negative liberty response would nevertheless require that a woman be allowed to decide to return to her spouse. Negative liberty would hold that to be free, a woman must decide for herself what she wants, and be allowed to act on it. Options are always available: if a police officer is reluctant to arrest, a battered woman should invoke citizen's arrest statutes and take advantage of other victims' rights to force the arrest. She should be aggressive with prosecutors in convincing them she is serious about prosecution.[28] If she lacks employment training, she should seek it out. The fact that finding and taking advantage of resources may be difficult, or require perseverance, does not mean doing so is impossible. It is ludicrous to say that forcing her to abandon the batterer makes her freer, because her ability to make and act on her choice is the only criterion for determining her freedom.

Such a response is particularly adopted by the legal system in the United States, which emphasizes individual responsibility for private and personal preferences. Courts often reject women's claims of self-defense for killing their abusers on grounds of individual, rationalist responsibility (that is, the women should have left, instead of killing their men). In such rejections, courts refuse to admit expert testimony on battered women's syndrome because of its implication of diminished responsibility[29] and frequently fail to account for women's social role as mothers, a role that belies the notion of isolated individual actors.[30]

That such moves seem to harm women's opportunities for individual agency does not negate the fact that these responses are *based on* those same negative liberty principles of individual agency; nor does it negate the fact that these very same principles are vital to feminism. For instance, agency and choice are key to many feminist political issues such as abortion. Indeed, respect for individual battered women's choices and decisions is key to the feminist shelter movement; as Jillian Riddington notes, "Returning home is always [an option] and the decision to do this is respected."[31]

Perhaps the key difficulty of the negative liberty response is its reliance on an overly individualistic concept of choice. Its concept of agency denies the complex emotional *and structural* factors that take away many of a woman's choices, that make her *feel* as if she has no choice. It also denies that leaving is not a complete solution: where will she go when it is time to leave the shelter? Will leaving prevent her *spouse* from seeking to control her? For many women leaving does not end their vulnerability to violence. Indeed, Mahoney suggests that leaving may *precipitate* violence; what she calls "separation assault" involves the use of violence by the rejected male partner "to block her from leaving, retaliate for her departure, or forcibly end the separation."[32] The high incidence of separation assault, and the greater severity of these assaults, could easily induce a woman not to press charges or leave for fear of retaliation.

Thus both negative and positive liberty responses seem inadequate. Negative liberty downplays the complexity and even subtlety of the barriers to women's freedom, while positive liberty runs the danger of second-guessing women's desires. What is required, I maintain, is a reunderstanding of liberty that acknowledges positive liberty claims about internal barriers and the need for community and relationship, while also acknowledging negative liberty's focus on external barriers and its central claim that a woman has to make her own choices. But it goes beyond both of these models to recognize what domestic violence particularly highlights: namely that choices are so deeply, fundamentally and complexly constructed for women that the conventional understandings of liberty and of restraint found in the positive–negative debate are inadequate to address women's experiences.

Obstacles to Freedom: Rethinking "Internal" and "External"

The construction of women's choices occurs on at least two levels. The first, obvious level refers to the choices available. In addition to the obvious restrictions placed on women by their partners' violence, police routinely fail to respond to calls for help, or to arrest abusive husbands, displaying dismissive attitudes toward "family disputes" and women complainants. Even when police seek to support women, broader institutional parameters systematically remove women's choices. For instance, police who discourage a battered woman from pressing charges by pointing out that the abuser will be released on bond or bail in a few hours are not necessarily trying to intimidate the woman: they may be stating a fact about the legal system's failure to take domestic violence seriously.[33]

Prosecutors allow battered women much more discretion in deciding whether to prosecute than they do in other violent crimes, thus making such women more vulnerable to ongoing threats from their attackers.[34] If a case makes it to court, judges may abuse discretion by trivializing the violence, doubting women's accounts, making the violence appear mutual, or excusing men on weak grounds.[35] They may also routinely grant child custody, or at least generous visitation rights to male abusers, which may prevent the woman from moving out of state or even out of town. If a judge refers a case to arbitration to resolve disputes over custody or visitation, the battered woman must negotiate in an ongoing relationship with the abuser in a context where losing her children to him is a frightening and all-too-common reality.[36] At the same time, women's responsibility for children can heighten barriers to leaving, such as lack of financial resources.

Many of these obstacles, the products of broadranging sexism and classism, are further exacerbated by racism. Arrest rates for sexual assault are known to be lower when the victim is Black than when she is white, and racism in the legal system and courts can work against women of color in pernicious ways. African-American women in particular may be reluctant to call police or press charges because they do not wish to subject either themselves or their abusers to the racism of the US criminal justice system.[37] They and other women of color may also be censured by the broader community as "traitors to the race." Community norms in Latina, Asian and Aboriginal communities present further sanctions on women seeking security, such that leaving the spouse entails leaving the community.[38]

Women of color are also more vulnerable in white-dominated courtrooms. It is not merely that white judicial systems are being racist in failing to understand non-white cultures, nor that women's experience of culture is "different," but that whites *use* "culture" and racism to *express* sexism: as Sherene Razack puts it, white courts use the notion of "culture" to excuse domestic violence in "a process whereby white patriarchs bond with brown patriarchs."[39] Patriarchs of all racial groups overlook the possibility that women's experience "counts" as part of "culture."

At a more basic level, language barriers and illiteracy will make it difficult for some immigrant women to find out about available resources, let alone take advantage of them. Furthermore, while the Immigration Act of 1990 amended the requirement that abused immigrant women remain married to US citizens for a minimum of two years, the conditions for proof of victimization are such that many immigrant women cannot meet them. And of course, many women are married to undocumented workers, and are thus afraid to call the attention of legal authorities to themselves and their spouses.[40] Finally, racism exists within the battered women's movement itself, which may not wish to highlight cultural differences in domestic violence either (misguidedly) to undercut racist stereotypes or to ensure funding from legislators who are much more worried about "their" women.[41]

In the face of such sweeping bias, women's choices are severely constrained. Women's desires and preferences not to be beaten are not validated, and are even resisted, by those in positions of power and authority. Beyond this, what is viewed as a choice, and what is not, is constrained and constructed for women on a more subtle level. For women in the above scenarios, returning home is viewed as a choice, an autonomous act of agency, though paradoxically made by someone who is not recognized as fully human. Women who decide not to press charges are then chastised by attorneys and judges who fail to acknowledge fear and financial dependence as real motivators. These women may be viewed with humorous contempt by police, who believe they understand all too well, and have their stereotypes about women confirmed. Psychotherapists view returning as evidence that women want to be in these relationships.[42]

Yet male abusers are seen as acting unfreely in a myriad of ways. Men who "enter therapy . . . as a condition of 'getting her back'" or "because their wives . . . were threatening to leave" see themselves as coerced rather than as choosing between two unsatisfactory options.[43] Nor is men's violence viewed as a choice: men routinely blame their violence on alcohol, on women's "nagging," their "ugliness" or deficiencies as wife and mother.[44] And of course such men rarely see that they have chosen to subscribe to rigid sex-role values that legitimize violence, but rather consider such values to be a factual account of the natural order of things.[45]

The construction of choice in this way is obviously counterfactual; men's social, economic, and physical superiority allows them to make choices and act on them far more than women. Women who are afraid, economically dependent, and viewed with prejudice by those from whom they seek help are effectively incapacitated from acting on their preferences. If this happens over a long enough period of time, it may even affect those preferences, and construct these women into people who think of themselves as others, particularly the batterer, see them. As work on colonization reveals, the more complete and effective a system of oppression is, the less aware of it *as* oppression its victims are; a truly successful system of oppression will encode itself into the world-view of the colonized, become reality, and construct their inner visions of themselves, social and political relations, nature, and the world.[46]

Given such a situation, the apparent contradiction of violence on the one hand, and love and care on the other – including the abuser's profuse apologies, remorse, lavish gift-giving and increased care and attention following an incident of violence[47] – will produce a "cognitive inconsistency"[48] which women try to overcome, "creating a fiction of normality"[49] by trivializing the violence, focusing on the positive aspects of the relationship, or believing the abuser when he promises "it will never happen again." Women are reluctant to give up their homes or possessions which represent substantial investments of labor, money, time and emotion. They may also feel they have paid for these items in part by being victimized by violence, such that having to abandon these things victimizes them in a second way. Such investments provide women with additional motives to believe promises of reform.[50] Finally, the cultural construct that women are socially responsible for men's emotional lives ensures that a batterer's remorse, appeals to sympathy, and shifting of blame to his victim effectively make women perceive themselves as culpable.

In the position of the oppressed within patriarchy, then, the construction of women's choices occurs at many levels in women's lives, from the most systemic and public to the most intimate and personal. A feminist approach, however, allows us to see how even the supposed intrapsychic phenomena are culturally mediated and created. Many of women's so-called internal barriers are in fact externally generated by a structure that has women's subjugation at its core. The pervasiveness of this subjugation makes it at once difficult to identify and yet central to women's lack of freedom. In a society that tacitly condones domestic violence by making resources for battered women a low funding priority and by the ineffective actions of courts and police, battered women's feelings of shame and guilt are predictable responses. But their sources are not just internal.

In order to assess women's struggle for agency and freedom, we need to start from the perspective of a battered woman. From this perspective, feminists could adopt an "expanded" negative liberty approach by modifying the concept of "external barrier" to include many aspects of the cultural landscape that may, from a masculinist perspective, seem natural or given. In this light, the ultimate barrier to women's freedom would be patriarchy, or the social, legal, and economic power that men are accorded over women, and which validates individual men's choices to use violence as a means of control. This larger repressive context sets the terms for specific barriers that individual women experience: any individual battering incident, for instance, or police failure to arrest, or courts' failure to convict, or the absence of women's shelters can be seen as *barriers* to women's free agency if we locate them in a larger repressive context. In this view, women's freedom would require ending violence *and* its ideological support.

As long as society does not recognize and support that goal, however, it is up to individual women to manage and cope in the best way they can. But this shift from "choosing" to "coping" radically changes our view of women's freedom and unfreedom. For instance, strategies such as complying with the batterer's demands, passively enduring the beating, continuing to live with the abuser, and even denying fear and dependency, may be seen as the only available options; what looks like complicity or "masochism" may in reality be a form of resistance, management, or just plain survival. Such a view of agency does not mean that such women do not feel fear, that they want the beatings, or that they are free; but it shifts the source of "unfreedom" to the social context in which such women make their choices and decisions.

Yet even if we accept this generous expansion of negative liberty as an important *starting point,* this cannot be where a feminist theory of freedom *ends,* because the unfreedom of battered women cannot be explained entirely in terms of external barriers. Not all men batter women, not all battered women stay with their abusers, and the reasons for such differences cannot simply be reduced to external factors. Even Kathleen Barry, who asserts that "90 percent of battered women would leave if resources were available," indicating a negative liberty view, nevertheless lists "fear of loneliness," "stigma of divorce," and belief that the batterer will reform, as reasons for women's not leaving.[51] To insist that such beliefs and values are only external barriers – that is, not women's "true" beliefs but only the products of patriarchy, "false consciousness" – turns women into victims once again by second-guessing their "true" desires and motivations.

Expanding the notion of "external barrier" to create a more inclusive notion of negative liberty thus also ironically robs women of agency; by saying that *everything* in the patriarchal order is a barrier to women's freedom, possibilities for free action within those parameters disappear. Women who subscribe to traditional roles, or who stay with mates who have exhibited some violence, are by this view unfree because they are externally restrained, whether they realize it or not. The attempt to develop an expanded model of *negative* liberty by completely externalizing the barriers to women's freedom thus ironically returns us to the problems of *positive* liberty.

Accordingly, feminist freedom must retain some essential features of positive liberty from the start. Thinking about freedom from the perspective of battered women suggests that while removing external barriers is crucial, it may not be enough, because what these barriers have already constructed as internal identity may remain. Indeed, any focus on external barriers will be weakened without attention to the internal. This is acknowledged in ideas such as "learned helplessness," where it is precisely the persistance of male violence and the unresponsiveness of police, family, and courts that makes women's shift from "escaping" violence to "coping" with it so understandable; when women see no escape, their goals and choices are bound to accommodate such perceptions to maximize survival.[52] Without seeing the ways in which the relationship between the "inner" self and the "outer" environment must be redefined and reconceptualized, a focus on external barriers reduces the complexities of intimate violence to the very same individualist, rationalist assumptions which are blamed for Western liberalism's inability to respond adequately to women's needs.

Feminist Freedom: Theory and Practice

Thus we must acknowledge not just that what is often called an "inner barrier" is culturally mediated and externally generated, but also understand the *interaction* of "inner" and "outer" in order to reconceptualize the meaning and relationship of those terms. Inner and outer are not mutually exclusive, but interdependent in meaning and in practice. A feminist conception of freedom requires us to acknowledge how external factors influence and generate inner feelings and motives, as well as how those inner feelings act on and influence the external world. If we are who we are through social relations, then as Vaclav Havel argues, people who adapt to oppressive conditions "help create those conditions. . . . They are objects in a system of control, but at the same time they are its subjects as well."[53] This duality of oppression is key to understanding battered women's (un)freedom: for if battered women are the most obvious subjects of this "sytem of control," then they have the power to change it.

Indeed, in a final sense, *only* battered women can change it: in the current context of reluctance to make battering men change their behavior, in most cases battered women must separate from their abusers.[54] But given the difficulties I have noted in doing this, and the ease with which battered women's responses can be and have been misinterpreted by courts and social agencies, battered women must also become active agents and participants in prosecution, advocacy, lobbying, testifying, and legislating. Such an approach fully acknowledges that women's subjective experiences are responses to oppressive and restrictive conditions; but it also acknowledges their capacity to see that and to take action. Women are not responsible for their battering. But they are responsible for and to themselves.

Paradoxically, however, because of the trauma of violence, a battered woman may not be able to do all this. Women's exercise of agency and freedom thus requires the help of others; the positive liberty focus on the potential for others to help one realize one's true self and desires is important to retain. Mary Ann Dutton and many other feminist therapists argue that a feminist approach to therapy involves empowering women to see their options realistically, as well as to struggle to increase and maximize those options. She suggests that such therapy is vital to battered women's ability to see beyond the intensely limiting context of their abusive relationship and to envision a different way of living and responding.[55] Rebecca and Russell Dobash, in spite of their emphasis on external barriers, similarly highlight the need for and success of feminist communities in helping battered women overcome the deep emotional and psychological damage done by intimate violence. Such community, marked by a profound egalitarianism among women, including staff, is a hallmark of "activist shelters," where battered women take part in collective decision-making and responsibility for the shelter's daily operation.[56]

The lesson such experiences offer to a theory of freedom is that if barriers to women's freedom lie in the broad cultural and ideological meanings attributed to women's identity, then eliminating such barriers and reconstituting that identity requires us to shift the entire cultural context within which we live. In a sense, shelters do precisely that: they provide safe, woman-identified spaces within which individual women can reclaim and rename their experiences. This space, though temporary, begins the process of freedom: even one visit to a shelter provides some women with the power they need to end their partner's violence, or the self-validation to leave for good.[57]

Thus a feminist theory of freedom can learn much from the experiences of battered women. While the interrelationship of theory and practice is accepted wisdom among feminist scholars, feminist theory, particularly in the (loosely defined) areas of freedom and autonomy, is often abstracted from the material experiences women confront. By locating theory in the concrete conditions of women's lives such as battering, however, we can see that existing conceptions of freedom are both inadequate and gender biased. Yet it would be foolish for feminists to reject the concept of freedom as liberal illusion. Rather, we must reclaim it and rename it in order to reconstruct the world in our own image, just as battered women must do with their lives.[58] The experiences of battered women suggest that positive liberty's community orientation is highly relevant: the freedom of self-definition and empowerment requires the interaction and support of a "community of women" to provide meaningful choices and options. Yet the point remains from negative liberty that the battered woman has to be able to seek out such help. She has to be willing to engage in supportive relationships. And she must make choices and decisions herself.

In turn, this feminist conception of freedom can also help battered women; by challenging the language of internal and external boundaries, by identifying the ways in which what is called internal is externally generated and mediated, a feminist theory of freedom can help battered women gain a more complex understanding of their experiences, and validate their desires not to be beaten. Formulating a theory of freedom out of and in response to the concrete experiences of women will help us not only to understand those experiences more fully, but to understand *why it is so difficult to understand them*: why the conceptual vocabulary and epistemological assumptions of the existing discourses skew our inquiries to emphasize certain questions (Why didn't she leave?) while obscuring others (Why is he violent? Why didn't anyone help?). This shift in perspective can help policymakers see inadequate resources and institutional response as barriers to women's freedom, and can stimulate the provision of resources and the alteration of existing policies in social agencies and the legal system. Theory can thus influence practice in important, and potentially revolutionary, ways.

208 *Nancy J. Hirschmann*

Notes

Research for this paper was conducted as a Fellow at the Bunting Institute of Radcliffe College, and funded by a grant from the American Council of Learned Societies. An earlier, longer version of this paper appeared in *Frontiers: A Journal of Womens Studies*, vol. 16, no. 1, 1995.

1 See Nancy J. Hirschmann and Christine Di Stefano, eds, *Revisioning the Political: Feminist Reconstructions of Traditional Concepts in Western Political Theory* (Boulder: Westview Press, 1996); Nancy J. Hirschmann, *Rethinking Obligation: A Feminist Method for Political Theory* (Ithaca, NY: Cornell University Press, 1992); Susan Moller Okin, *Justice, Gender and the Family* (New York: Basic Books, 1989); Carole Pateman, *The Sexual Contract* (Stanford: Stanford University Press, 1988); Kathleen Jones, *Compassionate Authority: Democracy and the Representation of Women* (New York: Routledge, 1992).
2 Isaiah Berlin, "Two Concepts of Liberty" in Berlin, *Four Essays on Liberty* (New York: Oxford University Press, 1971), pp. 122–3.
3 Charles Taylor, "What's Wrong With Negative Liberty?" in Alan Ryan, ed., *The Idea of Freedom: Essays in Honor of Isaiah Berlin* (New York: Oxford University Press, 1979), p. 177.
4 Ibid.
5 Richard Flathman, *The Philosophy and Politics of Freedom* (Chicago: The University of Chicago Press, 1987).
6 Hirschmann, *Rethinking Obligation*, Chapters 1 and 2.
7 Diana Coole, "Constructing and Deconstructing Liberty," *Political Studies*, 41 (1993), pp. 83–95.
8 Zillah Eisenstein, *The Radical Future of Liberal Feminism* (New York: Longman's, 1981); Jean Elshtain, *Public Man, Private Woman: Women in Social and Political Thought* (Princeton: Princeton University Press, 1981).
9 Angela Brown, *When Battered Women Kill* (New York: MacMillan, 1987); Diana Russell, *Rape in Marriage* (Bloomington: Indiana University Press, 1990), esp. Ch. 7; Lenore Walker, *Terrifying Love: Why Battered Women Kill and How Society Responds* (New York: Harper and Row, 1989).
10 Mildred Pagelow, *Woman-Battering* (Beverly Hills: Sage, 1981).
11 Russell, *Rape in Marriage*, p. xx.
12 Martha R. Mahoney, "Legal Images of Battered Women: Redefining the Issue of Separation," *Michigan Law Review*, 90, 1 (1991), pp. 1–94.
13 Wendy Hilberman, "Overview: 'The Wifebeater's Wife' Reconsidered." *American Journal of Psychiatry*, 137, 11 (1980), p. 1336.
14 Walker, *Terrifying Love*, pp. 51–2; Brown, *When Battered Women Kill*, pp. 30–2.
15 Michele Cascardi and K. Daniel O'Leary, "Depressive Symptomatology, Self Esteem, and Self-Blame in Battered Women," *Journal of Family Violence*, 7, 4 (1992), pp. 249–59; Mary Ann Dutton, *Empowering and Healing the Battered Woman: A Model for Assessment and Intervention* (New York: Springer, 1992).
16 Richard Gelles and Claire Pedrick Cornell, *Intimate Violence in Families* (Newbury Park: Sage, 1990), p. 77; Pagelow, *Woman-Battering*.
17 Mahoney, "Legal Images of Battered Women," pp. 10–18.

18 Rosemary Ofeibea Ofei-Aboagye, "Altering the Strands of the Fabric: A Preliminary Look at Domestic Violence in Ghana," *Signs: Journal of Women in Culture and Society*, 19, 2 (1994), pp. 924–38. See also Sherene Razack, "What Is to be Gained by Looking White People in the Eye? Culture, Race, and Gender in Cases of Sexual Violence." *Signs: Journal of Women in Culture and Society*, 19, 2 (1994), pp. 894–923.

19 Jan Hoffman, "When Men Hit Women," *New York Times Magazine*, Feburary 16, 1992, pp. 23–72.

20 Erin Pizzey and J. Shapiro, *Prone to Violence* (London: Hamlyn, 1982).

21 Robyn Norwood, *Women Who Love Too Much* (New York: Pocket Books, 1985); N. Shainess, *Sweet Suffering: Woman as Victim* (New York: Pocket Books, 1984).

22 In R. Emerson Dobash and Russel P. Dobash, *Women, Violence and Social Change* (New York: Routledge, 1992), p. 215.

23 Susan Schechter, "Building Bridges Between Activists, Professionals, and Researchers" in Ellen Bograd and Kirstie Yllo, eds, *Feminist Perspectives on Wife Abuse* (Newbury Park: Sage, 1988), p. 310.

24 Pagelow, *Woman-Battering*, p. 159.

25 Erin Pizzey, *Scream Quietly or the Neighbors Will Hear* (Hillside, NJ: Enslow Publishers, 1977), p. 6.

26 Dobash and Dobash, *Women, Violence and Social Change*, p. 81.

27 See Hoffman, "When Men Hit Women."

28 La casa de las Madres, "Legal Rights of Battered Women" in Donna M. Moore, ed., *Battered Women* (Beverly Hills: Sage Publications, 1979), pp. 145–89.

29 Walker, *Terrifying Love*.

30 Mahoney, "Legal Images of Battered Women."

31 Jillian Riddington, "The Transition Process: A Feminist Environment as Reconstitutive Milieu," *Victimology*, 2, 3–4 (1978), p. 570.

32 Mahoney, "Legal Images of Battered Women," p. 6.

33 Pagelow, *Woman-Battering*, pp. 79–80.

34 Kathleen Ferraro, "Cops, Courts and Battered Women," in *Violence Against Women: The Bloody Footprints*, eds P. Bart and E. Moran (Newbury Park: Sage Publications, 1993); Brown, *When Battered Women Kill*, pp. 168–70.

35 See particularly Walker, *Terrifying Love*, pp. 68–9, and Russell, *Rape in Marriage*, p. xix.

36 Hilary Astor, "Violence and Family Mediation: Policy," *Australian Journal of Family Law*, 8 (1994), pp. 3–21; Mahoney, "Legal Images of Battered Women."

37 Kimberlé Crenshaw, "Mapping the Margins: Intersectionality, Identity Politics, and Violence Against Women of Color," *Stanford Law Review*, 43 (1991), pp. 1241–99. See also her essay in this volume.

38 Nilda Rimonte, "A Question of Culture: Cultural Approval of Violence Against Women in the Pacific-Asian Community and the Cultural Defense," *Stanford Law Review*, 43 (1991), pp. 1311–26; Razcack, "What Is to Be Gained."

39 Razack, "What Is to be Gained," p. 902.

40 Crenshaw, "Mapping the Margins." See also Narayan's essay in this volume.

41 Ibid.

42 Pagelow, *Woman-Battering*, pp. 69–70, 78–9.
43 Larry Tifft, *Battering of Women: The Failure of Intervention and the Case for Prevention* (Boulder, CO: Westview Press, 1994), p. 82; Pagelow, *Woman-Battering*, p. 105.
44 David Adams, "Stages of Anti-Sexist Awareness and Change for Men Who Batter," in Leah J. Dickstein and Carol C. Nadelson, *Family Violence: Emerging Issues of a National Crisis* (Washington, DC: American Psychiatric Press, 1989); James Ptacek, "Why Do Men Batter Their Wives?" in Yllo and Bograd, *Feminist Perspectives on Wife Abuse*, pp. 133–57.
45 Tifft, *Battering of Women*, p. 11.
46 Albert Memmi, *The Colonizer and the Colonized*, trans. Howard Greenfield (Boston: Beacon Press, 1967).
47 Lenore Walker, *The Battered Woman Syndrome* (New York: Springer, 1984).
48 Dutton, *Empowering and Healing The Battered Woman*, p. 68.
49 Tifft, *Battering of Women*, p. 62.
50 Brown, *When Battered Women Kill*, p. 36.
51 Kathleen Barry, *Female Sexual Slavery* (New York: New York University Press, 1984), p. 171.
52 Walker, *Terrifying Love*.
53 Vaclav Havel, *Living in Truth* (London: Faber and Faber, 1987), p. 52.
54 Tifft, *Battering of Women*, p. 80.
55 Dutton, *Empowering and Healing the Battered Woman*.
56 Dobash and Dobash, *Women, Violence, and Social Change*, pp. 86–8.
57 Judy Woods Cox and Cal D. Stoltenberg, "Evaluation of a Treatment Program for Battered Wives," *Journal of Family Violence*, 6, 4 (1991), pp. 395–413.
58 See also Nancy J. Hirschmann, "Toward a Feminist Theory of Freedom," *Political Theory*, 24, 1 (1996), pp. 63–84 and "Revisioning Freedom: Relationship, Context, and the Politics of Empowerment," in Hirschmann and DiStefano, *Revisioning the Political*.

Suggestions for Further Reading

Ackelsberg, Martha, *Free Women of Spain: Anarchism and the Struggle for the Emancipation of Women* (Bloomington: Indiana University Press, 1991).

Addelson, Kathryn Pyne, *Impure Thoughts: Essays on Philosophy, Feminism and Ethics* (Philadelphia: Temple University Press, 1991).

Allen, Anita, *Uneasy Access: Privacy for Women in a Free Society* (Totowa, NJ: Rowman and Littlefield, 1987).

Anzaldúa, Gloria, *Borderlands/La Frontera: The New Mestiza* (San Francisco: Spinsters/Aunt Lute, 1987).

Anzaldúa, Gloria, ed., *Haciendo Caras: Making Face, Making Soul* (San Francisco: Aunt Lute, 1990).

Apthekar, Bettina, *Tapestries of Life: Women's Work, Women's Consciousness, and the Meaning of Daily Experience* (Amherst: University of Massachusetts Press, 1990).

Arendt, Hannah, *The Human Condition* (Chicago: University of Chicago Press, 1958).

Baier, Annette, *Moral Prejudices: Essays on Ethics* (Cambridge: Harvard University Press, 1994).

Benhabib, Seyla and Drucilla Cornell, eds, *Feminism as Critique* (Minneaopolis: University of Minnesota Press, 1987).

Binion, Gayle, "Human Rights: A Feminist Perspective," *Human Rights Quarterly*, 17.

Bookman, Ann and Sandra Morgen, eds, *Women and the Politics of Empowerment* (Philadelphia: Temple University Press, 1988).

Bumiller, Kristin, *The Civil Rights Society: The Social Construction of Victims* (Baltimore: Johns Hopkins, 1988).

Butler, Judith, *Gender Trouble: Feminism and the Subversion of Identity* (New York: Routledge, 1990).

Butler, Judith and Joan Scott, eds, *Feminists Theorize the Political* (New York: Routledge, 1992).

Chodorow, Nancy, *The Reproduction of Mothering: Psychoanalysis and the Sociology of Gender* (Berkeley: University of California Press, 1978).

Collins, Patricia Hill, *Black Feminist Thought* (Boston: Unwin Hyman, 1990).

Crenshaw, Kimberlé, "Demarginalizing the Intersection of Race and Sex: A Black Feminist Critique of Antidiscrimination Doctrine, Femininist Theory, and Antiracist Politics," *University of Chicago Legal Forum,* 1989.

Davis, Angela, *Women, Culture and Politics* (New York: Vintage, 1990).

Diamond, Irene and Lee Quinby, eds, *Feminism and Foucault: Reflections on Resistance* (Boston: Northeastern University Press, 1988).

Dietz, Mary, "Citizenship with a Feminist Face: The Problem of Maternal Thinking," *Political Theory,* 13, 1 (1985).

Eisenstein, Zillah, *The Radical Future of Liberal Feminism* (New York: Longman's, 1981).

Elshtain, Jean Bethke, *Public Man, Private Woman: Women in Social and Political Thought* (Princeton: Princeton University Press, 1981).

Etzioni, Amitai, *The Spirit of Community: Rights, Responsibilities and the Communitarian Agenda* (New York: Crown Publishers, 1993).

Ferguson, Kathy E., *The Feminist Case Against Bureaucracy* (Philadelphia: Temple University Press, 1984).

Fineman, Martha Albertson, *The Illusion of Equality: The Rhetoric and Reality of Divorce Reform* (Chicago and London: University of Chicago, 1991).

Fineman, Martha Albertson, *The Neutered Mother, the Sexual Family, and other Twentieth-Century Tragedies* (New York: Routledge, 1995).

Finley, Lucinda, "Breaking Women's Silence in Law," *Notre Dame Law Review,* 64, 5 (1989).

Fox-Genovese, Elizabeth, *Feminism Without Illusions: A Critique of Individualism* (Durham: University of North Carolina Press, 1991).

Fraser, Nancy, *Unruly Practices: Power, Discourse, and Gender in Contemporary Social Theory* (Minneapolis: University of Minnesota Press, 1989).

Frug, Mary Joe, *Postmodern Legal Feminism* (New York: Routledge, 1992).

Frye, Marilyn, *The Politics of Reality* (Freedom, California: The Crossing Press, 1983).

Gilligan, Carole, *In a Different Voice* (Cambridge: Harvard University Press, 1982).

Glendon, Mary Ann, *Abortion and Divorce in Western Law* (Cambridge: Harvard University Press, 1987).

Glendon, Mary Ann, *Rights Talk: The Impoverishment of Politics* (Cambridge: Harvard University Press, 1991).

Gordon, Linda, ed., *Women, the State and Welfare* (Madison: The University of Wisconsin Press, 1990).

Gordon, Linda, *Pitied But Not Entitled* (New York: Basic Books, 1994).

Greenawalt, Kent, *Law and Objectivity* (Oxford: Oxford University Press, 1992).

Grimshaw, Jean, *Philosophy and Feminist Thinking* (Minneapolis: University of Minnesota Press, 1986).

Grossberg, Michael, *Governing the Hearth: Law and Family in Nineteenth-Century America* (Chapel Hill: University of North Carolina Press, 1985).

Gunew, Sneja and Anna Yeatman, eds, *Feminism and the Politics of Difference* (London: Allen and Unwin, and Boulder: Westview Press, 1993).

Gutman, Amy, "Communitarian Critics of Liberalism," *Philosophy and Public Affairs* (Summer 1985).

Hanen, Marcia and Kai Nielsen, *Science, Morality and Feminist Theory* (Alberta: University of Calgary Press, 1987).

Harrington, Mona, *Women Lawyers: Rewriting the Rules* (New York: Knopf, 1994).

Hermann, Anne C. and Abigail J. Stewart, *Theorizing Feminism: Parallel Trends in the Humanities and Social Sciences* (Boulder: Westview Press, 1994).

Hirschmann, Nancy, *Rethinking Obligation: A Feminist Method for Political Theory* (Ithaca: Cornell University Press, 1992).

Hirschmann, Nancy and Christine Di Stefano, eds, *Revisioning the Political: Feminist Reconstructions of Traditional Concepts in Western Political Theory* (Boulder: Westview Press, 1996).

hooks, bell, *Feminist Theory: From Margin to Center* (Boston: South End Press, 1984).

Kittay, Eva Feder and Diana Meyers, eds, *Women and Moral Theory* (Totowa, NJ: Rowman and Littlefield, 1982).

Koven, Seth and Sonya Michel, *Mothers of a New World* (New York: Routledge, 1993).

Kymlicka, Will, *Contemporary Political Philosophy* (Oxford: Clarendon Press, 1990).

Laclau, Ernesto and Chantal Mouffe, *Hegemony and Socialist Strategy: Towards a Radical Democratic Politics* (London: Verso, 1985).

Lorde, Audre, *Sister/Outsider* (New York: Crossing Press, 1984).

MacKinnon, Catherine, "Feminism, Marxism, Method and the State: Toward Feminist Jurisprudence," *Signs: Journal of Women in Culture and Society*, 8, 4 (1983).

MacKinnon, Catherine, *Feminism Unmodified* (Cambridge: Harvard University Press, 1987).

Minow, Martha, "Interpreting Rights," *Yale Law Journal*, 98 (1987).

Minow, Martha, *Making All the Difference: Inclusion, Exclusion, and American Law* (Ithaca: Cornell University Press, 1990).

Moon, Donald, *Constructing Community* (Princeton: Princeton University Press, 1993).

Moraga, Cherríe and Gloria Anzaldúa, eds, *This Bridge Called My Back: Writings by Radical Women of Color* (New York: Kitchen Table Press, 1983).

Morrison, Toni, ed. *Race-ing Justice, En-gendering Power* (New York: Pantheon, 1992).

Nelson, Barbara and Najma Choudhury, eds, *Women and Politics Worldwide* (New Haven: Yale University Press, 1994).

Nicholson, Linda, ed., *Feminism/Postmodernism* (New York: Routledge, 1990).

Noddings, Nel, *Caring: A Feminine Approach to Ethics* (Berkeley: University of California Press, 1984).

Okin, Susan Moller, *Women in Western Political Thought* (Princeton: Princeton University Press, 1979).

Okin, Susan Moller, *Justice, Gender and the Family* (New York: Basic Books, 1989).

Olsen, Frances, "The Family and the Market: A Study of Ideology and Legal Reform," *Harvard Law Review*, 96 (1983).

Olson, Frances, "Statutory Rape: A Feminist Critique of Rights Analysis," *University of Texas Law Review*, 63 (1984), p. 387.

Pateman, Carole, *The Problem of Political Obligation: A Critique of Liberal Theory* (Berkeley: University of California Press, 1985).

Pateman, Carole, *The Sexual Contract* (Stanford: Stanford University Press, 1988).

Pateman, Carole, *The Disorder of Women* (Stanford: Stanford University Press, 1989).

Patton, Paul, ed., *Nietzsche, Feminism and Political Theory* (New York: Routledge, 1993).

Pennock, J. Roland and John W. Chapman, eds, *Anarchism*, Nomos XIX (New York: New York University Press, 1978).

Phelan, Shane, *Getting Specific: Postmodern Lesbian Politics* (Minneapolis: University of Minnesota Press, 1994).

Phillips, Anne, *Engendering Democracy* (Cambridge: Polity Press and University Park: Pennsylvania State University Press, 1991).

Phillips, Anne, *Democracy and Difference* (University Park: Penn State University Press, 1993).

Posner, Richard, *Sex and Reason* (Cambridge: Harvard University Press, 1992).

Rawls, John, *A Theory of Justice* (Cambridge: Harvard University Press, 1971).

Regan, Milton C. Jr, *Family Law and the Pursuit of Intimacy* (New York: New York University Press, 1993).

Rhode, Deborah, ed., *Theoretical Perspectives on Sexual Difference* (New Haven: Yale University Press, 1990).

Rich, Adrienne, *Of Woman Born: Motherhood as Experience and as Institution* (New York: Norton, Bantam, 1976).

Robson, Ruthann, *Lesbian (Out)law* (Ithaca: Firebrand Press, 1992).

Ruddick, Sara, *Maternal Thinking* (Boston: Beacon Press, 1989).

Sandel, Michael, *Liberalism and the Limits of Justice* (Cambridge: Cambridge University Press, 1982).

Sargent, Lydia, ed., *Women and Revolution* (Boston: South End Press, 1981).

Sarvasy, Wendy, "Beyond the Difference versus Equality Policy Debate: Citizenship and the Quest for a Feminist Welfare State," *Signs: Journal of Women in Culture and Society* (Winter 1992).

Saxonhouse, Arlene, *Women in the History of Political Thought* (New York: Praeger, 1985).

Shanley, Mary Lyndon, *Feminism, Marriage and the Law in Victorian England* (Princeton: Princeton University Press, 1989).

Shanley, Mary Lyndon and Pateman, Carole, eds, *Feminist Interpretations and Political Theory* (Cambridge: Polity Press, 1991).

Shklar, Judith, *American Citizenship: The Quest for Inclusion* (Cambridge: Harvard University Press, 1991).

Smart, Carol, *Feminism and the Power of Law* (New York: Routledge, 1989).

Smith, Barbara, *Home Girls: A Black Feminist Anthology* (New York: Kitchen Table Press, 1983).

Spelman, Elizabeth, *Inessential Woman: Problems of Exclusion in Feminist Thought* (Boston: Beacon Press, 1990).

Stanworth, Michelle, ed., *Reproductive Technologies: Gender, Motherhood and Medicine* (Cambridge: Polity Press, 1987).

Tong, Rosmarie, *Feminist Thought: A Comprehensive Introduction* (Boulder: Westview, 1989).

Tronto, Joan, *Moral Boundaries: A Political Argument for an Ethic of Care* (New York: Routledge, 1993).

Villmoore, Adelaide, "Women, Differences, and Rights as Practices," *Law and Society Review*, 25, 2 (1991).

Waldron, Jeremy, ed., *Theories of Rights* (Oxford: Oxford University Press, 1984).

Walzer, Michael, *Spheres of Justice: A Defense of Pluralism and Equality* (New York: Basic Books, 1983).

Weisberg, D. Kelly, *Feminist Legal Theory: Foundations* (Philadelphia: Temple University Press, 1993).

Weiss, Penny and Marilyn Friedman, eds, *Feminism and Community* (Philadelphia: Temple University Press, 1995).

Weitzman, Lenore, *The Marriage Contract: Spouses, Lovers and the Law* (New York: Free Press, 1981).

Weitzman, Lenore, *The Divorce Revolution: Unexpected Social and Economic Consequences for Women and Children in America* (New York: Free Press, 1985).

Williams, Patricia, *The Alchemy of Race and Rights* (Cambridge: Harvard University Press, 1991).

Yeatman, Anna, *Postmodern Revisioning of the Political* (New York: Routledge, 1994).

Yellin, Jean F., *Women and Sisters: The Anti-Slavery Feminists in American Culture* (New Haven: Yale University Press, 1989).

Young, Iris Marion, *Justice and the Politics of Difference* (Princeton: Princeton University Press, 1990).

Index

Note: **Bold** type indicates contributions to this volume Legal cases shown in *italics*.